Lands and Peoples

THE WORLD IN COLOR

VOLUME III

THE GROLIER SOCIETY

NEW YORK   TORONTO

P

Volume III

TABLE OF CONTENTS

SHEPHERD OF CENTRAL GREECE

Only about one-fifth of the soil of Greece can be planted to crops, but the arable land is farmed with skill. Large areas, however, are better suited to the raising of sheep and goats, and there are more sheep and goats in Greece than people. This shepherd with his staff wears the traditional tunic, tight trousers and turned-up slippers with pompons.

THE GREEKS OF TODAY

Modern People in a Land of Ancient Culture

The Greek people have the oldest recorded history of the European nations, and the Greek language today, though its form has changed in many ways, is obviously the tongue used by Homer, who lived about 1000 B.C. The Greeks, or Hellenes, besides being unequaled in art and literature, were also clever and brave warriors. They were not, however, a united nation, but merely a collection of city-states which combined only in times of stress. It was not until 1832 that, for the first time, this race of ancient culture became a united nation. Today it is a monarchy. Here we shall learn something of modern Greece, with the exception of Athens, which is so important historically as to deserve a separate chapter.

THE very mention of the name Greece brings to our minds that country of long ago in which the best in art and literature was produced. Most of us know little of the Greece of today and were we to go there, we would probably neglect the present in order to reconstruct those scenes of long ago.

A map shows us that Greece is a peninsula extending into the Mediterranean at its easternmost end. While the Mediterranean forms its southern boundary, two upraised arms of that great sea, the Ionian Sea and the Aegean Sea, determine its western and eastern limits. To the north are the Balkan countries of Albania, Yugoslavia and Bulgaria.

One notices that the Grecian peninsula is in two parts and that the southern portion seems to dangle from the mainland by a mere thread of territory, the Isthmus of Corinth. It is really severed entirely for a canal is cut through to give trade ships a shorter route.

Although the west coast consists of high mountains with no harbors, the east coast is full of bays and havens for ships. Nearly all the large towns—Athens, the capital and most important city, Piraeus, the chief port, and Thessaloniki (Salonica), a thriving town in Macedonia—are on the eastern side of the country. In this respect Greece differs from Italy, whose principal cities, with the exception of Venice, lie on the western coast. The mountain barriers to the west and north and the fine natural harbors on the east made Greece from the very beginning a maritime country. Trade was carried on in the earliest days with the Aegean Islands, with Africa and with Asia, and the contacts thus made with older and more civilized countries had no little influence on the civilization of Greece.

The approach by water to the eastern side of Greece is through the Aegean Archipelago, and the scenery which it presents is unmatched in any other part of the world, for the sea is studded with many islands and groups of islands, varied in shape and size and color, rising out of the purple-blue waters. In ancient days, some of these islands were separate states and commerce as well as warfare was carried on among them.

When the history of Greece opens, many centuries before the birth of Christ, this land was known as Hellas and the people were called Hellenes. Their own explanation of their origin is not unlike our story of Noah and the Ark. Zeus, "father of gods and men," had brought about a flood in order to destroy wicked mankind, but Deucalion and Pyrrha, who had been forewarned, survived this catastrophe. In order to repeople the earth Deucalion and Pyrrha were commanded to throw stones behind them and for each stone Deucalion threw, there sprang up a son and for each one that Pyrrha threw, a daughter. One of the sons was called Hellen and it was from him that the Hellenes or Greeks were descended. Historians believe, however, that tribes of Indo-European origin came down from the north and the east and made this land their home.

These Hellenes did not exist as a nation, but were split up into many little states

RUINS OF THE GREAT AMPHITHEATER AT EPIDAURUS

The ruins above, unearthed by the Greek Archaeological Society, are the outstanding example in existence today of a Greek theater. Although the actors performed on the circular stage that we see far below, this huge theater, built by the famous architect Polyclitus, was so constructed that all the 16,000 spectators, even those seated farthest away, could hear every word of the plays. On the plain beyond the theater is the ruined temple of Esculapius, the god of healing. Invalids flocked here during the yearly festivals in his honor to beseech him for a divine cure.

6

THE WHITE TOWER NEAR THE HARBOR OF SALONIKA

Probably dating back two thousand years, the ancient tower still guards the modern port of the second largest city of Greece. Salonika (Thessalonike), in Macedonia, was founded during the fourth century B.C., and St. Paul later found Christian converts there. Today it is an important trading center and seaport of the Aegean and Mediterranean seas.

usually with a city as a centre. The geography of Greece partly explains this lack of unity, since it is divided into small sections by the great mountain ranges, and each of the sections had a ruler, laws and customs of its own. There was little sympathy between the city-states, as we call them, and the record of their relations with each other is one of jealousy, quarrels and wars.

In the fifth century B.C., the Persians, who at that time made up the most powerful nation in all Asia, came to Greece with a mighty army to subject these people. Even the danger of conquest failed to unite the Greeks, for they became allies only to defeat the enemy and immediately after, again went to war among themselves.

The greatest of the city-states was Athens, capital of Attica, which at its zenith was a great sea-power, and the home of literature, of art and of learning —that wonderful culture which we associate with ancient Greece. The story of Athens, however, we shall reserve for the following chapter.

West of Athens was Bœotia with

Thebes as its capital and in the extreme south, known as the Peloponnesus, was Sparta, noted for its courageous warriors. So great was the Spartan desire for supremacy that they killed all the babies who did not measure up to their standard of physical fitness and trained the surviving male children in hardship and endurance in preparation for military life. Thus Sparta became a powerful state. These three were the most important although there were over 150 in all, counting the many island states.

Alexander the Great succeeded in conquering the city-states, but even he failed to weld them into a nation. They fought for him and helped him to conquer all the parts of Asia and Africa that were then known. At his death, however, in 323 B.C., his vast empire was broken up and about 200 years later Greece was taken by the mighty Roman Empire. Greece later became a part of the Byzantine or Eastern Roman Empire, whose capital was at Constantinople. This might be called a Greek Empire, for so great was the influence of the Greeks on their Roman conquerors that Greek became the official language. In the fifteenth century, the Turks broke into Europe, conquered the country and held it until the nineteenth century, ruling the people very harshly and very badly. It was not until 1832 that Greece shook herself free from them and, helped by Great Britain, France and Russia, was recognized as an independent kingdom with a Bavarian prince as king. Since then, there have been many political changes. In 1924, Greece became a republic, but disorderly uprisings frequently occurred. A royalist party gained control of Parliament in 1933, and the King returned to the throne in 1935.

War Years and After

After conquering Albania in 1939, Italy invaded Greece in 1940. The Greeks fought off the enemy for six months, but fell to the Axis in 1941.

The German occupation was brutal. It lasted three and a half years and during that time 400,000 Greeks died of starvation. Many resisted with constant guerrilla warfare, and many were killed for their valiant show of patriotism.

British troops invaded Greece and with the resistance troops drove the Germans from the land by November 1944. In withdrawing, the German Army looted villages and executed thousands.

Unfortunately the guerrillas did not lay down their arms upon the defeat of Germany. Fighting continued against the new Greek Government, with neighboring states sending aid to the rebels. Not until 1949, after American aid had arrived, were the guerrillas defeated and peace restored to the peninsula.

The havoc wrought by the German occupation and the civil war has kept Greece from achieving a decent standard of living. The country has suffered from inflation, a shortage of machinery and poor transportation. Though these conditions have been relieved to some extent by outside aid, the country's greatest source of income—export trade with central Europe—has as yet not been restored.

Nevertheless, Greece was able to send men to fight alongside the United Nations troops in Korea. And there are other signs of recovery. The Greek merchant marine now ranks tenth in the world. Roads, railways, airfields, bridges, ports and canals have been built.

Agriculture the Chief Occupation

Greece is mainly an agricultural country, although mountains cover four-fifths of its surface. The rivers are small and often dry up, and the rainfall is scanty. There are great stretches of undeveloped and uninhabited land and many of the hills are bare, but there are large tracts covered with forests and olive groves. The plain of Thessaly is the granary for the rest of the country, while the slopes and hills in the vale of Sparta are covered with orange and lemon groves and vineyards. Grape-currants, tobacco and wheat are also grown, and sheep-raising is carried on extensively.

Until recently there were few factories, and goods were made in little neighborhood shops. Industry is developing, however, and olive oil, wine, textiles, leather and soap are made. Since the coming of the refugees, rug and carpet factories have been started, for many of them had been weavers in Asia Minor. There are a few cotton, silk and woolen mills, and many flour mills.

Marble, in great quantities, is supplied by Greece's mountains. Dazzling white marble of the finest kind from the Island of Paros, and Mount Pentelicus, marble veined with blue or green, black marble and marble in colors, the same that the ancient Greeks and Romans used for their statues and buildings, still supplies Greece and other countries. There is considerable iron, copper and zinc, but since there is no coal and little wood for fuel, the ores are scarcely worked.

Old Customs Preserved

If we go to any of the districts situated in the heart of the country we shall see the peasants wearing the national costume, living their lives in the manner of their forefathers and keeping up old customs. Even in many of the larger towns, particu-

© E. N. A.

ATHENS, since ancient times the most famous of Hellenic cities, is situated in Attica on and around a group of hills. It is about three miles from the coast and five miles from its port, the Piraeus. As we stand upon the northern ramparts of the Acropolis, or citadel, we look west-wards across the city towards the Theseum to the distant hazy Poikilon Hills. Athens was made the capital of Greece in 1833 after the War of Independence, and has since grown rapidly in size and importance, but its chief attraction is in its historic ruins.

A GIRL OF THE GREEK VINEYARDS SHOULDERS A LUSCIOUS BURDEN

The most valuable grape of Greece is the currant—not the currant of jams and jellies, but a kind of raisin that takes its name from the Corinth region where it grows in abundance.

10

A BUMPER RICE HARVEST WHERE ONCE THERE WERE SALT FLATS

Marshall Plan aid has turned a wasteland into fertile fields near the mouth of the Spercheios south of Lamia.   The modern reaper cuts the stalks, husks the kernels and sacks the rice.

THE TRUSTY MULE, A FAMILY TREASURE IN A MOUNTAINOUS LAND

To market, to church or to the fields, the Greek farmer packs his mule and is off.   His slow ride is bumpy, to be sure, but is a safe one without a worry about engine or tires.

SPARTA was once the chief city of the Peloponnese, and its inhabitants were famous throughout Greece as warriors of great fortitude. Even today when we wish to pay great tribute to a man's endurance we say that it is Spartan. There are, however, very few traces left of the grandeur of ancient times, and on the hillsides, where stood the greater part of old Sparta, are modern houses, many tall cypress trees and rich orchards. Modern Sparta, built in the early nineteenth century, is hardly more than a small town. It occupies the southern hills within the walls of the old city.

12

THE METEORA MONASTERIES in Thessaly are all perched on the summits of high pillar-like rocks such as this one. They were built in the Middle Ages, when their impregnable positions ensured the safety of the monks, and visitors and provisions were drawn up in a basket lifted by a windlass. At the present, most of them have been abandoned.

THE SEVERELY SIMPLE GRAY LIMESTONE PALACE AT ATHENS

The Royal Palace, completed in 1838, is not a beautiful building. But it marks an important turning point in the history of Greece. In 1833, when Athens was selected by the newly established Greek kingdom as the site for its capital, there was nothing here but a few fishermen's huts which stood around the base of the Acropolis with its remnants of ancient glory.

larly on market days, we may still see the native dress—the men in their full short linen kilts, or fustanellas, the women in their beautiful dresses with richly decorated bodices and aprons. It is very pleasant to pay a visit to these people for they are most hospitable and kind and take a great interest in foreigners.

They are, perhaps, seen at their best when at their daily work or enjoying their simple pastimes. How simple their pleasures are is indicated by an ancient custom which still survives at Tenos. This is known as the "evening sitting" and is nothing more than a meeting of groups of people after the day's work is done to listen to the older folk telling stories, which they relate night after night with a gusto that makes them sufficiently exciting to hold the attention of their audience.

The Greeks are very fond of their old customs, and of none more than their ancient dances. These are danced both by the peasants and by the more educated people at the balls in the large towns. In order to preserve these dances at least one or two are performed at the beginning or end of every ball, and in the army and navy only these national dances are permitted.

Birthdays, as we know them here, have little significance in Greece. Their place is taken by what are termed "name days." Most Greeks are called after some patron saint, and when a saint's day comes round all people bearing his name take occasion to celebrate. Friends call and offer presents of flowers and cakes just as we receive presents on our birthdays.

It is interesting to know that the many

14

COLORFUL GREEK EVZONES GUARD THE ROYAL PALACE IN ATHENS

In a strictly military sense, the evzones are simply riflemen. But their history is as colorful as their uniforms. Traditionally, the members were recruited from the mountains and trained from an early age to be fierce, valiant fighters. They are famous for their heroism and wear with pride the full circular skirts and tufted shoes of their regiment.

15

© E. N. A.

RUINS OF ANCIENT CORINTH, which in olden days was the most prosperous and one of the fairest of Greek cities, dot the slopes beneath the rock of the Acrocorinth or citadel. The seven columns that we see in the center of the photograph are all that remain of the once splendid temple of Apollo, now surrounded by other ruins. A few miles away there has sprung up a new city of Corinth which, although its trade brings it considerable prosperity, does not enjoy the commercial greatness that belonged to the ancient city visited by St. Paul.

16

THE TEMPLE OF APOLLO at Corinth, which we saw in the distance on the page opposite, is the most impressive ruin now standing among the remains of that ancient city. Even these seven battered columns, each of which is carved from a solid block of stone, enable us to imagine the splendor of the temple as it originally stood. Situated on the narrow isthmus that joins the Peloponnese peninsula to the Greek mainland, ancient Corinth was the most convenient centre in the Mediterranean for trade from the east and the west.

17

FARMING—HEARTBREAK STYLE

Agriculture is the principal occupation in Greece, although only about one-fifth of the land is arable, and the civil war reduced even that area temporarily. Modern methods of irrigation will undoubtedly be an important factor in increasing production. The farmer shown above is engaged in the backbreaking task of operating his old-fashioned irrigating apparatus by hand.

WOOL MUST BE DRIED GENTLY IF THE YARN IS TO BE STRONG

Modern equipment is difficult to get in Greece, even for those who can afford to buy it. So many farm women dry wool for their homespun clothing in the open air and sunshine.

customs concerning weddings are quite different from those which exist in this country.

A marriage in Greece is often an elaborate affair. The wedding ceremony generally takes place in the home instead of at a church and, in the country districts, it is often preceded and followed by a long series of formalities, which vary in different parts of the country. For instance, in some districts the bride has to observe various customs with regard to the gathering together of the articles required for her future home, and then she retires to the house of her parents, pretends she does not want to be married and resists the efforts of her friends to bring her to a more reasonable frame of mind. She maintains this attitude for as long as is the custom of the district, until finally the bridegroom comes with his relatives and carries her away by "force." Even when she arrives in her own home she is obliged to spend several days performing various ceremonies and giving presents to the relatives and friends who throng around her till the proper time arrives for them to leave her alone with her husband.

BOISSONNAS

VILLAGERS OF ZEMENON, led by priests, walk slowly homewards over the winding hill path in the calm evening. All the women and children are dressed in their holiday clothes—brightly colored dresses and hoods—and one of the men wears the white fustanella or short linen kilt of the Greeks. The bearded priests, who are of peasant stock, are permitted to marry. The curious, tall hat with the brim at the top instead of round the head, worn by the one who is second from the right, is part of the conventional garb of the Greek priests.

BOISSONNAS

NEMEAN PEASANTS drive a team of horses and mules yoked together over the wheat to separate the grain from the ears. Behind them are three pillars, all that remain standing of the famous old temple of Zeus, "ruler of the universe." These peasants may not have heard the legend, but a story runs that a ferocious lion once ravaged the Nemean valley until it was slain by Hercules, who afterwards wore its skin. In ancient times, famous games were held every two years at Nemea, and athletes came from all over Greece to compete in them.

KOSTICH

MENDING NETS IN A SUNNY HARBOR ON RHODES

Sponge divers are mending their nets, while the boats ride high in harbor. In ancient days the trading ships of the Rhodians freely roamed the Mediterranean; and Rhodians founded colonies in Asia Minor, in Sicily, Italy and as far away as Spain. Almost 2,000 years ago the people of Rhodes set up a maritime code that has influenced maritime law down to the present day.

A NEW VILLAGE, NEA ARACHOVA, COVERS THE SCARS OF WAR

Marshall Plan aid helped to build the sturdy brick homes of Nea (New) Arachova. The old village, badly damaged during World War II, lies in the shadow of Mount Parnassus, sacred shrine of the Muses, nine goddesses of song and poetry and of the arts and sciences. Farther along the slope of Parnassus are the ruins of Delphi, ancient home of a famous oracle.

The position of women in Greece has, in the past, been an inferior one. Women did most of the work but were limited in their freedom and, even among the upper classes, conversed only among themselves. During recent years this has completely changed, and, although they still maintain control of the home, they have now entered various professions formerly reserved only for men. Today they even compete with men for national office.

In spite of having been a part of the Moslem Turkish Empire for 400 years, the Greeks are Christians but they have many strange customs in connection with their religious festivals. Christmas and New Year's Eve are observed in a quiet manner, but at Epiphany the ceremony of blessing the waters is most unusual. This is especially true at Syra.

The night before the festival boys parade the streets with lanterns, singing

POPOFF

MACEDONIAN WOMEN, appareled in the beautiful dress of their district, suggest the barbaric splendor of Asia rather than the costume of the oldest state in Europe. Heavy embroidery in colors and a profusion of gold thread needlework represent many hours of painstaking effort, but what matters it, if the effect is such as these two women have produced.

CROOK

A WEDDING in Macedonia, a district in northern Greece, is an occasion for much festivity. Both the bride and bridegroom wear gay national costumes and, as a usual thing, the bride waits on the guests at the wedding breakfast as though she were a servant. In this case, she has presented the company with an embroidered handkerchief like the one she is carrying.

religious songs appropriate to the occasion, and early the following morning a service is held in the Church of the Transfiguration. At the conclusion of the service a procession is formed of priests accompanied by men bearing a cross tied with ribbons. They proceed down to the harbor and after the water has been blessed, one of the priests throws the cross into the sea, then numbers of men dive in and struggle for it. The one who secures the cross is regarded as being peculiarly lucky, especially if in the struggle the ribbons have been torn off. A similar ceremony is held at Athens, but, as the cross is only thrown into a reservoir, it naturally lacks the picturesqueness of the scene at Syra.

Easter is a great festival for then besides religious services, there are processions through the streets, houses are illuminated, and in country districts dancing takes place. On Easter Tuesday ancient dances performed by people in national costume are a great feature at Megara, and one of the peculiarities of the festival is that the women decorate themselves with old Turkish coins.

Interesting, indeed, are the monasteries —the Meteora in Thessaly, shown on page 13, and those at Mount Athos occupying the eastern prong of the Chalcidice Peninsula. Women and even female animals are not allowed there, and the monks (numbering nearly 5,000) manage the affairs of the community so efficiently that they have been granted an autonomous government.

We have often heard people describe a place as being "a perfect Arcadia," by which they meant, of course, that it was extremely lovely and quite unspoiled by man. Yet Arcadia is composed of rugged mountains, gloomy defiles and has a severe climate. This is how it came about.

The worship of the god Pan began in Arcadia, and from the hymn which was composed to him we learn that the piping and dancing, the nymphs and rustic gods and the country scene were really connected with early pagan ceremonies. It would appear, then, that the stern mountaineers of Arcadia, who had to fight hard for their living, imagined this beautiful land, and in their worship of Pan sang about the Arcadia for which they longed.

GREECE: FACTS AND FIGURES

THE COUNTRY

A peninsula lying south of the Balkan States; bounded on the north by Albania, Yugoslavia and Bulgaria, on the east by Turkey and the Ægean Sea, on the south by the Mediterranean Sea and on the west by the Ionian Sea. It includes about 220 islands, the largest of which is Crete. The mainland area is 42,427 square miles and the total estimated population is about 7,600,000, including the Dodecanese Islands ceded by Italy.

GOVERNMENT AND CONSTITUTION

A constitutional monarchy headed by King Paul I, who succeeded his brother, George II, in 1947. The years immediately following the end of World War II were followed by turbulent strife as extreme leftists carried on guerrilla warfare to upset the government.

COMMERCE AND INDUSTRIES

Agriculture is the chief industry and the land is largely in the hands of peasant proprietors. The total area, only one-fifth cultivable, is covered with mountains and occupied by lakes and wastelands. The chief crops are tobacco, currants, wheat, corn, barley, oats, olives, grapes, figs and cotton. The leading industrial products are flour, olive oil, textiles,

cigarettes, leather, machinery, chemicals and building material. Mineral deposits include lead, salt, lignite, emery and crude magnesite. The chief exports are tobacco, currants, wine and raisins, and the imports are cotton goods, woolens, coal, iron and steel, and machinery.

COMMUNICATIONS

There are 1,668 miles of railway. A canal 4 miles in length has been cut across the Isthmus of Corinth. Telegraph lines are 15,065 miles in length; telephone lines, 36,914 miles.

RELIGION AND EDUCATION

Greek Orthodox is the state religion but liberty is granted other sects. Education is compulsory between 7 and 12 years but attendance is not well enforced in the country. There are trade, agricultural and technical schools. Athens is well supplied with schools and has six of university rank, including the National University. There is also a university at Thessaloniki. The Ministry of Education has charge of the Service of Antiquities.

CHIEF TOWNS

Athens, capital, 1,130,591; Piraeus, 184,980; Thessaloniki (Salonika), 216,838; Patras, 88,-414; Rhodos, 55,181; Kavalla, 42,250.

WHERE BEAUTY REIGNS IN RUINS

Athens and Its Vestiges of a Glorious Past

In ancient times Athens was the most famous of the cities of Greece. To-day it is the capital of the modern state that bears the ancient name of Greece, but its glory lies mainly in the past. From the marble ruins of the Parthenon, which crowns the Acropolis hill, we look down upon the buildings of the modern city and sigh for the beauty that has been lost to the world in the destruction of the ancient buildings of Athens. Yet lovers of art and students of history will find in the city a source of endless joy. Even the ordinary visitor can hardly fail to be fascinated by this pleasant city and its fine situation, which has been said to rival that of Naples.

WE could, if we so desired, approach Athens by train. We should jolt into a vast modern station at the end of our journey in so commonplace a manner that it would be exceedingly difficult to believe ourselves actually in the famous city whose history is as glorious as that of the greatest empire. But let us rather make part of the journey in a steamer, which we shall imagine is now churning through the bright blue waters of the Saronic Gulf. We pass a tiny green islet crowned with the ruins of an ancient temple. Beyond is Mount Hymettus whence, long ago, honey was brought to the Athenian market—honey so fragrant that poets wrote in praise of it.

Let us keep our eyes fixed on the land for presently we see in the distance, across dull green trees, the ivory-tinted pillars of the Parthenon standing on the huge flat rock of the Acropolis. At its base are the white buildings of the modern city of Athens. Before long, our ship is in the harbor of the Piræus, the port of Athens, and we are ready to disembark.

Much that we see is modern and familiar. There are steamboats and tugs, wharves and warehouses, for the Piræus is itself a large and bustling town. Many of the ships moored to the quays are small, gaudily painted boats with large sails. These remind us that, in about 500 B.C., ships of much the same type traded with the Piræus, for even at that time it was the port of Athens.

But we cannot delay any longer by the waterside, for a train is waiting to take us to Athens—a distance of about five miles.

In the ancient days, these two cities were connected by massive walls, 16 feet wide and 30 feet high, running along each side of the road. Portions of them could now be seen if we were to go by motor or carriage along the beautiful boulevard lined with pepper trees, but if we did so we might be smothered in the dust that lies thick everywhere. Before we have been many days in Athens we shall have had enough experience of dust, and shall realize why there are so many prosperous bootblacks plying their trade in the streets.

The modern Athenians are not very different in appearance from the inhabitants of any other great city of western or southern Europe. Their clothes are lighter, of course, and their hats are generally broad-brimmed. But the short, voluminous kilts that constitute the Greek national dress (see page 42) are not commonly worn by the Athenian men, except perhaps on feast days and by some soldiers, for whom they are part of the regimental uniform. A fez may be seen occasionally and serves to remind us that we are on the threshold of the Near East. So do the many street merchants who try to sell us sweetmeats, flowers and an endless variety of cheap wares.

This Oriental atmosphere is especially noticeable in the meaner streets. Here we may see tinsmiths, cobblers and blacksmiths at work in their booths or in the open air. Cookshops abound, and we see that the food is often prepared in the streets. These establishments are very popular, and when a Greek from some country district visits Athens, he does not

HADRIAN'S ARCH stands close to Amalia Boulevard and was built by the Roman Emperor Hadrian, who did much to beautify Athens. He added a new quarter to the city which was named Hadrianapolis (City of Hadrian) and at the entrance stood this arch. The second story or "attica" was formerly filled with thin marble slabs which have long since disappeared.

© E. N. A.

GRACEFUL FIGURES support the roof of a portico on the south wall of the Erechtheum, a building constructed in the 5th century before Christ, which contained among other things the shrine of the guardian goddess of Athens—Athena Polias. The Erechtheum has since been put to many and varied uses, including a Christian church and a Turkish harem.

MODERN ATHENS AND LOFTY LYCABETTUS FROM THE STADIUM

The white marble stadium and its colonnade, built in the classical style in the nineteenth century,
add a touch of old Athens to a panorama of the new city's parks and buildings.

THE LIGHT BOATS OF FISHERMEN IN THE HARBOR OF PIRAEUS

Five miles from Athens is the ancient port of Piraeus, the capital's outlet to the sea. Precious little
of the classical past remains in this thriving center of industry and trade.

FOR THE ENRICHMENT OF THE PRESENT—THE ART OF THE PAST

The Academy of Art and Science in Athens is a re-creation of ancient building styles. Its marble is from the same source—the Pentelic quarries—as the stones of the Parthenon.

THE ACROPOLIS, or Citadel Hill, dominating the surrounding plain made an ideal spot to the early Greeks for building temples to their deities. In the centre background is the Parthenon, dedicated to Athena with Mount Lycabettus at its right, while to the left is the Temple of Erechtheus. Farther to the left is the Propylæa, which was the ceremonial approach

to these temples. Beneath the Acropolis are the ruins of the Odeum, or Concert Hall, where Athenian playgoers gathered to witness dramatic performances. In the building, erected by Herodes Atticus, a wealthy Athenian, the seats rose in semi-circles up the side of the Acropolis, giving accommodation to 5,000 spectators.

ATHENS, MOTHER CITY OF GREECE, REFLECTS A GLORIOUS PAST

Modern Athens spreads out in a jumble between the Acropolis, heart of the ancient city, and Lycabettus, the nine-hundred-foot summit that looms up in the background.

34

GENNADIUS LIBRARY, AT THE CENTER FOR AMERICAN STUDIES OF GREEK ARCHAEOLOGY AND CIVILIZATION

At the foot of Mount Lycabettus and facing Speusippus Street, in Athens, is the library of the American School for Classical Studies. The ground on which the beautiful building stands was donated by the Greek Government. Completed in 1926, the gracious structure was made possible by contributions from America. Its most striking feature is the slender columns with Ionic capitals. Within the library there is a valuable collection of rare manuscripts relating to the Byzantine Empire and to ancient and modern Greece, the gift of Dr. and Mrs. Johannes Gennadius.

© E. N. A.

THE PROPYLÆA, viewed from the northwest, seem to command the Acropolis. On the right, standing on a bastion flanking these imposing and stately ruins, is the temple of Athena Nike. Its date is uncertain but it was reconstructed in 1835 with the fragments of the original building. Like the Propylæa it is of Pentelic marble, and the sculptured frieze depicts a council of the gods. The Propylæa were begun in 437 B. C. on the foundations of an older gateway and are composed of a series of vestibules and doorways, which gave entrance to the Acropolis.

AROUND THE PARTHENON, lie shattered columns and weather-worn stones, each of which could tell a romantic story of the vanished glory of ancient Athens. In the central aisle of the Parthenon is a space paved with dark-colored stone, on which formerly stood a famous gold and ivory statue of Athena of colossal proportions, probably designed by Phidias

usually stay at a hotel, but at a rooming house that supplies him only with sleeping accommodation, for he prefers to buy his meals at the eating place that looks the most attractive.

In the more prosperous districts there are splendid stores and handsome offices, apartments and mansions. The streets are lined with trees unfamiliar to us, and there is an abundance of excellent cafés. To them the Athenians flock to discuss the latest political news and to argue interminably over affairs of state. It is this love of arguing and freedom of speech that has much to do with the political unrest in Greece.

As might be expected in a city so full of remains of the past, there are exceedingly interesting collections of antiquities in Athens. Many glorious works of art are to be seen in the Acropolis Museum, which has a collection of sculptures found on the Acropolis, and the National Archæological Museum is a vast treasure-house of all that throws light upon the ancient history of Greece. These ancient monuments are kept in repair by a special department of the Greek government while institutions supported by the French, Americans, British, Italians, Germans and Austrians aid in archæological research so that we are coming to know more and more about the ancient Greeks and their culture.

It must not be thought that where learning is concerned Athens is always looking back to vanished glories. It is not only the capital of Greece and the seat of government, but it is also the national center of learning. There are six schools of university standing which provide for advanced education and there are numerous schools for special training. A walk along University Street will soon

EWING GALLOWAY

IMPRESSIVE REMAINS OF THE SHRINE OF THE DELPHIC ORACLE

In a grotto nearby the oracle sat upon her tripod stool. When asked for advice, she stroked a laurel branch, inhaled a vapor and chanted messages inspired by the god Apollo.

THE THESEION, STAINED BY WEATHER AND AGE TO A GOLDEN HUE

On a small rise north of the Areopagus, meeting place of the ancient court of Athens, the Theseion stands out as a reminder of the architectural genius of the Greeks. Like the Parthenon, it is in the Doric style and its beautiful marble is from the Pentelic quarries.

convince us that the modern Athenians have a love for culture and are certainly progressive.

Their good taste, too, is shown in the architecture of the Academy of Science—a really noble building of classical plan, faced with gleaming white Pentelic marble such as was used in the ancient buildings. This institution does all in its power to encourage scientific studies in Greece. Another imposing building, constructed on the same lines, is the well-equipped National Library which has a very fine reading-room. Very different in outward appearance, however, is the University, which is gaudy in the bright sunlight and not at all in harmony with its surroundings.

Some of the schoolboys are educated for the Church, and these we easily recognize, for they look very like young monks. Their hair is long but is usually bunched under their hats.

As we stroll past the schools and colleges of modern Athens, we remember

that the city was famous for its learning more than four hundred years before Christ. Here the great philosopher, Socrates, taught. Here, too, his most famous pupil, Plato, also a teacher of philosophy and one of the most profound thinkers that the world has known, established his school, the Academy, early in the fourth century B.C.

But the history of Athens is not altogether a record of peace and the advance of enlightenment. Time has not been the only destroyer of the splendors of ancient days. The Persians took and sacked the city in 479 B.C., but they were driven out, never to return to Greek soil. As a protection from further invasions, the Athenians built strong walls about the city and then proceeded to construct new buildings. Many of the fine temples, which we can see in ruins to-day, were erected. Pericles was then the head of the Athenian state and this period (445 B.C. to 431 B.C.) has come to be known as the Golden Age, for he did all in his power to make Athens

FROM THE PARTHENON, the Temple of Athena, which is situated upon the summit of the Acropolis, we can look down upon modern Athens. The temple was built between 447 and 438 B. C., and is the most perfect monument of ancient Greek art. It remained almost intact until 1687, when it was seriously damaged by the explosion of a powder magazine.

the intellectual leader of the city-states. The other states were jealous and this brought about the Peloponnesian Wars which resulted in the defeat of Athens. Although Athens was occupied by the Romans after their conquest of Greece in 146 B.C., they did not prove destructive. It was after the capture of the city by the Turks in 1458 that most damage was done, much of it, regrettably, by Greek guns. In 1833, when Athens became the capital of united Greece it was little more than a hamlet standing amid glorious ruins. Despite all that has been done in modern times to make Athens a great city, these remains are still its most impressive feature. Let us climb the Acropolis to the Parthenon, a ruined temple of the goddess Athena. We can easily imagine how majestic it must have been when it was unstained by the weather and gleamed with painted decorations, when all its carvings were perfect and its pillars of marble were white and unchipped and when, above all, the huge ivory and gold statue of the goddess stood in its place.

Marvels of Artistic Craftsmanship

But the statue is gone. Much of the sculpture has been broken or removed to museums, and the pillars have suffered from bombardments. Yet even to-day the plan of the building, the height and symmetry of its columns and the power and beauty of such of its reliefs as remain, convey an impression of incomparable magnificence. It is a most inspiring illustration of the spirit of ancient Athens.

The Parthenon was the holiest shrine in the city, but not by any means the only splendid one. On the Acropolis are also the remains of the Erechtheum, a very wonderful temple containing beautiful statuary; and to the south of the Propylæa, which was the ceremonial approach to the Acropolis, is an exquisite ruined temple to Athena Nike.

From the hill we can see the Theseum, which is probably the best preserved ancient temple in all Greece. Its form shows that the Theseum was planned by an architect of great genius whose every thought was concentrated upon making

the building a masterpiece of art. Great sculptors executed the vivid carvings that adorn it, and each one of the craftsmen, too, who labored on its marble pillars, now shining like gold in the sunlight, must have been something of an artist. Altogether, if we are willing to learn, the Theseum can teach us more about Greek art in a day than all the textbooks that were ever written, for it is the result of an endeavor to erect a temple whose every detail should be ideally beautiful.

Remains That Tell of Greek Life

From the Acropolis we also notice the fifteen tall columns of the temple of the Olympian Zeus that are still standing. It is later in date than the Parthenon or the Theseum, which are almost contemporary, and it was one of the largest Greek temples ever built. According to a legend, it stands on the spot where the waters of the Flood disappeared into the earth.

Other remains tell us something of the different aspects of ancient Athenian life. There is the Stadium, for example, in which athletic contests were held. It is interesting to remember that it was here that the Olympic games were held when they were revived in 1896. But, however popular the sports in the Stadium might be with the people of Athens, they were not nearly so important as the performances in the theatres.

Two Theatres of Ancient Athens

The modern Athenian, like most other people, goes to see plays mainly for amusement; in ancient Athens, however, as in all Greek states, the drama had a religious significance. Plays were acted in honor of the god Dionysus, and this explains why the greatest theatre of ancient Athens is named the Dionysiac.

It lies at the base of the Acropolis and we can still survey the ruined stage and vast, semicircular "orchestra" from one of the many tiers of seats, although these date from Roman times. They are of limestone—except the seats of honor, which are of marble, richly carved. Here throngs of eager citizens watched the famous tragedies of Æschylus, Sophocles

TANGERINES SPREAD UPON PALM LEAVES TO TEMPT THE PASSER-BY

A wrinkled fruit vendor of Greece waits patiently at the edge of the curb for customers to purchase his freshly picked and juicy merchandise. Tangerines are also called mandarins.

THE ANCIENT TEMPLE OF ATHENA STILL RISES ABOVE ATHENS

The marble columns of the beautiful Parthenon high on the Acropolis once sheltered a huge statue of the mythical goddess.   Modern Athens has widened out from the base of its famous hill.

43

and Euripides, now enjoyed throughout the civilized world, when they were performed for the first time. We may visit another immense theater, too, the marble-built Odeum. This was erected at a much later period (160 A.D.) by a wealthy friend of Hadrian, Herodes Atticus, in memory of his wife.

As we walk about the city we pass the Tower of the Winds, where observations of the weather were made in ancient days. Not far away is the site of the Inner Kerameikos, or Agora, where Athenian municipal affairs and much business were transacted. Beyond it, again, is the Street of the Tombs, once lined from end to end

with monuments to the dead. Some magnificent examples still stand today, but alas! how few. Here we will leave Athens with the thought that if these commemorate private individuals, the city itself might be considered as one vast monument commemorating all the forgotten Athenians, by whose aid so much beauty was created. Modern Athens, with a situation that rivals even that of Naples on its famous bay, is truly charming. We cannot fail to enjoy, too, the unaffected manners and real hospitality of the true Athenian, but when we think of this Greek city it is to the wonderful Athens of old and to its people that our thoughts turn.

THREE LIONS

PRESENT-DAY GREECE IS ACUTELY INTERESTED IN ITS OWN PAST

Broken fragments of statues and buildings, excavated from the surrounding countryside, are brought to a workshop in Athens to be carefully studied and, if possible, restored.

ALBANIA AND ITS MOUNTAINEERS

The Land of the Eagle People

Albania is a rocky country with narrow valleys, volcanic mountains in the south and coastal plains in the west. The rivers are short and the roads are few and poor. The Mediterranean climate and the soil are suitable for farming but modern methods are unknown and production is low and uncertain. Poor transportation and ancient methods have also prevented the profitable use of Albania's mineral wealth. Only through outside help has the little country been able to make anything at all approaching a decent livelihood from her resources. But this foreign aid—from Italy before World War II and from the Soviet Union since—has meant more profit to the outsider than to the Albanians and has led to a loss of independence.

ALBANIA occupies a portion of the territory along the eastern coast of the Adriatic Sea. Only 10,632 square miles in area, this tiny country has enjoyed less than thirty years as a completely independent nation. After centuries of domination by the Turks, Albania secured her independence in 1912. In 1939, Italian troops marched into Albania. Since that time the country has never been free again. After World War II, a republic was established; but the Communist Party, which gained control, is under the influence of Moscow.

Albania, or Shqypnië, as the map will show us, is an oblong country with many rugged mountains, especially in the northern part. Some of the peaks of the Prokletia, or Accursed Mountains, reach over 7,000 feet in height, and the scenery is equal in beauty to any in Europe. These, as well as the mountains of the east, form a natural frontier between Albania and its neighbors, Yugoslavia and Greece. There are mountains, too, in the south, though not so high or so continuous as those of the north. In the centre is a plain, while the coast is bare and rocky alternating with marshy plains. Rivers, few in number, rise in the mountains and flow toward the sea, but of these the only one navigable is the Boyana (or Bojana) which connects Lake Scutari with the Adriatic.

Dividing Albania almost in two parts is the river Shqumb which seems to separate it also in climate and people. North of it, the winters are colder and the land less cultivable. The people have become

COUNTRY HOUSE BUILT FOR DEFENSE

Albania has ever been a land of brigands, and these and the inconveniences of the family feud have made it necessary that remote houses among the hills shall resemble fortresses.

hardier, sterner, and different in temperament from those in the south. They call themselves Ghegs. The climate of southern Albania resembles that of the south of Italy, and the people living there, called Tosks, are lively, talkative and affable. These people differ too in the manner of dress for the Tosks still wear the fusta-

Black Star

A DASHING YOUNG MAN OF ALBANIA

With his ornaments, braid-trimmed vest and plaid sash, he is ready to make merry at a wedding festival. Albanian men used to wear red fezzes; but since being freed from Turkish rule, they wear white ones.

selves, should be more backward than any other Europeans, for they are one of the oldest peoples on that continent. So early was their beginning that history and even legend does not tell when they arrived in the Balkan Peninsula. They are thought to be descendants of the earliest Aryan immigrants whom the ancient Greeks described as barbarous since they were non-Hellenic. They were a tribal people, and the succession of invaders who swept over the land subdued some, while other tribes, taking protection in the mountains, were able to resist.

This territory was part of the Roman Empire when in the fourth century A.D. that great empire was divided. Albania was then assigned to the Eastern or Byzantine Empire, the capital of which was in far-away Constantinople. There followed a period of invasions during which Goths, Slavs, Bulgars and Sicilians came but left few marks of their influence. Through it all, the Albanian people have remained Albanians and have retained their own language, customs and manners. In the fifteenth century, there was a brief period of native rule under Scanderbeg (George Castriota) who became lord of Albania and who to this day is their national hero. When he died, there was no one to take his place, and his country was bequeathed to the Venetians who, it was hoped, would hold back the Turks then pushing further and further into Europe. The Venetians failed. Albania was conquered by the Turks and was held until 1912 as a province of the Ottoman Empire. Because of its distance from Constantinople and the fact that most of the people accepted (at least in name) the Mohammedan religion, Turkey paid little attention to the Albanians. As a mark of favor, many of them were taken into the Turkish army and a few of them, such as Mehemet Ali who became famous as a

nella, or pleated white linen skirt, while the Ghegs usually wear trousers. Both, however, are seen wearing the Moslem fez.

Except for Durrës (Durazzo), which is being fully equipped, the harbors of Albania have been little developed. There is one railroad, twenty-two miles long, which connects Tirana, the capital, with Durrës. Passable roads link the few towns. However, in many places transportation is still by means of pack ponies and donkeys, especially in the mountains to the north. There are ten regular air routes in service.

It is, indeed, strange that the Albanians, or Eagle People, as they like to call them-

WEATHER-WORN CHURCH OF THE GREEK ORTHODOX FAITH

The tile roof and heavy stone walls, so typical of the Mediterranean region, offer protection against the hot summer sun; and the interior offers comfort to the followers of the Eastern Greek Church. The building has a look of repose and quiet endurance though it shows the scars of centuries. A rather unusual feature is the many-sided tower that crowns the top.

47

WHERE OLD AND NEW MINGLE, IN ALBANIA'S CAPITAL

Looking down this street in Tirana, the telegraph poles almost hide the old mosque, but you can see its slender minaret from which faithful Moslems are called to prayer. In many ways Tirana has the appearance of an ancient Moslem city. However, the street is well paved; and the buildings at the left, with their graceful, decorative balconies, are new.

viceroy of Egypt, made places for themselves in the history of Turkey or of Turkey's vast dominions.

During this period of Turkish domination the people were slowly developing a national feeling which did not make itself felt very strongly until the whole northern part of the country blazed out in revolt. For three years, from 1909–12, they fought for their freedom, and finally proclaimed their independence. They were recognized by the European powers. Having no outstanding person for a ruler, the place was offered to Prince William of Wied who had held his regal position for a few months only when World War I broke out and he was forced to take refuge in another country. Albania, then, with no one at its head, fell into a state of anarchy, and at the same time several contending armies were making use of the land as a battleground. The Albanians fought on both sides with equal enthusiasm, for they were concerned more with the actual fighting than with the interests involved. The end of the war saw them with an independent country but it also saw their land desolated. The process of reconstructing their villages and endeavoring to make the soil produce sufficient food

THREE LIONS

TAKING A MOMENT OF REST OUT OF LONG HOURS OF TOIL

Workmen relax on top of a load of produce they have been handling. In the background forest-clad mountains come down to meet the waters of Valona harbor, on the Adriatic Sea.

CARRYING THE DAY'S PURCHASES HOME FROM THE MARKET
The sure-footed donkey is a highly valuable means of transportation in Mediterranean countries
where streets are roughly paved and often too steep or narrow for any wheeled vehicle.

for their needs is occupying them even today.

The people have never produced a surplus of food. In fact, each family usually looks after its own needs, as most of them are engaged in agriculture of a primitive sort. It is the women who do most of the work, such as getting the firewood, carrying water, weaving, cooking and taking the small surplus to market.

The regard for women is higher than in most Mohammedan countries. A woman is safe in every way from the clans with which her family may be at feud, and safety is even accorded a man who may be accompanying her. In the country districts they often go unveiled, and some of them are very good to look upon. They are also much brighter and quicker witted than most Moslem women. Those who can afford it adorn themselves with embroidery and gold braid. Their

apparel, like that of the women in most Mohammedan countries, consists of pantaloons (of silk if possible), which are gathered in at the ankles with gold-embroidered ankle bands. With these is worn a blouse made with wide flowing sleeves, and this costume is further embellished by a jacket or bolero richly embroidered in gold thread and studded with imitation stones. Some of the embroidery which comes from Albania is very fine. Most of it is used at home, however, and very little ever reaches the world's markets.

A marriage in Albania is an interesting event. Children are betrothed when very young and marry as early as thirteen years. On the day of the wedding the bride, in apparent protest, is taken screaming and struggling from her father's house, and is carried by her brothers to the husband's family, who come to meet them at a place between the lands of the two tribes.

SOVFOTO

ALBANIAN FARM GIRLS GATHER A CROP OF WARM-CLIMATE MELONS

The mountains in the background show how rough and rugged the terrain of the little Mediterranean country is. Only a small portion of Albania's land can be used for crops and pasturage.

51

REFRESHING PAUSE IN THE DAY'S OCCUPATIONS

A street vendor gives two Albanian workmen an opportunity for a brief respite. From his rough
cart, he is dispensing what appears to be milk and bread—energy-giving foods anywhere.

It is not the custom for two people within the tribe to marry. On arriving at her husband's house, she takes a place in the corner and stands for three days and nights with her hands folded on her breast, her eyes downcast and without food or drink. In this way, the bride is a suppliant for the gift of fire, of life and of the mystery that continues the race. For six months, she must obey the commands of her elders and speak only when addressed and then some day when it is convenient she and her husband will go to the priest to be married.

A birth is none the less interesting for some ancient customs are still in use— customs that may be two thousand years old. When a child is born, cakes made of a mixture of flour, water and olive oil are fried and sent to the relatives and friends. Then etiquette requires that the relatives must call within three days. On the third day a banquet is given and pres- ents are brought to the mother. Accord- ing to a legend, on the third night after the child is born, three fairies appear carrying with them the skein of fate. The first spins the thread, the second measures it off on the spinning-wheel and the third cuts the thread with the scissors. Thus the destiny of the child is determined.

Due to the influence of the Turks, many of the Albanians, as we have said, became Moslems. Now about two-thirds of them call themselves Moslems, although they are not very strict about their religion, and have a tolerance for the Christians, as the Christians have for them, that is not found elsewhere—certainly not in the Near East. One will find the Christians using a prayer rug, and Moslems observing Roman Catholic feast days. But the Albanian is first of all an Albanian and no religion interferes with his own standard of right and wrong. Taking revenge when revenge is due is a matter of necessity to an Albanian,

SOVFOTO

"LIQUID GOLD" GUSHES FROM A PIPE IN AN OIL FIELD

The mountainous little Balkan country has been able to produce enough petroleum for its own use in recent years. There is a pipeline from its principal fields to the seaport of Valona.

and this has often brought about feuds among the various tribes.

In the old days Albania had a peculiar legal system called "the law of Lek." Lek was a fifteenth-century tribal chieftain who wrote down the unwritten laws of his people. The law of Lek placed great emphasis on the virtues of hospitality and of keeping one's promised word. Most of the law, however, was concerned with rules for conducting the feuds. By a certain kind of pledge, for instance, some persons were granted protection during the quarrels. This applied especially to boys under sixteen years of age and to women. A man accompanied by a woman would be safe.

Up until the early 1900's, the beys (Turkish governors) were the aristocrats of Albania. They lived in the hills in feudal splendor. King Zog, who reigned from 1928 until 1939, was the only Albanian monarch the country ever had.

The Albanian language, which has survived so many centuries, has ever been a puzzle to philologists. Unlike the Greek or Slav of the neighboring countries, it is thought to have come from the primitive Illyrian, the language of Macedonia in the time of Alexander the Great. All attempts of the Serb, Greek and Turk have failed to destroy the Albanians' love for it. Once, in southern Albania, where some of the people are Greek Orthodox Christians, the priests taught that it was useless to pray in Albanian for God could not understand it. The Turks forbade giving instruction or printing books in the language but books were printed abroad and smuggled in.

What education the people had was chiefly gained in the schools started by the

SOVFOTO

A JEEPLIKE TRUCK RECEIVES CARGO FROM A COASTAL STEAMER

The ship is docked at Durazzo, Albania's chief port, which is on the north shore of the Gulf of Durazzo, a little arm of the Adriatic. Most of the city's trade is with ports of other Balkan countries—offering olive oil, grains and tobacco in exchange for manufactured articles. Durazzo has a beautiful location, on a rocky promontory just south of Mount Durazzo.

ON A COBBLE-STONED SQUARE IN TIRANA

Once the red fez was the national headdress of the Turks and some other Moslem peoples. Since the 1920's its use has declined, but it is still to be seen in Albania. This family group (both husband and wife in baggy trousers) is perhaps from the country, spending a day in Tirana, the capital. At the right of the picture are arches of a famous old covered well.

55

Austrians and the Italians, each of whom had an eye to annexing the territory. Students who could afford it were sent away to Vienna or Paris or to the American School in Constantinople for advanced training but a vast majority of the people were totally illiterate. In the few years following her independence Albania set up several hundred primary and a few secondary schools. Primary education was free and compulsory, but there were not enough schools for the people within the age limits and the law was not enforced.

Albania's industries are little developed, each family generally providing for its own needs. Cattle-raising is the most important activity, and receives special attention. In the mountain pastures, goats and sheep graze. The chief dairy product is cheese. It is a staple of diet and an item of export. Tobacco is grown in sufficient quantity for shipment abroad.

Mineral resources, excepting oil, have been largely neglected. But Albanian crude-oil production was the sixth highest in Europe before 1940.

Between the two world wars, Italy had a strong influence on affairs in Albania. Italian businessmen built up the petroleum industry and financed other plans. But Italy wanted mostly to rule the Balkans. In 1939 she invaded Albania as a first step in this direction. For five years thereafter Albania was occupied by either the Italian or the German army.

After liberation in 1944, the new Communist Government turned to Yugoslavia for the help that Albania once had received from Italy. In 1948, however, when Yugoslavia broke with the Cominform (Stalin's international propaganda organization), Albania chose to side with Russia and abandon her treaties with Yugoslavia. As a result, Albania has been in a precarious position. Though dominated by Russia, she is outside the iron curtain and cut off from sources of food and raw materials.

ALBANIA: FACTS AND FIGURES

THE COUNTRY

A communist republic since the end of World War II, Albania is bounded on the north and east by Yugoslavia, on the east and south by Greece and on the west by the Strait of Otranto, the Adriatic Sea and Yugoslavia. The area of the country is 10,629 square miles, and the latest estimate of the population is 1,175,000.

GOVERNMENT

For centuries a semifeudal state under Turkish rule, Albania proclaimed its independence in 1913 and was a principality or aristocratic republic from then until 1928, when the President made himself King Zog I. His government included an elected chamber and a Cabinet. Zog was driven out by Italian invasion in 1939, when the King of Italy became King of Albania. German occupation replaced Italian in 1943, and a regency was set up. Albania was proclaimed a republic in 1946, and an all-communist Government fashioned a Soviet-type Constitution.

COMMERCE AND INDUSTRIES

Before World War II, the country had but 10% of its land under cultivation; animal husbandry was the principal industry. Number of livestock—mostly sheep and goats—is nearly 3,000,000. Principal crops are corn and wheat. Like other East European communist countries Albania has emphasized the development of manufacturing. The Government claims large postwar increases in the production of food, textiles, leather footwear, building materials, tobacco, chemicals and electric power. Considerable mineral resources include deposits of copper, oil, chromite, bitumen and salt. Trade with Italy, Yugoslavia and Great Britain, once considerable, has virtually stopped as a result of Albania's close ties with the Soviet Union.

COMMUNICATIONS

There are motor roads connecting all the principal towns, and three railroads have been built since the end of World War II. Communications in the mountainous interior are primitive. Principal and most modern port is Durrës (Durazzo). There are 7 radio transmitters (state owned) and 12 daily newspapers.

RELIGION AND EDUCATION

About 70% of the people are Moslems, 20% Orthodox Catholic and 10% Roman Catholic. Clergy and church leaders have been forced to submit to state control. Adult education is encouraged as part of state effort to reduce illiteracy; 10% to 20% of the people are now literate. There are about 2,200 elementary schools as well as secondary, teacher training, medical, trade, agricultural, art and technical schools.

CHIEF TOWNS

Tirana, the capital, has a population of 64,000; Scutari, 35,000; Koritsa, 25,000; Elbasan, 17,000; Durazzo, 16,000; Valona, 16,000; Berat, 13,000; Argyrokastron, 12,000.

THE FOLK OF YUGOSLAVIA

Among the Serbs, Croats and Slovenes

Yugoslavia (sometimes spelled Jugo-Slavia) is a Balkan state that was created at the end of World War I by uniting Montenegro and portions of the old Austro-Hungarian Empire with the kingdom of Serbia. Most of the inhabitants of this mountainous region are Southern Slavs, but in the northern regions there is a large number of Germans and Hungarians. Perhaps the most interesting people are the inhabitants of Montenegro, the Black Mountain. Montenegrins are Serbian highlanders who successfully resisted the Turks for five centuries while peoples around them were subdued by the fierce conqueror. In this chapter we shall read about these proud mountaineers and the other inhabitants of Yugoslavia and of this country which faces the Adriatic, stretching from Albania to the Alps.

YUGOSLAVIA, the land of the Southern Slavs, is made up of several countries and peoples. It includes Croatia, a part of the region known as Macedonia and also Slavonia, Bosnia, Herzegovina, Dalmatia, Slovenia, Serbia and Montenegro. This varied country was formerly called the kingdom of the Serbs, Croats and Slovenes, all of whom, racially, are Slavs, and it was created at the end of World War I by uniting Montenegro and part of the former Austro-Hungarian Empire with the old kingdom of Serbia.

Montenegro, formerly an independent kingdom, is the most interesting part of Yugoslavia, and its people are renowned for their bravery and love of independence throughout the whole world. Surrounded by powerful enemies, only the excessively mountainous nature of their country and their own courage have preserved the independence of the Montenegrins.

Let us imagine a land consisting almost entirely of naked rock with rugged mountains stretching as far as it is possible to see, a land hot in summer and bitterly cold in winter—that is Montenegro, the Black Mountain. It is difficult to believe that people can dwell amid such desolation, yet a splendid and freedom loving race has made this barren land its home.

After the Turks had defeated the Serbians at Kossovo, 1389, the Montenegrins retired to the mountains and became an independent people. The Mohammedan Turks at that time had a vast empire in Asia, but not content with this, they sought to conquer Europe. They swept through what is now Albania, Bulgaria, Rumania and Serbia, and then, confident of victory, sent an army to conquer the people of the Black Mountain.

The Montenegrins had to withdraw from the fertile land about Lake Scutari and, retreating into the mountains, founded their capital on the plain of Cetigne, or Cetinje. The Turks soon marched after them, but behind every rock stood a Montenegrin ready to shed his blood for his country. Charge after charge was repulsed, and regiment after regiment of Turks had to admit humiliating defeat.

There were large numbers of Turks to every Montenegrin but in spite of overwhelming odds, Montenegro was never conquered. For five centuries these two nations fought till at last the gallant and undefeated Montenegrins were protected from Turkey by the principal European powers. Thus, this little nation came about, and so it is no wonder that today the men walk with the proud step of conquerors. They are fine looking, too, as many of them are very tall, often exceeding six feet.

The Montenegrin gentleman wears a gorgeous and picturesque costume. A brightly colored coat hangs from shoulder to knee, and is open in front to display a beautifully embroidered waistcoat and baggy breeches tucked into high, Russian boots. A scarf encircles his waist, and in it are stuck a revolver and a whole armory of knives. Upon his head is worn a "kapa," or cap, of black with a crimson

HOLBACH

THE NARENTA VALLEY is one of Bosnia's most beautiful districts. Sometimes it narrows to a deep gloomy ravine, but often, as here, near Jablonica, green fields, fruitful orchards and groves of chestnut-trees line the banks of the river. As the whole course of the river is through mountainous country, the valley is usually narrow and is hemmed in by rugged peaks. For only ten miles, near its mouth, is the Narenta navigable, but the pathway it has cut through the mountains enables Serajevo to communicate with the Adriatic coast.

HOLBACK

THE SHEEP MARKET of Jezero is not held in the village, but in a pleasant meadow beside the River Pliva. There, the Mohammedan villagers—for the inhabitants of Jezero, like many other Bosnians, adopted the religion of their former conquerors, the Turks—drive their horned and long-fleeced flocks. The Pliva, just below Jezero, widens into a chain of small lakes and at Jajce, six miles below the point that we see here, falls over ninety feet into the River Vrbas, forming a beautiful cascade which is considered one of the finest in all Europe.

THE REPUBLIC OF YUGOSLAVIA

top, symbolic of the blood shed for freedom. The peasants dress similarly, only the materials are much coarser.

The Montenegrin is seldom to be seen without his gun, the symbol of his hard-won freedom. The late King Nicholas of Montenegro often used to stop one of his subjects in the street in order to examine his rifle, and if it were dirty, which was very seldom, the punishment would be severe. When a Montenegrin is happy or excited he discharges his gun into the air, which is naturally rather alarming.

Cetinje, the capital of Montenegro, has no port of its own, but does its shipping through Cattaro, on the coast, a town which possesses a wonderful natural harbor of indescribable beauty. The harbor is land-locked except for a narrow opening into the Adriatic Sea. There are several of these beautiful lake-like inlets along the coast, and they have been compared with the fjords of Norway.

The port of Cattaro itself is full of interest. It is so closely ringed by the mountains that it can scarcely find room beside the waters of the gulf. In the streets we may see Montenegrin peasants who have brought their market produce down the long zigzags of the "Stairs of Cattaro," a road carved out of the face of a mountain and the only way into Montenegro from the west.

Cetinje is really not very interesting, except from an historical point of view. There are no imposing buildings and we see no crowds in the streets. The market square is a feature of Cetinje, as it is of all Montenegrin towns, but there are no shops as we know them—in fact there is not a large glass window in the whole town. One sees many cafés and everywhere the colorful clothes that the people love to wear.

A characteristic of the Montenegrins is their absolute honesty. To be called a thief is a terrible insult, second only to being called a coward. They are a strong and hardy people, although they exist on a frugal diet of salted fish, called scoranze, potatoes, heavy bread made of rye or corn, and cheese.

On this simple fare, however, the Montenegrins perform wonderful feats of endurance and never show fatigue. Unfortunately, however, the men despise all manual labor and are content to sit about and dream of their victories. We may see old women and young girls toiling up a rocky path with buckets of water—which is sometimes more precious than wine for the spring may be a two hours' journey away—while near by may be sitting two handsome warriors who will never attempt to help these tired women, not even if they be their own sisters or mothers.

Christmas is a great festival in Montenegro. On Christmas Eve ivy branches are hung over the doors in order to bring good luck. Everyone is gay, songs are sung and revolver shots fired all day long. Easter is also a great festival all over Yugoslavia, and there is much rejoicing and feasting.

The Montenegrins are fond of family life and are devoted to their children, who are brought up very strictly and are taught to be brave and manly. Girl babies are counted as a misfortune because they are unable to fight. Once women were not counted in the census, which included only those able to bear arms for their country.

The Serbians, unlike the Montenegrins, were unable to hold out against the Turks, and for 345 years, they formed a pashalik, or province, of the Ottoman Empire. However, they had not given up their dream of a nation of Southern Slavs and they were frequently at battle with their oppressors until about 1830 when they became an autonomous state. Their history from then on did not run smoothly for there were constant upsets due to internal politics and there were wars with Turkey

THREE LIONS

A FARMING SCENE on the broad, flat Posavina Plain of central Yugoslavia. Lying along the banks of the Sava River, this area constitutes some of the country's richest farmland.

© E. N. A.

ABOVE JAJCE, the capital of medieval Bosnia, the River Pliva is a rushing torrent interrupted by many rapids. The people who dwell in its fair, green valley realize the strength and usefulness of the swift stream, and so it has many a mill-wheel to turn before it reaches Jajce, a steep-roofed hill-top town which looks down on the river valley.

"HALF ORIENTAL, half Italian and wholly Herzegovinian" is a phrase that has been used to describe Mostar with its many minarets and red-roofed white-walled houses. It lies in a beautiful and fertile valley between the hills of Hum and Podvelez, towards the latter of which we are looking. In the right background is the Greek cathedral.

ARGOSIES OF OLD SET OUT FROM THE HARBOR OF DUBROVNIK

Broad beaches and architectural riches attract tourists from all over the world to this loveliest of spots on the Dalmatian coast of the Adriatic. Known through most of its history as Ragusa, Dubrovnik was long a republic and the port for overland trade to and from Constantinople. Modern docking facilities make it one of Yugoslavia's busiest ports.

again, resulting in complete independence in 1878. Wars with their neighbors, the Bulgarians, followed, then came the Balkan wars and the murder of the Archduke Francis Ferdinand at Serajevo, which touched off the World War of 1914-18. After these years of struggle, Serbia finally came to realize the "Great Serbian Idea" upon the establishment of the new state of Yugoslavia, land of the southern Slavs.

The population of Yugoslavia has increased at one of the fastest rates in Europe. And about three out of four persons live on small farms, working with very crude implements. Indeed, farmers in some of the remote parts of the country have never used anything more modern than a wooden plow.

Less than one-fifth of the land is really fertile, and the good farming region—the north and east—is the most densely populated section of the country. Consequently, Yugoslavia is always dangerously close to famine. When crops fail, people go hungry.

Yugoslavia has been a communist state since World War II. The Yugoslav Government now invests large sums of money to build heavy industries in the cities. It feels that industry can, first of all, supply the tractors and trucks that are needed so badly on the farms. In fact, Yugoslavia has need of modern machinery in every field of manufacture. Increased production in industry will call for more workers; many young men and women will leave the farms and villages and go to the cities to earn the high wages that are promised them there.

These changes have undoubtedly affected the daily lives of the Serbs, Croats, Slovenes and others who make up the Yugoslav nation. In the old days these groups fought among each other bitterly, but city life has a tendency to break down barriers of prejudice. Though it is at odds with the Soviet Union, Yugoslavia is still a communist country and controls every facet of the lives of its people.

When a young Serbian goes to ask a girl to marry him he takes two friends and brings a flat cake made of wheat and a bunch of flowers. One of his friends

MACEDONIAN MOSLEMS GATHER ROUND THE FOUNTAIN OF A MOSQUE

At the entrance to a mosque in Skoplje, capital of Yugoslav Macedonia, several fezzed loungers pass the quiet time of day.   More than one Yugoslav in ten is of the Mohammedan faith.

BUSHBY

THE RIVER NARENTA divides Mostar into two parts, but most of the chief buildings are on the left, or east, bank. The several minarets that over-top the houses show that Islam has here a strong hold—indeed half the population are Mohammedans. This is not surprising as the town was the Turkish headquarters in Herzegovina. Nevertheless, Mostar is also the seat of a Roman Catholic and of a Greek Bishop. The town dates from Roman days and commands the principal pass between the interior and the sea.

HOLBACH

AN OLD BRIDGE with a single, graceful arch spans the River Narenta and has provided Mostar with its name—"most" meaning "a bridge" and "star" meaning "old." Like the two gate-towers that guard its approach, it is said to be of Roman origin, but it really dates from the fifteenth century. A new bridge is used by vehicles in crossing the river

THE HORNS AND DRUMS OF THE GIPSY BAND SERENADE A BRIDE

A wedding party is not a wedding party in the western Macedonian village of Galicnik without the gay music of the gipsy bandsmen who are ever willing to lend their talents. Galicnik is on the Radika River in the high cattle-raising country near the border of Albania. The principal occupation of the villagers, aside from herding, is the making of cheese.

carries a pistol, for any joyful event is announced by the firing of rifles or pistols. After every convention has been carefully observed, the young man is encouraged by the father of the girl to come and ask for his bride. If he is successful, he pays a sum of money to show that he has bought her.

The marriage service usually takes place on a Sunday, but the celebrations often begin as early as the preceding Thursday, when special wedding cakes are prepared in the bride's and bridegroom's houses.

On Saturday the dowry is taken to the bridegroom's house. On Sunday the bride is decked with orange blossoms, and a coin is hidden in her hair, to prevent her ever wanting money in after life. The couple are presented with crowns of flowers or metal; they then walk with the priest three times round the altar, while the guests sprinkle them with raisins, sweets and nuts. Although the Serbs, Croats and Slovenes are not rich, there is always plenty of food at the wedding feast.

The costumes of the peasants are picturesque although in most parts of Serbia they do not display the desire for color seen throughout the Near East. White or gray linen clothes are worn by both men and women, and during the cold weather, they put on tweeds or woolen clothes and thick sheepskin coats with the fleece inside. The national costumes vary according to religion and locality. The Mohammedan men, for instance, wear a fez and the women wear baggy trousers.

There is beautiful scenery in Serbia, especially along the Danube, and a large part of the land is covered with splendid forests. We may sometimes come upon a gipsy camp, but though the gipsies occasionally settle down, forming separate camps or villages, they usually prefer a wandering life. They are generally admirable musicians, and almost every town possesses a gipsy band.

Croatia and Slavonia were freed from the Turkish rule in 1718 by the Austrians and, except for a brief period during which they were under French rule due to Napoleon's conquest, they remained as Austrian possessions until the end of World War I.

A GREAT INDUSTRIAL PLANT THAT CONVERTS COAL INTO COKE

Only brown coal is mined in Yugoslavia, and some is imported from other lands. In large, modern factories, such as the one shown here, the coal is made into coke, one of the most important fuels of the twentieth century. Much of Yugoslavia's coke is consumed by the country's rapidly expanding iron, steel and allied industries.

CROATIAN LOVERS are seen here wearing their holiday best to celebrate a feast day. Then both men and women array themselves in bright-colored clothes, often of silk, on which much hand-work has been lavished. The Croats, like the Serbs, are mostly Slavs by race, but differ in their modes of living and in their religious beliefs.

THIS YUGOSLAVIAN GIRL is posing in a gaily colored peasant costume typical of those which were once worn in her native Serbia, today a part of the Federation of Yugoslavia. After posing for this picture she returned to her work in the fields. There is still little industrialization in Yugoslavia, and farm women must work hard, raising crops by primitive methods.

SERBIAN WOMEN DRAW WATER FROM AN OLD VILLAGE FOUNTAIN

Serbian housewives fill earthen jugs, metal pots and a sprinkling can at the village fountain. It is their chief source of water for all washing, cooking and drinking needs.

72

LUMBER WAITING TO BE PUT ABOARD SHIP AT SENJ

The small harbor town is on the Adriatic Sea in western Croatia. Senj is said to be the oldest town in the region, dating back to the Romans, and was once a hiding place for pirates.

HOUSEWIVES STOP FOR A MOMENT OF GOSSIP IN A SERBIAN TOWN

The houses of Galicnik follow the road that winds up the side of a steep hill. There is good pasturage on the slopes; and the making of cheese is a profitable occupation in the town.

Racially, they are the same as the Serbs but most of them are Roman Catholic by religion, while in other parts of Yugoslavia, the larger number are Greek Orthodox or Mohammedan. The peasants occupying Croatia and Slavonia are perhaps less prosperous than those of Serbia as the climate is more severe. Among the Karst Mountains they have sudden and violent climatic changes, and at times the "bora," a fierce northeasterly wind, sweeps over the land. The riverside districts are barren, monotonous steppes which are somewhat unhealthy, especially beside the River Sava, where marsh fevers are prevalent.

The Croatian homes are more primitive than those of the Montenegrins and Serbians, for many of them are merely rough huts of wood with thatched roofs. As in Serbia proper, there is no middle class between the peasants and the very few educated people, and those who do

the little trading that there is are mostly foreigners—Germans, Italians or Jews. Numerous gipsies wander from village to village, selling and buying horses.

The Croatian farmers produce corn in abundance and also cultivate wheat, oats, rye and barley, but much of the land is not fit for cultivation. The plum orchards of Slavonia are wonderfully beautiful when in blossom. Most of the fruit is dried, but some of it is made into a kind of homemade brandy which the peasants love. Many of the estates are planted with mulberry trees for feeding silkworms. Parts of both Croatia and Slavonia are covered by forests, and herds of swine feed in the oak and beech woods.

Dairy-farming and bee-keeping are other occupations, and horse-breeding is a flourishing industry. The farmers are constantly trying to improve their livestock by importing purer breeds.

KOSTICH

A SUNNY HARVEST MORNING IN A FIELD OF FLAX

The mist is rising in wispy clouds from the mountains beyond the meadow as the morning sun warms the ground. These women are at work early, gathering the flax and tying the stems in bundles. Flax plants must be harvested carefully by hand, for the fibers lose something of their spinning value if they are cut by a sharp instrument.

KOSTICH

GOTHIC SPIRES OF THE CATHEDRAL OF ST. STEFAN IN ZAGREB

The magnificent fifteenth-century edifice, which stands in the Main Square, is viewed from the Strossmayer Promenade in the old part of the city. Zagreb is the capital and cultural center of Croatia and is the second largest city in Yugoslavia. It is a trading and manufacturing town located on the abundant agricultural plains of the Sava River.

WHITE GEESE PLAY "FOLLOW THE LEADER" IN A SERBIAN FARMYARD

The geese furnish eggs, down and feathers as well as meat. High above the waddling fowl is an oddly shaped bird house or roost to entice small feathered visitors. For a time the Yugoslavian Government tried to collectivize farms on the Soviet model. In 1953, however, it gave up this plan and announced that Western types of agricultural co-operatives would be formed.

TROUT-FISHERMAN'S DELIGHT

Lake Ochrida (or Ohrid), in southern Yugoslavia and eastern Albania, is twenty-five miles long and as much as 938 feet deep in some portions. Nestled high in the mountains, this lake is breathtaking in its scenic beauty. Its waters abound with rare fish, notably salmon trout. Fishing nets can be seen hanging to dry from the poles on the beach at the right.

North of Croatia, parts of the former Austrian territory of Carniola, Corinthia and Styria have been united to form Slovenia, so named because it is inhabited by Slovenes. Here, these Slavonic people have lived since the seventh century and have retained a language quite distinct from that of their neighbors although it is related. They are mostly peasants, but they produce some tannin, and bentwood furniture is manufactured to a considerable extent.

Dalmatia, the most beautiful province of Yugoslavia, consists of a strip of coastland running down most of the eastern shore of the Adriatic Sea. No part of the Mediterranean shore, except the coast of Greece, is so deeply indented as the Dalmatian coastline, with its multitude of rockbound bays and inlets sheltered from the open sea by a barrier of beautiful rugged islands.

In calm weather the channels between the islands and the mainland resemble a chain of lakes. All along the cliffs are half-ruined castles and monasteries, which seem to cling to the rugged rocks and add to the beauty of a scene not easily forgotten. Although it is not so rocky as Montenegro, the country is everywhere mountainous.

The highlands of Dalmatia are composed of dry, barren limestone which is honeycombed with caverns and underground watercourses, into which all the rain immediately goes. Even the few surface rivers often suddenly disappear underground and do not reappear for many miles. Owing to this strange geological formation the peasants are only able to cultivate about one-tenth of their land.

The once famous forests of Dalmatia were either burned by pirates or were cut down to provide timber for shipbuilding, and all attempts to replant them have failed owing to the lack of soil and rain. The peasants rival those of Montenegro in courage and stature and are like them, too, in having an olive skin with dark hair and eyes, although sometimes

77

QUEUING UP AT A BUS STOP IN MODERN BELGRADE

The bus is an up-to-date one as are the apartment houses in the background. Though Belgrade is an old city, it has been transformed in the years since 1866, when it was finally freed from the Turks. Outside of Yugoslavia, it is still usually called Belgrade, but its official name since 1929 has been Beograd. It was once the capital of the Kingdom of Serbia.

one sees the fair type with blue eyes.

The people of Dalmatia are hardy fishermen, their fleets taking in large catches of tunny, lobsters and sardines. Dalmatia's coastal waters are also rich in coral and sponges.

Across the Dinaric Alps from Dalmatia stretch the rugged limestone plateaus that form the region of Bosnia and Herzegovina, two states with long histories of subjection to a number of countries. They were finally united as one province by Austria-Hungary in 1878 and became a part of Yugoslavia in 1918.

The Hard Lot of the Farmer

Herzegovina and western Bosnia are poor farming lands. The valleys cut out by the Bosna and Vrbas rivers are fertile, but the yield of crops is low. Methods of cultivation are ancient. The poor mountain roads have kept the peasants from contact with the outside, and very near starvation year after year.

The northern and eastern parts of Bosnia are more fortunate. Here broad plains watered by the Sava and the Drina make farming easier and more productive.

There are also large mineral deposits scattered throughout the highlands of Bosnia-Herzegovina, and the tumbling mountain streams are great potential sources of hydroelectric power.

The greatest city of Yugoslavia is Belgrade—often called the northern gateway to the Balkans. Situated at the junction of the Danube and Sava rivers and commanding a rising bluff, it has been the center of trade for a rich region and a strategic site for military installations.

Building and Rebuilding

During World War I the city was occupied by Austrian troops. At the end of that war it became the capital of the new state of Yugoslavia. In the next twenty years the city was transformed and its population increased more than three times. Belgrade received a terrific bombing when the Germans occupied Yugoslavia in 1941; many buildings, such as the national library and the state theater, were destroyed or damaged. Most of them have been restored since or replaced with parks and houses.

We have seen that Yugoslavia has many problems. A high rate of farm production, for example, is a persistent requirement that is seldom met. Farm regions are overpopulated, and poor transportation makes the introduction of scientific methods and the distribution of goods extremely difficult.

During the 1920's improvement was hampered by hostility between the Croats and Serbs, who could not seem to work together in Parliament. Strong measures were taken by the King to control the situation. He closed Parliament and imposed military rule, which forbade the printing and reading of pamphlets likely to inflame regional ill will. Eventually the King restored order and brought the Croats and Serbs together. A period of recovery at the close of the decade was the result of this co-operation.

The Effects of Depression

Yet prosperity was cut short by the great depression of the 1930's. Yugoslavia, like all the countries of Europe, could find no markets for the products of industry. There was widespread want and unrest. In order to keep the country from complete collapse, the Government was forced to borrow money from Germany.

Later, however, Germany made Yugoslavia pay heavily for this indebtedness. In 1941 the Germans needed to send troops and materials to Africa, and demanded passage through Yugoslavia. When the Yugoslavs refused, Hitler ordered the invasion of the country and air raids on Belgrade. The entire country was occupied within ten days.

During the four-year occupation that followed, two groups—one led by the Serbian patriot Mihailovitch; the other by Josip Broz, or Tito, a Croatian Communist—waged telling warfare against German and Italian troops. Yet because the resistance groups differed in political ideals they could not present a united front to the enemy. Indeed, part of their time was spent in attacks upon each other. In 1944 the Allied governments openly supported Tito rather than Mihailovitch, upon the assumption that Tito waged more effective resistance to Hitler's troops.

Tito fought alongside Russian troops when they invaded Serbia in 1944 and also helped repulse the forces of Mihailovitch. When the war ended Tito set up a communist government. In 1946 he enacted a constitution modeled after the Soviet pattern. Mihailovitch was executed for collaboration with the Germans, and church leaders were imprisoned.

As time went on, Tito balked at Russian leadership. In 1948, his Government was banned from membership in the Cominform, the Soviet propaganda agency. From then on Yugoslavia was forced to make her way without the help of her former allies. She was shut off from trade on the Danube and was constantly fearful of attacks on her borders. The Government, therefore, eased its early hostility toward the West. Loans were obtained from the United States and a trade agreement was made with Britain.

Tito's tight grasp on the affairs of the entire population relaxed. Drought in 1949 and 1950 prevented further collectivization of farms. The Government continued to watch its large investments closely, but it gave local governments more authority than before in the regulation of social as well as industrial affairs. Elected representatives of labor began to take part in settling disputes and in planning production.

YUGOSLAVIA: FACTS AND FIGURES

THE COUNTRY

Yugoslavia has been both a monarchy and a republic since its formation at the end of World War I. At the end of World War II, it became the Federal Peoples Republic, composed of the 6 republics of Serbia, Croatia, Slovenia, Montenegro, Macedonia and Bosnia-Herzegovina, and the 2 autonomous provinces of Vojvodina and Kosovo-Metohija. It is bounded by Austria and Hungary on the north, by Rumania and Bulgaria on the east, by Greece on the southeast, by Albania on the south and the Adriatic Sea and Italy on the west. During World War II, the country was overrun by the Germans and partitioned among Germany, Italy, Hungary and Bulgaria. The Germans were driven out by the Russian Army in 1944. Its area is 99,069 square miles and the population is 16,338,500.

GOVERNMENT

The constitution provides for an elected parliament which elects a Presidium for 4 years. The Presidium elects two houses, the Federal Assembly and the House of the Peoples, for 4 years each. The president of the Presidium is the head of the state. The Government is communist though anti-Russian.

COMMERCE AND INDUSTRIES

Agriculture occupies about 70% of the population. Besides corn, wheat, oats, barley and rye, there are grown large quantities of grapes, plums, apples, pears, olives, sugar-beet and tobacco. Cocoon production is important. Fishing and the raising of livestock are carried on extensively. There is a large forest area. Minerals including lignite, iron, copper ore, gold, lead, chrome, antimony and cement are abundant but little developed. Oil is found to some extent. The chief industries are flour milling, brewing and distilling, cotton-spinning and weaving, tanning, boot-making, pottery and iron-working. Carpet-weaving (notably at Pirot) is an old industry. Meat-packing is a growing industry as is also cardboard- and paper-making.

The chief exports are wheat, timber, livestock, animal products, corn and eggs, and the imports are cotton and cotton goods, metals, machinery, chemicals and mineral oil.

COMMUNICATIONS

Total railway mileage, 7,010, mainly state-owned. Roads aggregate about 25,000 and are largely in an indifferent state. There is a navigation syndicate controlling the rivers Danube and Sava. The total length of navigable waterway is 1,200 miles. There are 12,000 miles of telegraph and 150,000 miles of telephone line. Air service connects Belgrade, Zagreb, and Skoplje.

RELIGION AND EDUCATION

About 48% of the population belong to Greek Orthodox Church, 37% are Roman Catholics, 2% Protestants and 13% Mohammedans. All ecclesiastical officials are controlled by a Minister of Public Worship. There is complete freedom of conscience. Primary education free and compulsory, under Ministry of Education. There are veterinary, law and engineering schools and universities in Belgrade, Ljubljana, Skoplje, Subotica and Zagreb.

CHIEF TOWNS

Belgrade, capital, 450,000; Zagreb, 325,000; Ljubljana, 130,000; Sarajevo, 125,000; Subotica, 115,000; Skoplje, 95,000; Novi Sad, 80,000; and Rijeka, 75,000.

THE BULGARS AT HOME

A Peasant People and Their Historic Land

The story of the Bulgarians is one of centuries of almost continuous warfare. It began almost as soon as the original Bulgars (they later mixed with Slavs) arrived from Asia in 679 A.D. and occupied part of the Balkan Peninsula. After enduring Turkish misrule from 1396 to 1878, the Bulgarians at last won independence in 1908. Then they were caught up in the terrible conflicts of World Wars I and II. Both of these wars ended, for them, in disaster and defeat. World War II was scarcely over when, in September 1946, the Bulgarians ousted their nine-year-old King, Simeon II, and established a republic. They drew up a constitution modeled after that of the Soviet Union, and their Government is now controlled by the Bulgarian Communist Party.

IF we glance at a map of Europe we shall see that Bulgaria forms a part of the Balkan Peninsula. It is wedged between Greece and Turkey on the south, and Rumania on the north, the republic of Yugoslavia on the west. The eastern boundary is formed by the Black Sea.

Sofia, the capital and largest city, lies between two mountain ranges in the heart of the Balkans. It has a population of about half a million people. Sofia is the major center of transportation, manufacturing and commerce. Its educational facilities include a university, a polytechnique institute and schools of various types ranging from academies of science and art to schools of physical education and military tactics. These, together with an opera house, theaters, a library, an astronomical observatory and museums, make the capital also a cultural center of Bulgaria.

Among its architectural masterpieces are the cathedral of St. Alexander Nevski, the hero-saint of Bulgaria, built by subscription of the peasants at a cost of $5,000,000, and the chapel of St. George, the oldest building in Sofia. There are several mosques, the only remnants of the days when Bulgaria was the Turkish province of Roumelia. These include the Banya-Bashi mosque, a minaret still used for Moslem worship, and the Black Mosque that was converted into a church. Sofia was rebuilt in 1880, and today it bears little resemblance to the Turkish town which it replaced. It has broad, tree-bordered avenues, public parks and modern buildings.

Yet despite its prosperous appearance, it gives unmistakable evidence of being the capital of a war-weary country that has been twice defeated. It is no longer the spruce capital of the early twentieth century. Its shops and restaurants have lost their sparkle; its air of buoyancy is gone.

In 1912 Bulgaria, flushed with successes in the first Balkan War, was at the height of her power. She had united with Greece, Serbia, Rumania and Montenegro to throw off the Turkish yoke but, after their victory, they were not able to come to any agreement about the division of the territory newly acquired from Turkey. War broke out among the countries so recently allied—that is, Bulgaria attacked the Serbs and the Greeks, and the second Balkan War in 1913 ended in utter defeat for Bulgaria.

Then, in 1914, came the World War and her ruler, King Ferdinand, again failed to justify himself as one of the wisest of the Balkan sovereigns for, after a year's hesitation and intrigue, he suddenly threw in his lot with the Germans and Austrians. The Bulgarian people paid heavily for the two errors of royal judgment. Not only did they lose several thousand square miles of their fertile lands but they were faced with a crushing war debt which would take years of hard work to lift.

Unable to cope with the rising discontent, Ferdinand gave up his crown, and was succeeded by his eldest son, as King Boris III, who assumed the powers of a dictator. But whether they had king or dictator was of little concern to

81

A LAKE SCENE IN THE BRACING AIR OF THE RHODOPE MOUNTAINS

The picturesque Rhodope range, with its evergreen forests and peaks more than nine thousand feet high, starts in southern Bulgaria and extends into the northeastern corner of Greece.

CURIOUSLY FASHIONED ROCKS NEAR BELOGRADCHIK IN BULGARIA

High in the Balkan Mountains of northwestern Bulgaria, not far from the Yugoslavian border, eroded rocks like grim giants watch over the ruins of an old fortress.

most of his subjects. Boris died under somewhat mysterious circumstances in 1943, after a conference with Adolf Hitler. Since the war's end Bulgaria has been governed according to the Soviet pattern.

In Sofia there is a Bulgarian National Museum which contains what will one day be a complete record of Bulgarian history. Let us stroll round the rooms and reconstruct from the coins, weapons and pottery, the story of this ancient people. The Bulgarians are the descendants of certain Mongol tribes, who originally came from Asia. They reached Europe during the seventh century and united with a large number of Slavs already living in the Balkans. They seized upon lands to the north of the Danube, the great river of Central Europe. Soon they spread southward, and their turbans, decorated with fluttering horse tails, caused terror wherever they appeared.

Their history consists of a succession of wars against and in alliance with that last outpost of ancient civilization—the Byzantine Empire whose emperors, taking shelter behind the mighty walls of Constantinople, trembled at the sound of the Bulgar war horns. The Emperor Nicephorus was slain in 809 by their Tsar Krum who, so it is said, fashioned his enemy's skull into a drinking-cup.

A later ruler, Simeon, seems to have been just such a man as King Alfred, so famous in English history. He wrote books in the Slav language, and his skill as a statesman and his valor as a warrior have passed into legend. Three times the silver armor of his bodyguard appeared before the walls of Byzantium, or Constantinople, and he took toll of all the merchandise passing from Europe into Asia. This was no small bit, for in the words of a contemporary writer: "Greece sends her silks, her wines, and her fruits; Asia her dyes and her perfumes, her precious

stones, her white peacocks with gilded feet; Bohemia her swan-necked steeds; Russia her furs and her wax, her honey and her slaves."

In 1018, however, Bulgaria was occupied by the Byzantine Emperor Basil II, a cruel man who received, owing to his massacres, the nickname of the "Bulgarian Slayer." The Balkans have been the scene of much cruelty but none more terrible than one act of Basil's. Having captured an entire army of 15,000 men, he blinded them all and sent them back to their leader, King Samuel. The unfortunate king fell into a swoon and died.

European

CLEARING SOFIA OF WARTIME RUBBLE

The story of the next three hundred years is one of continual warfare with the Serbs and with the dying Byzantine Empire. A great change, however, was taking place. The Turks were spreading over Southeastern Europe, and Bulgaria, because of its position, was the first country to be conquered.

In 1396, it became the Turkish Province of Roumelia, and its position remained unchanged until toward the end of the nineteenth century, when Russia appeared as the champion of the oppressed Slavs in Europe. Then in 1878 after a short but decisive war, the Bulgars were free once again after nearly five hundred years of Moslem misrule.

Hereafter the story is one of steady progress, though there is little love lost

IT WAS ROSES, ROSES, ALL THE WAY

The rose garden in which this girl stands probably covers many acres. From the petals of the blossoms is distilled the oil, or attar, of roses that is exported to perfume makers. Formerly, many billions of roses were produced each year in Bulgaria, but the industry has declined since synthetic perfumes have largely replaced flower scents.

INTO THE BOILING KETTLE GO MILLIONS OF ROSE PETALS

Making attar of roses is an important industry in the Sofia region of Bulgaria, and thousands are employed on the rose plantations. Attar, a fragrant oil that comes to the surface when the petals are boiled in water, is a costly ingredient of perfumes and cosmetics. More than two hundred pounds of petals may be used to produce only an ounce of the attar.

CATHEDRAL COMMEMORATES RUSSIAN HERO-SAINT

Sofia is the site of the new Cathedral of St. Alexander Nevski, consecrated in 1924. The Russian hero received his surname to commemorate his victory on the Neva in 1240. The Russian church canonized him. Peter the Great honored his patron saint, in the 18th century, by building a monastery on the battle site and by creating the order of the Knights of St. Alexander Nevski.

between the various Balkan nations. In both World Wars these countries have neither aligned themselves against a common enemy nor remained neutral, but have fought among themselves. Border territory is likely to change hands during periods of international crisis, and the Balkan map does not remain fixed for very long.

Through all this welter of fighting and fear of war the Bulgar peasant has gone on driving his team of slow oxen or buffaloes across his fields. He, like the Dane, is a small holder, as most of the farms are from one to six acres.

The Bulgarian farmer has all the peasant virtues and defects. Though he and his forefathers have worked on the land for centuries, he has taken a long time to discover that the old ways are not always the best. Until quite recently his farming methods were as primitive as his great-grandfather's, but, nevertheless, he has always raised fine crops of wheat, corn, barley and oats. Tobacco, too, is cultivated to a great extent and forms a most important article of export. Around Sofia, where there are sugar refineries, the sugar-beet is grown.

The Bulgar, though he is quite a picturesque person, has not such a lovable nature as have others of the Balkan peoples. Frugal and taciturn, he has not the cheerful air of the Rumanian nor the expansive hospitality of the Serb.

As someone has said: "Put a Bulgar and a Montenegrin in a palace, and the Bulgar will look the peasant he is, while the Montenegrin, who has never bowed his neck to a conqueror, will look like a nobleman." But put them in a desert and the Bulgar will make it a garden of roses, while the other watches him work.

Elementary education in Bulgaria is free and obligatory for the youth but two-thirds of the population are peasants, who mostly live far away from the towns and are too much occupied with work to send the children to school regularly. Nevertheless, these hard-working farmers are the backbone of the Bulgar republic.

THE IMPOSING HOME OF OPERA IN BULGARIA'S CAPITAL CITY

Late in the nineteenth century, Sofia was rebuilt almost completely and the opera house dates from that period. It is a copy of the ancient classical style, with Ionic columns and a triangular pediment above the entablature. The building is embellished, however, in accordance with the rather fussy taste that frequently prevailed in the 1800's.

AN EQUESTRIAN STATUE DOMINATES A SQUARE IN SOFIA

To the right of the statue is the Moscow Cinema, which features Russian films. There is a star near the roof and the upper stories are probably offices for Soviet Union representatives.

AN ORNATE PUBLIC BATH IN SOFIA IN THE MIDST OF A PARK

Public baths are quite common in cities and towns of Europe, a custom left over from the days of ancient Rome. The conveniences of modern plumbing are lacking in many old buildings.

MOHAMMEDAN ARCHITECTURE AT ITS SIMPLEST—SOFIA'S MOSQUE

Recalling the long rule of the Ottoman Turks over the Bulgarians is the Banya Bashi mosque at Sofia. The single minaret has a dramatic effect, lending distinction to a simple design.

89

MONKS OF BULGARIA are known as the "Black Clergy," because they wear long robes and tall caps of dead black. Those we see here dwell in a beautiful flower-decked monastery near Tirnovo, the ancient capital of the kingdom. Most Bulgarians are by religion, members of a national form of the Orthodox Eastern Church.

THE ISKER VALLEY is for a considerable distance a dark and gloomy gorge through the mountains. At other parts it is wider and in the north, near the junction of the Isker River and the Danube, it is about two miles broad. The surrounding hills afford pasture for many sheep, whose wool is converted by the peasants into brightly-dyed cloth.

FASHION NOTE IN MILLINERY

The holiday costume in northern Bulgaria features a hat made from a kerchief smartly draped and tied and wreathed with flowers. Blouse and jacket are richly embroidered.

If we go on a railway journey through the Rhodope Mountains, which lie to the south of the Balkan Range, we shall see some magnificent scenery. These Rhodope Mountains are extremely beautiful and thrust their peaks above the forests and the vineyards that grow on their slopes. There are great gorges through which the rivers dash headlong to the sea, and in the dark pine forests that cover the hillsides we might expect to find those lost princes and green-winged dragons that figure so largely in the romantic old folk tales and ballads the Bulgarian shares with the Serbs and other Slavic neighbors.

Harvest Songs and Dances

In the autumn, when the grain has ripened, the Bulgarian peasant and his whole family almost live in the fields until the harvest is in. Then the harvest songs and dances enliven the villages. Young and old join in the fun. Dances are of various kinds, but the chief one is the *hora,* the national dance of Bulgaria. Any number of people can take part in this. Dancers join hands, or else each dancer places a hand upon the shoulder of his neighbor in front. A step is taken to the left and then three to the right. To the drone of a *gaida,* or bagpipe, the mass of dancers assumes the form of a serpent that coils and uncoils.

It is interesting to note that the bagpipe is a very ancient instrument, known to the Greeks and Romans. It has long been a favorite of Balkan peasants for whom it renders plaintive notes or stirring military airs or wildly gay melodies.

When the winter winds howl about the little lonely mountain cottages, the Bulgar peasant, snug by the fire, whiles away the long evenings telling old tales to amuse his children. Some of these stories are about peasants who marry beautiful fairies, only to see their brides vanish up the chimney on the wedding night. Others are of princes who fly as eagles and of women who are changed into swallows.

Prince Marko, Superman of the Slavs

Many wonderful tales are told about Prince Marko, son of a Serbian King. Marko actually lived in the fourteenth century; but the Serbs and Bulgarians and other Slavs have made him a legendary figure. In the stories, he resembles King Arthur, the English hero, or, perhaps, more exactly Paul Bunyan, early American Superman. Marko, in story and poem, lives for three hundred years; he rides a horse that is a hundred and fifty years old; his feats of strength and valor are prodigious if not supernatural; and he always uses his powers to comfort the sorrowful and free the oppressed. His great enemies are the Turks, and many of Marko's storied exploits are against Turks trying to bring Slavs under their yoke.

In spite of all the glamour that surrounds him, Marko is always a sad figure, a prince cheated of his throne.

There is not sufficient space here to tell

BULGARIAN WOMEN PLANTING FLOWERS ALONG THE PUBLIC STREET

In Bulgaria, it is up to the women to keep their towns beautified. This picture, taken in Karlovo, shows a group hard at work cultivating beds of flowers in the public square.

THE FOUNTAIN used to play an important part in many customs of Bulgarian village life. Into it, for instance, a bride would throw a coin as an offering to the water nymphs. But such quaint customs, like the peasant costumes of the past, are gradually being discarded under the changes imposed by the communist-dominated Bulgarian Government.

THIS FRUIT-GATHERER is returning home with her baskets full to overflowing. There are many types of Bulgarian national dress. This is the one that is worn round Kostenetz, a village in the south-west, at the foot of the Rila Mountains. The two young girls whom we see on the opposite page drawing water are near neighbors of this girl.

THREE R'S IN BULGARIA

These girls are attending school in Ustove village in the Bulgarian countryside. The Government has reorganized the educational system along the same lines as those of the Soviet Union. Education is free, and children between the ages of seven and fifteen must attend school. There are schools at all levels, from kindergarten through the university.

of his many feats of daring against the Turkish invaders, but the story of his passing is well worth the retelling. In his castle the aged Prince Marko lay on his couch of hides, dreaming of old wars and of the brave days of his youth. To him there came an old friend, Philip the Hungarian, fresh from the Turkish wars. He told Marko that the way of fighting had changed.

"Old Marko," he cried, "do you know what has befallen the world? Men are making little tubes of iron. In that tube they put a black powder and a little ball. Out it flies. It strikes a man and away flies his soul."

But old Prince Marko laughed. "How can a little tube kill a man? Why, then a coward could slay a hero! With this right hand I have slain three sultans! Bring me a tube and I will catch the ball and throw it back to you." One of Philip's soldiers fired his rude matchlock and Marko's right hand was shattered.

Then seeing that the times were changed and being weary of the world, the old warrior mounted his horse and rode away into the mountains where, to this day, the peasants believe he sleeps till his country has need of him.

The national religion of the Bulgarians is Eastern Greek Orthodox. The small remaining minority comprises Moslems, Roman Catholics and Protestants.

The constitution "guarantees" freedom of worship, but in this respect it is honored more in the breach than in the observance. In 1949, fifteen Protestant clergymen were tried, convicted and sentenced to fines and imprisonment on the grounds of allegedly conspiring and conniving with the United States and Great Britain against the state. In the same year, it was decided to outlaw Catholic missions and missionaries, and their properties were forfeit to the state. And in 1950, the Turks accused the Bulgarians of the mass expulsion of Moslems. A law was introduced to

96

provide for the prosecution of clergy found guilty of activities against "public order and morality" and against "democratic" institutions.

Churches may no longer maintain schools, hospitals or social agencies, which are now operated exclusively by the state.

Education is compulsory for children from seven to fifteen years of age. Reorganized on socialist lines in 1950, it follows the Soviet line. A census taken in 1934 showed roughly 63 per cent of the population to be illiterate. It is claimed that under the present system of schooling, the number is being sharply reduced. There are schools at all levels, from kindergarten through the university.

To increase the number of "intellectuals" among the people, a group of workers were permitted, in 1950, to enroll in the universities on the basis of preparatory courses arranged especially for them. Factory workers have not been overlooked in the state educational program, and short courses have also been introduced into the various factories.

APARTMENTS FOR BULGARIA'S WORKERS

Below are new apartments built for Bulgarian workers. In 1946, Bulgaria became a Soviet-type republic, and production was reorganized under the familiar Five Year Plan arrangement. One phase of the planning calls for improved living standards under which the people would receive a larger share of the total goods produced than in the past.

SOVFOTO

GABROVO ON THE YANTRA, a tributary of the Danube, is not really the poverty-stricken, tumbledown place that it appears to be in this photograph, for it has turned its poorest, though perhaps most picturesque, side to the camera. It is a thriving little town of ten thousand inhabitants, most of whom are engaged in the manufacture of woolens, cutlery, pottery or gold embroidery. It possesses six bridges over the river, more if we count such flimsy, wooden structures as the one across which these men are walking.

© E. N. A.

98

99

THE RILA MONASTERY, though most of its buildings are only a century old, is of ancient origin. In the ninth century a hermit, Ivan Rilski, dwelt among the Rila Planina, or Rila Mountains. He was venerated as a saint, and a monastery was later erected over his cell. That monastery has been rebuilt and enlarged until it has grown into the great building we see here, which includes within its high walls a church—building with domes on the left—a tower and an ancient armory. It is considered very holy by the Bulgarians.

AT TROYAN, QUAINT APARTMENTS OVERLOOK THE GENTLE OSAM

Ducks waddle in the rocky headwaters of the Osam as it flows beneath the bracketed tenements of Troyan, a health resort and woodworking center on the slopes of the Troyan range.

A SUNNY PAVILION AT STALIN (VARNA), A SEASIDE RESORT

On a narrow sandy stretch between the Stalin Gulf and the Black Sea is the busy port of Stalin.
Its mineral baths and pleasant beaches make it a Mecca for Russians on holiday.

101

THIS RIVER-CARVED GORGE made by the Elli Dere through the Rhodope Mountains of Bulgaria offered man a grade upon which he constructed a good roadway, while the river serves as a means of transporting the timber from the forest-clad slopes. The scene too is one of great beauty and grandeur, which one may contemplate as one drives along.

POPOFF

THE DUPNITSA GATE of the famous Rila Monastery is curiously painted in bright colors and frames a delightful view of the steep, beech-clad slopes of the Rila Mountains. The monastery, the religious centre of Bulgaria, is in a valley nearly 3,900 feet above the sea. It shelters a community of about 200, but can accommodate about 2,000.

Another important production is silk. There is considerable mineral wealth, but it is little exploited. Industry also is not highly developed, largely because of lack of capital. Among the more important industries are the weaving of textiles, flour-milling and the making of pottery, wines and cigarettes.

We have already told how the defeat of Bulgaria in the second Balkan War and in World War I left the state impoverished. World War II proved to be no less disastrous to the Bulgarians. Though neutral at first they soon joined Germany in the fight against the United States and Britain. When Russia declared war on Bulgaria in 1944, Bulgarians immediately begged for an armistice, which was granted in September of 1944.

After the defeat of Germany, the Communists in Bulgaria began their drive to control the country by gaining a hold on the Fatherland Front, the leading political coalition in the country. Parties outside the coalition were at first represented in Parliament, but in very small numbers. They had no Cabinet positions. In 1945 the Western Allies demanded that democratic elections be held before they would make a peace treaty.

But Bulgaria ignored the demand. A plebiscite in 1946 abolished the monarchy, and, in the elections for Parliament that followed, the Communists gained virtual control of the government. Yet there was a semblance of democracy; the opposition was allowed a few seats in Parliament. Britain and America signed the peace treaty in September 1947. The Communists then held trials and executions of opposition-party leaders. Finally, at the close of 1947, a Soviet-type constitution was drawn up. The Communist assembly soon passed laws taking over banking, industry and agriculture.

It can be seen that the story of Bulgaria since World War II has been much like that of other iron-curtain countries.

BULGARIA: FACTS AND FIGURES

THE COUNTRY

Became a republic by popular vote in 1946. It is bounded on the north by Rumania, on the east by the Black Sea, on the south by Greece and Turkey and on the west by Yugoslavia. As a result of the treaty of Craiova, signed with Rumania on September 8, 1940, Bulgaria gained Southern Dobruja, increasing both her population and area. The total area now is 42,796 square miles; population 7,022,206.

GOVERNMENT

Bulgaria declared war on the United States and Great Britain (but not on Russia) in 1941. In 1944 she declared war on Germany and signed an armistice agreement with Russia, the United States and Great Britain in the same year. The monarchy was abolished and a republic was established in 1946. However, in the following elections, the Communists gained control. At the end of 1947, a constitution modeled on that of the Soviet Union was drawn up.

COMMERCE AND INDUSTRIES

More than two-thirds of the population are engaged in agriculture. Most are peasant proprietors holding small farms from one to six acres. Wheat and corn are the principal crops but fruit, wine, cotton, tobacco, sugarbeet, roses and sunflowers are also important. Stock-raising is carried on extensively. Industries are not much developed. They include flour-milling, sugar-refining and the manufacture of woolen goods. Coal and iron are found in quantities, but there are deposits of copper, lead, iron, zinc and silver which are little worked. Exports are tobacco, wines, iron, wheat, hides and attar of roses; the imports are textiles, metals, machinery, hardware, chemicals, motor vehicles, mineral oils and cereals.

COMMUNICATIONS

Railways (2,211 miles) are owned and operated by the state. There are 372 miles of telegraph line, excluding that owned by railroads, and 13,208 miles of telephone line.

RELIGION AND EDUCATION

Most of the people belong to the Greek Orthodox Church. There are some Mohammedans and Roman Catholics. Elementary education is compulsory and free between the ages of 7 and 14. There are special factory schools and vocational courses and 11 universities and colleges, including the University of Sofia. Education is patterned along Soviet lines.

ESTIMATED POPULATION OF CHIEF TOWNS

Sofia, capital, 434,888; Plovdiv, 125,440; Varna (renamed Stalin in 1949), 77,792; Russe, 53,420; Burgas, 43,684; Pleven, 38,997; Stara Zagora, 37,057; Sliven, 35,553; Shumen, 31,169; Yambol, 30,311; Pazardjik, 30,430.

THE REPUBLIC OF RUMANIA

Modern Life in a Province of Ancient Rome

For centuries Rumania was practically unknown to the peoples of western Europe, and the country became an independent kingdom only in 1877, after having suffered Turkish misrule for many years. Though their country was laid waste during the World War of 1914–18, the Rumanians acquired much new territory and they strove earnestly to make a united kingdom of it. The second World War, in which Rumania was a more or less unwilling Axis partner, brought the Rumanians nothing but woe. At the war's end they had to give up considerable territory to Bulgaria and Hungary. Soon afterwards Russia extended her sphere of influence across Rumania.

THE beginning of Old Rumania (many Rumanians still speak affectionately of the Old Kingdom) appears to date from the expeditions made by the Emperor Trajan against the Dacians about 106 A.D. Trajan celebrated his victories over them by erecting a column, at Adam Klissi in the Dobruja territory, similar to the well-known Trajan's column in Rome. Many Roman colonists came to settle in the newly conquered fertile country, and thus it quickly became one of the most prosperous of all the Roman colonies. It was then known as "Dacia Felix."

It suffered terribly under the hordes of Goths who swept down upon the land in the third century. Some historians believe that the Daco-Romans retired to the Carpathian Mountains and, as the Goths did not pursue them, they lived there almost forgotten. There they formed themselves into a permanent nation with a language and a civilization that was far above that of the barbarians which later surged in from all sides. Others think that the main part of the population retired south of the Danube, but later returned to re-occupy the land. The territory between the Carpathians and the Danube has passed from one invader to another, but none succeeded in wiping out the people as a national body. Their own proverb exactly describes their national experience: "The water passes, but the stones remain."

There developed in this territory two large principalities, Wallachia and Moldavia, each of which tried separately to free itself from its oppressors, the Turks, who had conquered the country in the fifteenth and sixteenth centuries. It was not until 1859, however, that they united and gave the present name to the country. The people declared their independence from Turkey in 1877.

About the middle of the nineteenth century, Rumania was powerfully influenced by France. The educated classes sent their children to French schools, and French became the official language which was used in international negotiations. Napoleon III spoke of Rumania as "France's Latin sister" and encouraged the Rumanians to repel Turkish and Russian attempts to acquire political influence. Members of the younger generation who had gone to Paris came back with many French ideas, especially about education. An education act, passed in 1864, made education free and elementary education compulsory. But because there were few schools and not nearly enough teachers, the majority of the peasants remained illiterate, as they are even to this day, in spite of the act.

A slight knowledge of Latin will, however, be quite sufficient to prove how right the Rumanians are in claiming their language to be of Roman origin. There are many Latin terms and words in their language, although there is a larger percentage of Slavic with numbers of Turkish, Greek and Magyar words. The sound of it is not unlike Italian, and in poetry it is exceedingly musical.

There are two distinct and opposite types even among pure Rumanians. One is fair and blue-eyed, and the other is as

RUMANIA FROM SOVIET RUSSIA TO THE DANUBE AND FROM HUNGARY TO THE BLACK SEA

THRESHING TIME IN TRANSYLVANIA

The great Transylvanian plain is a rich, well-watered area; but the people have been backward in adopting modern farming methods. The scene above is typical—the grain is hauled by a team of slow-going oxen to an old-fashioned thresher in the field. The Rumanian Government has promised to mechanize the country's agriculture.

TIMBER FROM THE CARPATHIAN SLOPES

Though agriculture is the mainstay of the country, Rumania has many other fine resources. There are wide forests, rich oil and gas deposits, gold, silver, copper, iron, lignite and salt. Since Rumania became a satellite nation of the Soviet Union (in 1948), the people of the Western world have not been able to learn very much about her.

BRINGING TO THE SURFACE THE RICHES THAT LIE UNDER RUMANIAN SOIL: AN OIL FIELD AT PLOESTI

Rumania's most important source of mineral wealth is oil, although production has slackened in recent years. Ploesti, second city of Rumania, is an important center of the oil industry. During the early years of World War II, the rich Ploesti oil fields fueled the German war machine.

dark as the Italian people. Both types are tall, hardy, and proud of their race, and have a very keen sense of nationality, for every child is taught that he is a descendant of the ancient Roman colonists. The size of Rumania, however, has changed several times during the twentieth century. When it had the largest territory, after 1919, the population included many Magyars, Russians, Germans and Bulgarians.

A Land of Varied Resources

Rich in timber, rich in minerals and especially so in petroleum, Rumania is also one of the greatest grain-producing regions in Europe. The soil is fertile and there is plenty of rainfall. Even though agricultural methods are still rather primitive and the yield per acre is low, large quantities of wheat and corn are grown. The chief food of the poorer farmers is a corn-meal pudding called *mamaliga*. Plums are a special crop, from which a drink called *tuica* is made.

The main artery of trade is the Danube River, by which cargoes—mostly petroleum, grains and timber—are brought down to be loaded on sea-going vessels at Brăila and Galati, the two most important river ports. The Danube has one serious disadvantage for trade, however; it is either frozen or in danger of freezing during most of the winter. Then transportation must rely on the network of railroads and highways, which was greatly enlarged and improved in the years between the two world wars.

Rumania's only port on the Black Sea is Constanta. It has a modern harbor that can accommodate the largest ocean vessels. It is also the end of a pipe line that brings petroleum from the oil fields, which center about Ploesti, about 140 miles northeast of Constanta. Near the port are two seacoast summer resorts, Mamaia and Eforia, as well as the famous mud baths of Takir-Ghiol.

Rumania's Changing Shape

In the early 1900's the shape of Rumania on maps was somewhat like a crescent with a deep hollow and blunted ends. It became almost a perfect oval with the territorial gains made in the first World War, which more than doubled its size. The Old Kingdom consisted of the provinces of Wallachia, Moldavia and the Dobruja. Greater Rumania included Bessarabia (from Russia), Southern Dobruja (from Bulgaria) and Bukovina, Transylvania and other large sections from Austria-Hungary.

The Rumania of today is still an oval, but a smaller one. The Southern Dobruja has been returned to Bulgaria; and Bessarabia is a part of the Soviet Union. The loss of these two regions cost Rumania almost half its coastline on the Black Sea, though neither the wide mouth of the Danube River nor the port of Constanta. Toward the west, however, Rumania has kept the southern part of Bukovina, and Transylvania, a high, fertile plain. Almost all the people of Transylvania are Rumanian, and Rumanians everywhere consider it the cradle of their stock. The country's present-day neighbors, therefore, are the Soviet Union, on the north and northeast; Hungary, on the west; Yugoslavia, on the southwest; and Bulgaria, on the south.

The Pride of the Rumanian People

The Danube is the joy and pride of the people, although they can claim only its lower course. It is truly a marvelous river. It is said to take its rise "in the courtyard of a gentleman's house in Germany," and it receives many tributaries as it flows through other countries before it reaches the Kazan Pass, where it passes through the Iron Gates and then comes into Rumania. It is at its narrowest and deepest in this pass. The submerged rocks that gave rise to the name of the Iron Gates have been cleared by dynamite to make a safe channel through which ships may go. When this great engineering feat was accomplished, it was made a ceremonial occasion, and its opening was attended by the emperor of Austria (Francis Joseph), who was then reigning, and the kings of Rumania and Serbia.

Although the Danube is not "blue," as the song describes it, it is far more mag-

SUNDAY AFTERNOON IN TRANSYLVANIA

Tidy main street in Rucar, a village in the Transylvanian Alps. The Sunday costume has a white kilt over tight trousers, a bell-sleeved blouse and sleeveless overjacket. Since the second century, when the Emperor Trajan conquered it, Transylvania has had a checkered career. Invading Romans, Slavs, Magyars, Saxons and others have left their imprint.

nificent and imposing than even the Rhine because of its stillness and breadth. It expands to a width of between two and three miles near Belgrade, and has islands and lovely reaches that give variety to it. The most famous bridge over the Danube in Rumanian territory is that at Cernavoda, which was completed in 1905. It carries the railway line from Bukarest, or Bucharest, to the Black Sea port, Constantza. The bridge is itself over twelve miles long, as it has to cross vast tracts of marshy land as well as water. Three arches of it were blown up by Rumanian soldiers in 1916 to prevent the advance of the enemy. We can imagine the grief they felt at having to destroy it. The restoration took five years. Work is underway on a Danube–Black Sea canal.

But let us leave the Danube to carry its huge burdens of timber and grain at its own dignified, if rather lazy, pace and fly northward. We shall pass over the capital, Bucuresti, which is also spelled Bucharest and Bukarest.

The city's favorite drive crosses Kisilev Park, which is styled after the Champs Elysées in Paris. It is typical of the

SOVFOTO

POSING IN FRONT OF AN OLD CHURCH IN A TRANSYLVANIAN TOWN

The church's roof of straw is the kind found on peasant houses in villages of the Rumanian province, and the gaily colored embroidery of the man's blouse is a sample of the needlework for which Rumanian women are noted. On the garments of men, women and children, even on sheepskin coats, they like to work rich, intricate patterns in red, gold, blue and black.

MODERN INDUSTRY IN RUMANIA. The Carbochim plants in Cluj supply electrodes, grindstones and silicon carbide to the nation's metallurgical and oil enterprises.

DYNAMO PLANT WORKERS in Bucharest. Rumanian industry is nationalized, and the Soviet Union makes decisions on plant capacities and distribution of their output.

EASTFOTO

A RUMANIAN GIRL DISPLAYS THE COTTON SHE HAS BEEN PICKING

She stands knee-deep in the midst of the ripened cotton plants to gather the valuable fiber fluffs. The field she has helped to tend is not far from Bucharest, in the flat, fertile lowlands of southern Rumania below the Transylvanian Alps. When the cotton has been carefully picked by hand it will be shipped to the city's textile mills to be processed into cloth.

SOVFOTO

TENDING A BUSY TEXTILE LOOM WITH SKILLFUL HANDS AND EYES

Textile mills are among the important enterprises in Bucharest, a manufacturing city as well as a capital. Extensive Rumanian farmlands furnish the mills with cotton, flax and wool.

THE SUN MUST DO ITS SHARE IN BLEACHING NEWLY WOVEN LINEN

In Rumania, where a vast majority of the people are engaged in agriculture, flax is one of the profitable crops, and processing and weaving its fibers into cloth is a gainful industry.

EASTFOTO

A TALENTED PLAYER OF RUMANIA'S FOLK MUSIC

Wearing the hand-embroidered blouse of his Transylvanian village, he is eager to interpret the traditional songs of his country. Rumanians are devoted music lovers.

roads and the chief terminal of the Rumanian air lines.

Burcharest lies in the midst of a vast plain, which swelters in the heat of summer and is lashed by bitter winds in winter. It is a fertile region, however—three-fourths of the Rumanians live on farms—and today maize (corn) has taken the place of wheat as the principal crop.

As far back as 1918, large land holdings were slowly being broken up and redistributed among the peasants. This process was speeded up after 1945, when the Communists gained control, and by 1949 all the great estates had disappeared. The Government then began to organize "Centers for Agricultural Machines and Equipment," similar to the machine-tractor stations of the Soviet Union. (The plain lends itself to large-scale farming, for which modern farm implements are necessary.) It is thought, however, that this plan has not been entirely successful and that production has suffered. Every phase of agriculture is subject to strict control under Rumania's masters, who work in close co-operation with the U.S.S.R.

On the small farms and in the little villages, the families usually occupy houses of a simple and hardy construction.

Upon four posts driven into the ground the builder places the roof. The walls are of clay and straw, and whitewashed when dry. Walls are brightened by gay bands of red or blue. The mud floor is as hard and smooth as timber. The cabin is divided into rooms. There will be a veranda gay with creepers, so that the home is quite picturesque outside and in.

The interior is bright with gay rugs and painted furniture and often with home-made embroideries and polished metals. It is only the better cottages, however,

wide boulevards crossing the city. The principal one is the Calea Victorei. Most of the streets would look familiar to Westerners, but here and there are curious little byways lined with bazaars which point up how close Rumania is to the Middle East.

Before World War II, Bucharest was a gay, cosmopolitan capital, with many theaters, motion-picture houses and cafés. Its gaiety and luxury vanished with the rise of the Communists, of course. Nevertheless, it remains one of the most important cities in this part of the world behind the iron curtain. It is the center of a network of at least eight rail-

which are so charming for there are others so poor as to be hardly fit to live in. Each village has a church and school and post office, and a well, which is the meeting place of the gossips and of sweethearts.

There is a great love for children in Rumania. An old proverb says: "A child is a blessing to any man's roof," and a large family is the pride of the parents. Children are useful, of course, as they start to work in the fields at a very early age—the girls gather the flax and fetch wool and the boys help with the plowing and reaping. Attendance at school is, however, steadily increasing.

Young and old are very fond of dancing. The young people will walk miles to a dance in a neighboring village, and the public dancing ground is of earth beaten smooth and hard and clean as a board. The girls wear ribbons, flowers and a smart though home-made dress. The young men a long, snow-white blouse, with a border richly worked in color, a sash of scarlet or embroidered leather and a sleeveless coat. They keep on their hats while they dance. All wear heel-less sandals. There is invariably a master of ceremonies, whose duty it is to see that the girls have partners—and no "sitting-out" is allowed. Music is usually furnished by the gipsies, or *tzigani*, of whom there are a large number in Rumania. They are quite distinct in race from the other people and although some live in settlements, they are mostly nomadic. The haunting strains of their melodies have an immense popularity with the Rumanians both in the country and in the towns.

The Rumanian peasant has no fear of having his house robbed. When he goes out he props a stick against the door to show he is not at home. It would be a serious breach of good taste to disregard this and enter. On the other hand it is not a crime to help yourself to his fruit or his grain, provided you do not take more than you need for yourself. It is

VIVID BALLS OF YARN DANGLE FROM A HAND LOOM

Several weavers work together on what will be a large carpet. Rumanian crafts are influenced somewhat by the Middle East. This shows in handwoven rugs, which may rival the true Orientals.

HARVESTING GRAIN IN TRANSYLVANIA

Late in summer, when the grain ripens, the plain of Transylvania is alive from dawn until sunset with men and women reapers. That season of the year is very warm on the plain, and this farmer wears light clothing, and a high straw hat to protect his head from the hot sun. In many parts of Rumania, the farmers still use old-fashioned, rather clumsy tools.

recognized as the right of the hungry to be fed, whether the host is at home or not.

The Rumanian woman has a busy life, especially after she is married. In addition to her housework, she has to collect and prepare all the material for spinning flax or wool. She spins and then weaves it on a hand loom, making the most beautiful materials in both light and heavy textures. The articles are also dyed and embroidered. The native love of color and design is clearly shown in this work. Many of the best pieces are taken to the towns for sale, but every home will be abundantly supplied with rugs and hangings, and the people are very fond of elaborately embroidered clothes. Everything, even pottery, is most lavishly decorated.

As we go north and cross the Carpathians, we come into quite a different type of country and to a people of quite an opposite character. On the farther side of the range the land is pastoral, of wild beauty and great charm. It is German, judging by the buildings, which are of stone and set in walled courtyards, and all as like one another as peas in a pod. The people are all alike, too, sturdy, stolid, not given to speech, but thrifty and most industrious. This is quite a contrast in disposition to the lively Rumanians we have left behind. It is a stretch of country surrounded by mountain peaks, called the Siebenburgen—the land of seven burgs or forts, or Transylvania, the land across the forest—that we come to now.

EASTFOTO

SEARCHING THE HORIZON FROM ATOP THE CARPATHIAN MOUNTAINS

Mountain-climbing vacationers in the southern Carpathians of Rumania examine the faraway valley with their field glasses. Their ascent was made easier by the cable chair that carried them up into the bracing air. This picturesque range of mountains is frequently called the Transylvanian Alps; some of its peaks are more than eight thousand feet in height.

EVERY RUMANIAN VILLAGE HAS ITS TRADITIONAL DRESS

Saliste, a Transylvanian village, was once well known for its elaborate costumes, its folklore and handicrafts. In times past needle arts and hand spinning took up much of the time of the women who created intricate embroidery designs and wove exquisite fabrics. The trousers of these men are of sheep wool; and the women's aprons, a fine black broadcloth.

HIGH IN THE BRACING AIR OF RUMANIA'S TRANSYLVANIAN ALPS

A vacationers' hotel, at an altitude of nearly five thousand feet and well above the winter resort town of Sinaia, looks out over the rolling, picturesque countryside of central Rumania. The Transylvanian Alps are really a part of the Carpathian range that extends into Rumania from the north. Some of its peaks rise eight thousand feet into the clouds.

THE GREAT DANUBE collects the drainage of an immense region, and flows in hollows between the Alps and the Jura, the Alps and Bohemia, the Alps and the Carpathians, and the Carpathians and the Balkan range. Between the two last is that famous section of the river known as the Iron Gates. The Danube has also created land where once was sea, for it has a wide delta, formed by the deposition at its mouth of sediment—the stones and soil it carried away when cutting through the mountains—picked up during its course of nearly 1,800 miles.

© E. N. A.

A RUMANIAN PEASANT FAMILY in the doorway of its thatched, wooden cottage. Changes in government mean little in the daily lives of farming people such as these. They live close to the soil in a yearly rhythm of sowing and harvesting. Flocks of sheep provide them with wool and sheepskin coats for the bitter cold of winter.

MODERN ARCHITECTURE IN BUCHAREST

Bucharest, nicknamed "City of Delight," used to be a gay city, full of color and life. Its people loved to be called "Little Parisians." Today such innocent frivolities are frowned upon. The modern street we show here, Calea Victorei, Street of Victory, received its name after the Battle of Plevna, in 1877, by which Rumania freed itself from Turkish rule.

Many of these settlers are Saxons, although where they came from is a mystery. In fact, it is so mysterious that legend has it that the founders of this "tribe," if we may so call them, were those children whom the Pied Piper decoyed from Hamelin town, and who, you will remember, entered the mountain after him and were seen no more by their parents and townsfolk. It is said that they came through the tunnel out into this fertile plain and have remained here ever since, self-supporting, producing everything they want, from nails to embroideries. They are their own carpenters and shoesmiths and tailors, their own weavers and potters and farmers. Truly, the Pied Piper did not leave them helpless if those children from Hamelin town grew up and founded a colony as prosperous as Transylvania is now!

This "land of a thousand beauties and a hundred hopes," as someone has styled Rumania, is a country full of the quaintest superstitions. Many of the peasants live in dread of "The Little People," or, as some call them, "The Good People." Many spells and incantations are practiced to induce these spirits to be merciful.

It would seem that "The Little People" have not lent kindly ears recently to the inducements of the Rumanian people, for their country has been beset with many difficulties both in war and peace. Forced to enter World War II on the side of the Axis, the Rumanians suffered heavy losses. After the war's end the country came under the domination of the Communists and today forms a part of the Soviet bloc of nations.

In times of national joy and national sorrow, too, the mountains are dear to the country folk of Rumania. They know and deeply love the passes, the mountain pastures, the secluded valleys and the defensible gateways to the plain.

RUMANIA: FACTS AND FIGURES

THE COUNTRY

Lies in southeastern Europe on the Black Sea. It is bounded on the north by Soviet Russia; on the east by Russia and the Black Sea; on the south by Bulgaria; and on the west by Yugoslavia and Hungary. Under the terms of the United Nations armistice Rumania agreed to restore Bessarabia and Northern Bukovina to Russia and they are now recognized as part of Soviet Russia. Southern Dobruja was ceded to Bulgaria. Area, 91,671; population, 15,873,000.

GOVERNMENT

With the abdication of King Michael (Mihai) in December, 1947, Parliament voted to abolish the monarchy and have a Constituent Assembly draw up a People's Republic constitution. It created a Soviet-like Presidium of 5 men. The National Assembly adopted a republican constitution, modeled on that of the Soviet Union, in 1948.

COMMERCE AND INDUSTRIES

Agriculture is the chief occupation, and the main crops are corn, wheat, barley, oats, rye, beets and tobacco. Forestry is carried on extensively especially in the Carpathians. There is much livestock. Petroleum wells and salt mines are worked, and other minerals include lignite, iron and copper ores, lead and antimony. Salt-mining is a state monopoly. Other industries are flour-milling, brewing and distilling. The chief exports are cereals, petroleum, timber, hides, wool, vegetable oils, wood manufactures, and the imports are manufactured goods (mostly textiles), machinery, automobiles, vehicles and chemicals.

COMMUNICATIONS

There are 5,962 miles of state-owned main rail lines; 94,189 miles of telegraph wire and cable; 91,327 miles of telephone wires. Airlines connect with European cities. Both the Black Sea and the Danube are important for commercial navigation.

RELIGION AND EDUCATION

Most of the population belong to the state church, namely Greek Orthodox with liturgy conducted in Rumanian language. There are also Roman Catholics, Protestants, Armenians, Jews and Mohammedans. Education is free and compulsory. There are special schools, including commercial, agricultural and polytechnic institutes, and 5 universities located at Bucharest (Bucuresti), Iasi (Jassy), 2 at Cluj, and Timisoara.

CHIEF TOWNS

Bucharest (Bucuresti), capital, population 1,041,807; (others estimated): Iasi (Jassy), 108,987; Galati, 93,229; Timisoara, 108,296; Cluj, 110,956; Ploesti, 105,114; Arad, 82,882; Braila, 97,293; Brasov, 85,192; Constanza, 79,716.

A PEASANT GIRL of Rumania returning from the well with a jar filled with water, greets
with a smile any chance wayfarer she may meet for she believes she will bring him
good luck. But should she meet anyone as she carries an empty jar to be filled, she
is sad and ashamed for then it is ill-luck that she brings. Such is the old superstition

126

THE CALUSARE, one of the national dances of Rumania, is usually performed by men. In gay costumes, decorated with fringe and tinkling bells at their knees, they dance in the open air at fairs and festivals to the music of the flute, the lute and the violin, played by ragged gypsy musicians. In another dance, the Hora, women also take part.

A PICTURESQUE SETTING ON THE SOUTHERN COAST OF CRIMEA

The Crimean Peninsula, extending into the Black Sea, is one of the beauty spots of Europe. Its southern shore, with its scenic cliffs and mild climate, is called the Russian Riviera.

RUSSIANS OF EUROPE AND OF ASIA

The People of the Steppes and Frozen Tundra

The old Russia, with its tsars, princes and peasants, disappeared in 1917 in one of the greatest political upheavals of modern times. In its place is the Union of Soviet Socialist Republics, with its bureaucrats and workers. Though the exchange promised much and brought some benefits to the Russian people, it has been at the terrible cost of even less freedom than they had before. Work, recreation, home life, the upbringing of children, the arts, thought itself—all are subject to rigid control. The individual counts for nothing; the state is all. This has happened in spite of the fact that the country is vast and there is enormous variety among its millions of people, from Slavs to Mongolians. Abundant man power, fertile soil and a wealth of mineral resources, including iron and petroleum, have helped to make the Soviet Union strong—though just how strong today the Western world can only guess.

RUSSIA is a strange blend of East and West. Now and then it splashes the pages of both European and Asiatic history with barbaric splendor. Scythians appeared beside the Black Sea in the days of ancient Rome; and later came men who rode like the wind—Mongols, Tatars, Cossacks.

To mention but a few of the many stocks who live today in the European part of Russia, there are the Karelians, or Eastern Finns, who inhabit the cold northwest; the Samoyedes, nomads of the northeast, who dwell also in Siberia; the Great Russians of the north, east and centre; the Little Russians of the south; the White Russians of the west; the Cossacks, a race of warriors who now dwell in Caucasia, that mountainous district of the south between the Black and Caspian seas; and the Tatars who also inhabit Caucasia, the banks of the Volga River and the beautiful, fruitful land north of the Black Sea. For generations Russia, at the cost of great suffering to herself, served as a buffer state, protecting the people of western Europe from the invasion of barbaric Asiatic hordes, Mongols and others, many of whom have now become part of Russia.

Russia in Europe is mostly plain. It has, of course, ranges of hills, but they are never very high. Its only mountains are those on its frontiers and those of rugged Caucasia. In the north, it reaches beyond the Arctic Circle; in the south it is in the same latitude as Italy. This southernmost part, especially the Crimea, which has been called the Little Paradise or the Russian Riviera, has quite a mild climate; but Russia, on the whole, being so far removed from any large stretch of water, has a very rigorous climate.

Little is known of the early history of the vast land we now call Russia. We are told that about the year 862 certain barbarous tribes sent to the Norsemen (whom they called the "Men of Rus") asking them to come and rule them. They came and established numerous independent principalities and built Kiev, Moscow and other cities. After about 350 years the land was invaded by hordes of yellow men from the East called Tatars, or Mongols, who ruled for more than two hundred years. During this period the Russian princes paid tribute to the Great Khan somewhere in Siberia.

The Mongol power weakened and the Russians under the leadership of the princes of Moscow threw off the Tatar yoke. Gradually the rule of Moscow became absolute, the boundaries of the kingdom were much extended, and serfdom was established, but the country remained a half barbarous, Oriental despotism far behind the remainder of Europe. Finally the royal line of Moscow ran out and there was a period of disorder. Then Michael Romanov was elected tsar, but it is with his grandson, known as Peter the Great, that modern Russia begins.

THIS RUSSIAN OF THE NORTH is both woodman and hunter, and thoroughly familiar with the habits of all the beasts and birds that live in the forest. Here we see him on the alert, as though he had heard a suspicious sound. Russia can, roughly speaking, be divided into two areas—the area of the woods and that of the plains. The woods extend from the north to the centre, and the plains from the centre to the south. The Russians are very fond of their forests and often used to build houses among the trees where they lived during the summer.

UKRAINIAN GIRLS not only are accustomed to work in their homes, but also toil hard beside the men in the fields for there is much farm work to be done in this rich agricultural land. Grain, vegetables and fruit grow in the fertile black soil in such great abundance that the region has long been referred to as the granary of Eastern Europe.

Sovfoto

HARVEST TIME ON A RUSSIAN COLLECTIVE FARM

In Russia to-day nearly all agricultural work is done on collective farms, that is where the farmers pool their labor and share a part of the crop.

Here are shown two of the women harvesters who have paused to read the field newspaper posted where all may read.

KOSTROMICHKA CATTLE ON A STATE FARM

The Kostromichka is a breed of milch cattle raised in the upper Volga region northeast of Moscow. State farms such as this usually have several hundred head of cows. Under a program begun around 1950, agricultural "towns," with 500 to a few thousand families, are taking the place of the old collective farms, which had 10 to 30 families.

This energetic ruler extended the boundaries, moved the capital from Moscow to the new city of St. Petersburg (which he built on land taken from Sweden), and attempted to make Russia a European rather than an Oriental state. It was a difficult task and success was not complete, but, at least, Russia never fell back to its former condition. Some of his successors were strong men and women and the power of Russia increased as time passed. The empire joined in the division of Poland, and also took much land from the Turk in the south, besides moving into Asia.

With the spread of education discon-

tent with autocratic rule grew stronger during the nineteenth century. Many who were suspected of plotting against the government were exiled to Siberia, but riots and assassinations continued. Finally Tsar Nicholas announced the establishment of a legislative body known as the Duma, which met for the first time in 1906, but was soon dissolved. A second Duma was also dissolved, but the third and fourth Dumas were less radical, and managed to escape dissolution.

The story of Russia in World War I is sad. Though the soldiers fought bravely, they were often badly led, and usually lacked the most necessary supplies.

THIS FAMILY OF KARELIANS is enjoying a picnic on the bank of a river not far from the town of Archangel. Near the man on the right is a copper samovar—the Russian hot-water urn that is used in making tea. The Russians drink enormous quantities of tea, usually without milk or sugar, but often with a slice of lemon. The Karelians are confronted by more unusual problems of position and natural environment than most civilized peoples. Karelia was annexed to Russia by Peter the Great in 1721. The people are one of the eastern divisions of the Baltic Finns.

IN THE DAYS of the tsars there were only about 3,000 miles of paved roads in all Russia. Rough and narrow tracks like the one above were common, and are still to be seen in some of the very remote districts. However, fine, modern highways are rapidly being constructed and motor vehicles are taking the place of these simple home-made sleighs.

135

Sovfoto

KERCHIEFED HEADS ARE STILL THE FASHION

The girl might almost be a model for the array of round little dolls, all exactly alike. Hand painted in bright colors, the vases and other articles as well as the dolls are made of wood. A factory of this kind is probably rather rare. The Government controls all industry and pays scant attention to products designed for amusement or decoration.

Finally in 1917 both people and army had become war-weary, and revolution broke out. The tsar abdicated but the provisional government was unable to maintain order and later the control was taken over by the Soviet of Workmen, Peasants and Soldiers, which declared for peace and the abolition of private property. Under Nicolai Lenin and Leon Trotsky, the new government was set up. Lenin died in 1924 and was succeeded by Josef Stalin. Trotsky was exiled and was assassinated in Mexico in 1940.

At first, the new Russia in Europe was considerably smaller than the old. However, the Russia of today, called the Union of Soviet Socialist Republics is a huge country which has expanded and extended its influence until it now covers more than half of Europe and an immense portion of Asia. Since World War II, many smaller countries of Europe have become parts of the Union, including Latvia, Lithuania and Estonia.

When the monarchy was overthrown and the Soviet government was established, naturally great changes took place. All power was placed in the hands of the workers and the property of the former business and professional classes was confiscated, and many of them fled the country. The cities, particularly, were

Sovfoto

A TRAVELING SHOP FOR BUSY HOUSEWIVES

The truck is fitted out as a regular store, with display windows at the rear. Halted in a near-by park, this shop serves people in Dnepropetrovsk, a large city in the east-central part of the Ukraine. Dnepropetrovsk is at the rapids of the Dnieper River, above the Dneprostroi Dam, one of the largest sources of electric power in the Soviet Union.

A MAIN STREET IN KIEV, CAPITAL OF THE UKRAINE

Kiev, on the Dnieper, is known in Russia as the "Mother of Cities," because of its great age. It was settled before the fifth century; by the thirteenth century it had become rich and powerful, and it was long the religious center of the Empire. Today Kiev is a bustling industrial town and a shipping port on the Dnieper, which flows into the Black Sea.

transformed, though the changes on the land have been hardly less striking Never before, perhaps, in the entire history of the world has so complete a transformation of an entire people taken place in so short a time.

For several years after the revolution Russia was engaged in wars with her enemies at home and abroad. When the Soviets had finally established their rule they found themselves masters of a country in ruins. Millions had been killed or had starved to death. The government controlled the country's resources, but commerce and industry were at a standstill.

During the first years food, clothing,

and other goods were very scarce, and not until 1928, with the inauguration of the first "five year plan," did the real turning-point come. This plan and those that followed it were something new in national policy. Every detail of industry and agriculture—even of cultural life— was planned in advance. It was laid down just how many factories should be increased, what crops should be sown. The whole population was put to work with a will to transform a huge but backward country into a modern industrial nation. Since the Russians lacked technical skill and experience, many foreign engineers and experts—among them many Ameri-

Sovfoto

A TROIKA IS STILL USEFUL IN DEEP SNOW

Russians call any kind of vehicle drawn by three horses abreast a "troika." It may be a sleigh or a carriage. Automobiles have taken the place of the old-time carriages; but when the heavy snows of the bitter winters come, sleighs still glide over country roads. This troika is coming through an evergreen forest in the Ivanovo region, northeast of Moscow.

cans—were imported during the early years. As time went on, the Russians gradually took over the work of designing and operating their own machinery.

Though in many respects the plans fell short of the mark set, the results on the whole were astonishing. Entire new industries were created. A network of electric power began to cover the land. Much-needed canals and other important public works were constructed, often with the labor of political prisoners. In some fields of production the improvement was very great. A tremendously powerful, mechanized Red Army was developed. Education was greatly extended. Where formerly the vast majority of the people had been unable to read and write, to-day illiteracy has been much reduced.

The People Tighten Their Belts

In order to make these things possible, the Soviet Government, dominated by the Communist Party, ruled the country with an iron hand. For many years the people had to tighten their belts and endure many hardships. All enemies of the regime were ruthlessly punished; but the Russian people had undergone centuries of oppression and poverty. Now they were made to believe that the sacrifices demanded of them were in their own interest, for the purpose of building up a better order of things.

There were several five-year plans, with goals set for industry, transportation and so on. However, the planning was interrupted by World War II, in which Russia suffered great damage. After the war, the Soviet Union threw all its efforts into restoring the shattered areas. When the United Nations was set up, Russia became a member with a permanent seat on the Security Council. Unhappily for the world, it has not been a co-operative partner. Disputes and deadlocks have been the rule, aggravating international tension. Even as the carefully selected spokesmen of the Soviet Union have talked "peace" loud, Communists have seemed bent on making any real peace impossible. The most flagrant example, of course, is Korea, where the Chi-

nese Communists have prolonged the conflict—evidently with the approval of the Soviet Union.

Though Russia has become a highly industrialized country, agriculture is as vital as ever it was under the tsars. For a long time, the peasants were the weak link in Soviet economy and not until after 1932 was there any real improvement in the agricultural problem.

The revolution gave land to the peasants, but farming was carried on by individual small land-holders, according to age-old, primitive and generally inefficient methods. Moreover the peasants could not sell their crops to the highest bidder. The government collected the entire surplus, often by forceful methods, paying far below the real value. As a result many peasants refused to raise anything beyond their needs, thus seriously endangering the country's food supply.

The Soviet plan for applying the revolution to the land was called the "collectivization of agriculture." It met with tremendous opposition, especially on the part of the moderately prosperous peasants called "kulaks." Not until there had been bloodshed and hundreds of thousands of these kulaks had been exiled did success begin to come.

Trouble in Agriculture

By the 1940's more than 90 per cent of Russian agriculture was being carried on in collective farms, where 10 to 30 families would work about 600 acres of land. A few years after World War II, the Government launched an even more extreme plan, the creation of agricultural "towns." Each was to contain several thousand persons and to be run by a bureaucratic caste. However, the "town" plan never got very far. According to the most reliable reports available, even the old collective-farm system was breaking down.

When Stalin died, in 1953, a severe crisis was brewing in agriculture. The chief causes seemed to be a shortage of manpower, poor condition of livestock, inefficient Machine and Tractor Service stations, and a tremendous burden of taxes on the farm workers. Letters smuggled

SOVFOTO

A SHEPHERD FONDLY PETS A PRIZE-WINNING ANIMAL

The shepherd's warm cap is no less fleecy than the coats of his charges. These sheep are a special breed developed in Russia and produce a semifine wool needed for some kinds of cloth.

APARTMENT HOUSES ON THE OKTYABRSKAYA, A STREET IN STALINGRAD

This view of Stalingrad, taken since the second World War, gives little indication that the city was reduced to a heap of smoking ruins in one of the most prolonged and fierce battles of all time. Stalingrad is on the lower Volga River, where it bends to the west; and the Germans hoped to cut the vital supply artery of the river at this point. The battle lasted from August 1942 until February 1943. Defeat of the Germans here marked the beginning of their decline in military power. The Russians took pride in rebuilding Stalingrad as quickly as possible.

out indicated that some areas were close to starvation. A soldier who had returned to a collective near Moscow wrote that "90 per cent of the farmers had no bread and lived on frozen potatoes and pancakes its way through a field of wheat, while only a mile away women are flailing grain as their ancestors did, centuries ago. Not far from Orel, in central Russia, a truck garden has water pumped to it through

SOVFOTO

WHERE NEVSKY PROSPECT CROSSES ANICHKOV BRIDGE, IN LENINGRAD

Nevsky Prospect is one of the principal thoroughfares in Leningrad and the most famous. For a time after the Revolution it was called October 25 Prospect. Some of the most imposing buildings of the days of the tsars still stand along this street, among them the baroque Stroganov Palace, and the Anichkov Palace. The latter is now called the Young Pioneers Palace.

made of minced grass with a small addition of flour." This situation may have been one of the reasons why the Malenkov regime was so quick to promise better living standards.

Russia is still a land of extreme contrasts. Jet aircraft fly over roads where an oxcart is the usual vehicle. The most modern kind of harvester may be eating high-pressure nozzles, like lawn sprinklers. Yet the women who live there must draw water, for household use, from a well and carry the buckets home suspended from a wooden shoulder yoke.

In the cities, numbers of apartment houses were hurriedly put up after the war. But conveniences such as electric lights and telephones are rather rare.

RIVER-BOAT PIER ON THE VOLGA AT KUIBYSHEV

At this point in its course—called the Samara Bend—the Volga is joined by the Samara River and is very broad. Along the water front of the city there are many wharves and extensive shipyards. Traffic on the river is heavy, and Kuibyshev has a large share in this activity. River boats leave its docks laden with grain, livestock and many kinds of manufactured goods.

HOUSES FROM TSARIST DAYS FACE REVOLUTION SQUARE

Like many other Russian cities, Kuibyshev (formerly called Samara) was made over in some ways and given a new name after the Communists came to power. Its modern development, beginning around 1900, was due to the fact that it was on the line of the railroads then being built into Asia. Today it is a center of heavy industry, with aircraft, locomotive and tractor factories.

HEAVY-DUTY TRACTORS lined up outside a manufacturing plant are part of the Soviet plan to mechanize agriculture. The tractors will be shipped to Russia's collective farms.

Stalingrad and some other badly destroyed centers got modern department stores that quite dazzle the eye. The average Russian, however, was much more likely to be found shopping in the old trading arcades that go back to tsarist days, with little choice of wares.

For years Russia paid little attention to foreign affairs. In August 1939, however, a non-aggression pact with Germany was signed. When Germany broke down resistance in Poland, Russia annexed over half of that state, and compelled the three little Baltic States, Latvia, Estonia and Lithuania, to allow the establishment of naval bases in their harbors. Next it was claimed that Finland was a danger to Russia and cession of territory was demanded. The Finns refused and for over a hundred days resisted the might of Russia, but in the end lost considerable territory. In 1940 Russia took complete control of the Baltic States and also took over Bessarabia and part of Bukovina from Rumania.

In spite of the non-aggression pact, Germany launched a sudden attack against Russia, in June 1941, which brought the Soviet Union into World War II on the side of the Allies. The high-water mark of the German invasion was the Battle of Stalingrad, where the Nazis were turned back after a fierce struggle. Eventually, in the closing days of the war in Europe, Red Army soldiers met Western Allied troops in Berlin. Germany was divided into four zones, with Soviet troops occupying the eastern zone. Here Communist influence became dominant. In Poland, Bulgaria, Rumania, Hungary and Czechoslovakia, the Communists also gained.

Before the Bolshevik revolution of 1917, religion played a great part in the life of the Russian people. The prevailing creed was that of the Russian Orthodox Church. Almost every cottage or house contained a corner with a small sacred picture or image, usually of the Virgin Mary or of one of the saints. Churches and chapels dotted the land.

REINDEER EAT LICHENS THAT GROW BENEATH THE SNOW

Reindeer can live where the land is always frozen, and in arctic places like northern Russia they are of great worth. They can draw sleds for long distances and can carry men or heavy loads on their backs, their sharp, cleft hoofs giving them firm footing on ice or in snow drifts. They also provide milk, meat, wool and leather for the people of these northern lands.

THEATER IN ARCHANGEL, NEAR THE WHITE SEA

Just below the great port city of Archangel the River Dvina empties into the White Sea. The Arctic Circle is only one hundred and fifty miles to the north, and the harbor at Archangel is frozen for a good half of the year; but it handles a great volume of traffic during the months when it is ice-free. Above is the Civic Theater, at the river's edge.

After 1918, the Communists separated the church from the state and the school from the church, and appropriated most of the church property. Freedom of worship was guaranteed in the constitution of 1936, but no church member may have a part in the Government. Atheism is taught in the schools. Among church-goers the Russian Orthodox Church has the largest following. Its two branches have headquarters at Moscow.

Peter the Great began to build his city in 1703 upon land taken from the Swedes. The ground was marshy and it was necessary to build the houses upon piles. Thousands of people from all parts of Russia were brought to the spot and forced to labor. So many died that there is an old saying that the city was really built upon bones. Under the succeeding tsars the city grew until the population was about a million and a half at the beginning of the first World War. The name was then changed to the Russian form Petrograd instead of the German St. Petersburg.

In 1918 the Soviet Government transferred the government to Moscow, and the former capital declined. In 1924 the name was changed to Leningrad, after Nikolai Lenin, founder of the U.S.S.R.

There was a general exodus from the city after 1918, and the population was at one time estimated as hardly more than half a million. However, between the two World Wars, the tide turned, and Leningrad is now the second largest city of the Soviet Union, with well over 3,000,000 population. It is a busy port and shipbuilding center.

A number of railroads converge at Leningrad, and the city is connected with Kronstadt, a port on the Gulf of Finland, by a sixteen-mile canal. Another canal system connects Leningrad with the White Sea, 141 miles away.

Russia is full of museums of every sort. In some, are works of art. In others, the life, customs and dress of every era are shown. There are exhibits of industrial processes and methods. All works of art in private hands all through Russia have been confiscated and placed in museums already existing or in others founded since the establishment of the communist regime. One of the most famous of Russia's museums is the Hermitage, in Leningrad; it contains a magnificent art and archaeological collection.

Originally built by Catherine II, it was reconstructed in 1840–50.

Moscow is connected by rail with Leningrad, the old capital of Russia, first known as St. Petersburg, then as Petrograd. We are told that this particular railway affords an example of the autocratic rule of the tsars. The railway was under construction when Nicholas I was on the throne. Difficulties arose as to the line it should follow; marshes were in the way and thick forest had to be penetrated, so that a very winding route seemed necessary. As the engineers were unable to agree upon the best route, the matter was referred to the Tsar who, it is said, called for a map, a pencil and a ruler. Taking the map, he drew a line from Moscow to Leningrad and stated that that was the route to be followed. This is why the railway runs so very straight.

Eastern Domes and Western Subway

During its history Russia has had five capitals, and Moscow has had that honor again since 1918. However, it is a very different city from what it was in the days of the tsars, though still a curious mixture of East and West. The onion-shaped domes of the old churches have a Moorish look; and at the other extreme is a modern subway, one of the Communists' showpieces, with marble stations decorated in stainless steel.

Just when Moscow was founded is uncertain. However, its 800th birthday was celebrated in 1947. It is first mentioned in the Russian Chronicles in 1147. It grew up on the main trade routes that led from Europe to the Orient and from the Baltic to the Caspian Sea. Mongolian hordes sacked it again and again. The Russians themselves set fire to their beloved city—"Little Mother Moscow"—in 1812 in order to prevent Napoleon from setting up winter quarters there, after his capture of the city.

Moscow is in the center of the great Russian plain, and is situated on seven low hills, rising in terraces from the high banks of the Moscow River, which winds across the city. The main part is on the north bank. Overlooking the river from Borovitzky Hill, in the very center of the city, is the vast Kremlin, or "Fortress." Wide streets radiate from it to the city's suburbs.

The ground on which the Kremlin stands is an irregular triangle, surrounded by a wall about 1¼ miles in circumference and from 14 to 20 feet thick and from 30 to 70 feet high. In the wall are 5 gates, and 19 towers, each one in a different style though all are generally pyramids in shape. The eastern and main entrance to the Kremlin, from Red Square, is the fifteenth-century Spasskiya Gate (Gate of the Redeemer), 205 feet high. Atop this gate is a belfry. For many years after the Revolution, the bells pealed forth the INTERNATIONAL at regular intervals. Napoleon entered from the Borovitzkiya Gate (Gate of the Woods), 62 feet high. Inside the walls are a bewildering number of buildings, including a vast palace, in a variety of styles—Byzantine, Renaissance, Baroque. Towering over all is the high dome of the Cathedral of the Assumption, begun in 1393. There is one thoroughfare, Communist Street.

Red Square, 900 yards long and 175 yards broad, is the center of political life. In front of the Kremlin gleams the polished red and black marble tomb of Lenin and Stalin, a communist shrine. On the other side from the Kremlin is the many-domed St. Basil's Cathedral, now a museum. Red Square frequently echoes to the sound of marching feet in the huge parades staged by the Government.

The Soviet Union in Asia

Let us now turn east and cross the Ural Mountains. The long north-south range marks the dividing line between the European and Asiatic parts of the Soviet Union. Soviet Asia includes Siberia (officially part of the Russian Soviet Federated Socialist Republic, the largest Soviet unit) and, in central Asia, five Soviet Socialist Republics, which we discuss in the next chapter. The name Siberia first came into use in the sixteenth century and was taken from a village, Sibir, on the Irtysh River.

A vast area of about five million square

148

A STEAMER AND GREAT LOG RAFTS BREAST THE MIGHTY VOLGA

Though most of the timber is destined for sawmills, some of the rafts are permanent and have houses on them. They provide shelter for the men who must keep the unwieldy logs in order.

149

BURIAT SHEPHERD AND HIS STEED

The Buriats live in north-central Asia, on either side of Lake Baikal. They are of Mongol origin, with high cheek bones, slanting eyes and sturdy frame. They gain a living chiefly by stock-raising, their occupation now being under strict Soviet supervision. The land of the Buriats is rugged and beautiful. Lake Baikal contains seals, as well as many kinds of fish.

WAREHOUSE FOR FURS IN THE FAR NORTH

Just across the Bering Strait from Alaska is the Chukotsky Peninsula, Russia's northeastern out-post. It is a chill region, bisected by the Arctic Circle and inhabited mostly by foxes, wolves and bears, and their trappers. Here a quantity of precious skins—polar fox and others—are sorted and processed. Furs are one of the Soviet Union's articles of export.

IN KHABAROVSK, EMBROIDERY IS A WORK OF ART

The women of Khabarovsk, in far eastern Asia, adorn their tunics, coats, gloves and even their fur footwear with lavish embroidery. Khabarovsk, on a cliff above the Amur River, has a cosmopolitan population, with Russians, Chinese, Koreans and others mingling on the streets. The city is cold for much of the year and clothing must be warmly padded.

miles, Siberia sprawls across the northern third of Asia, from the Urals to the Bering Sea. At least a quarter of Siberia is within the Arctic Circle. Off the desolate Arctic coast are the large islands of Severnaya Zemlya, Novosibirskiye (New Siberian Islands) and Wrangel. On the Pacific coast, practically encircling the Sea of Okhotsk, are the Kamchatka Peninsula, the volcanic Kurile archipelago and the island of Sakhalin.

Tundra, Taiga and Steppes

The Arctic shore is bleak tundra. Toward the south, the tundra merges into a region—called taiga—of swampy, evergreen forests. South of this are steppes—dry grasslands. Some of the world's longest rivers—Ob, Yenisei and Lena—flow north through Siberia, their lower courses frozen for nine months of the year.

Western Siberia—between the Urals and the Yenisei River—is largely a low, flat plain, drained by the Ob-Irtysh river system. East of the Yenisei, the land rises to form a great plateau, watered by the Lena. Eastern Siberia, still higher, is ridged with long mountain chains: Verkhoyansk, east of the Lena River; Cherski, farther east; Yablonovy, east of Lake Baikal; and Koryak, Kolyma, Dzhugdzhur and Stanovoi, guarding the Pacific coast. There are a number of active volcanoes among the mountains of the Kamchatka Peninsula. Siberia's southern frontier also is extremely rugged. Here the peaks of the Altai, Tannu-Ola, Sayan and Sikhote-Alin ranges mark the border with China and Mongolia.

Cold Pole of the World

The climate of Siberia runs to extremes—brief, hot summers and long, bitter winters. At Yakutsk, on the Lena, in summer the thermometer may shoot to above 90°. In the northeast, the region around Verkhoyansk and Oimyakon is sometimes called the world's cold pole. There the average temperature in January is between 60° and 65° below zero.

The earliest known people in Siberia were primitive tribes wandering the steppes. Later many of them were driven

north into the taiga by warlike Turkic and Mongolian clans, which thereafter occupied the grasslands. Descendants of these various groups still form the basic population of Siberia. Except when it interferes with the Government's plans, their nomadic way of life as herdsmen seems to be left undisturbed.

As early as the thirteenth century, Russian fur traders, seeking ermines and sables, penetrated northwest Siberia. Actual Russian conquest began in the 1500's and won through to the Pacific by 1640. It was during this period that the tsarist police began to use Siberia as a place of exile; the place itself provided punishment. Siberia acquired a reputation of human misery and brooding mystery.

Settlement under the Tsars

On the other hand, many parts of western Siberia were settled by free Cossacks and today seem little different from Russia proper. During the late 1800's so many gifted Russians were banished to eastern Siberia that such cities as Chita and Irkutsk became lively cultural and scientific centers, though hardly known to the world at large. After the Trans-Siberian Railroad was completed to the Pacific, in 1905, numerous Russian colonies sprang up along the right of way.

Industrial Development

So when the Soviet Government turned its attention east—ever on the search for untapped natural resources—it was not launching a completely new policy. Rather, it was speeding up a transformation that had begun under the tsars. Our information about present-day conditions is neither complete nor altogether reliable, but of one broad fact there can be no doubt: the industrial center of the Soviet Union has shifted east of the Urals. Magnitogorsk (at the south end of the range), with its furnaces and rolling mills, is the metal-working hub of the nation. Throughout Siberia the lifeblood of almost every large town is industry—manufacturing, mining or lumbering. The forests are immense and there is great mineral wealth. The Lake Baikal re-

WITHIN THE VAST KREMLIN at Moscow are chapels, palaces, barracks, offices and two cathedrals. A battlemented brick wall, more than a mile and a quarter in circumference, strengthened with towers, encloses the group of buildings. The structures are of all sizes, styles and ages, for each tsar seems to have added a church or a palace. The Kremlin was the ancient residence of the tsars. The Great Kremlin Palace occupies the site on which stood the old wooden and stone palaces of the tsars. It is now the seat of a government far different from the old.

A ROW OF SMALL HOMES IN A WORKERS' VILLAGE NEAR KAKHOVKA

Kakhovka is the center of a hydroelectric project on the Dnieper River in southern Ukraine. The region is a steppe, rich in the production of wheat, cotton, grapes and vegetables.

A MOSCOW FAMILY AT BREAKFAST IN A MODEST NEW APARTMENT

This family is indeed fortunate to have a new home. There is a continuing shortage of housing in the crowded capital and the growing industrial centers of the Soviet Union.

gion, the Lena and Kolyma valleys are rich in gold; Sakhalin Island has oil. In the Kuznetsk Basin (south-central Siberia), the Tunguska Basin, Lena Valley and Irkutsk and Transbaikalia areas, there are large coal fields. The Kuznetsk Basin and Transbaikalia also have important quantities of iron.

Yakutsk, Gold-mining City

Yakutsk, on the Lena River, may be taken as a fairly typical Siberian city. Around it are gold mines. There, also, intensive research is being carried on to find out how to grow such plants as corn and tomatoes in permafrost soil—below about four feet, the ground never thaws. Because of the permafrost, the city's water supply is limited and sewage disposal is a problem. The old houses, many of them dating from the late 1800's, are made of wood, with the fantastic gingerbread decoration of the period. Yakutsk has electricity, and practically every home has a radio—a necessity in this isolated spot. Otherwise, creature comforts are largely ignored. Perhaps the most striking feature of the city is the number of schools. It has no church.

Transportation Problems

Bicycles and motor bikes are used almost everywhere. Even if they were available, automobiles could hardly take the roads, which are usually muddy, pitted with potholes or frozen in jagged ruts. City streets are rarely paved. The Trans-Siberian Railroad serves only a narrow strip and has comparatively few branch lines, though more are being built and planned. To meet the need for getting over the enormous distances, the civil air fleet has a wide-flung network. A tiny hamlet may have a "hedgehopper" plane, connecting with major air routes.

The rivers, particularly the Lena, carry considerable traffic during the warm months. Then steamboats, on fairly regular schedules, ply the Arctic coastal waters and go far inland up the rivers. Outbound, they are laden with such welcome luxuries as fresh fruit. On the return voyage to northern European Russian ports, they may carry gold and furs.

The need to increase food production is one of the Soviet Government's most urgent problems and it is trying to develop the western steppes as a great breadbasket. In some places, especially along the course of the upper Ob, near Barnaul, the soil is rich. Lack of water is the biggest handicap. To overcome it, dams are being erected, for both irrigation and electric power. One of the largest of the dams is being constructed at Novosibirsk, where the Ob is a wide, muddy stream. This dam is supposed to be completed sometime in the early 1960's.

Secret Atomic-Energy Plants

It is surmised that at least two of the Soviet Union's largest atomic-energy plants are near Novosibirsk and Irkutsk. The latter city is on the Angara River, not far from Lake Baikal, and the water-power resources of the Angara are said to be tremendous. Norilsk, near the Yenisei River and close to the Arctic coast, made a sudden, mysterious leap in population during the 1950's. Always a mining town, there is reason for believing that it has become a center of uranium production.

Norilsk points up the dark side of Siberia that still exists. According to one report, at least 120,000 prisoners are toiling in the mines there. Soviet Asia is, in fact, the domain of the secret police, which "recruits" slave labor. The most notorious camps of which the outside world has heard are in the vicinity of Khabarovsk (on the Amur River, in the southeast), Yakutsk, Magadan (on the Sea of Okhotsk—25 per cent of the U.S.S.R.'s gold is supposed to be produced in this locality), Chita, Karaganda and Balkhash (the last two in the Kazakhstan republic).

Forced Migration

In addition to the miserable inmates of the prison camps, there are *spetsi*—a Russian nickname that refers to people who are forbidden to move from a certain city or area. They are in "forced residence." The *spetsi* include the victims of forced mass migration: a colony of Germans who long ago had their own republic on the

BECKETT

THE CATHEDRAL OF ST. BASIL (Vasili the Beatified) stands at the southeast end of the Krasnaya, or Red Square, in Moscow, presenting an extraordinary appearance with its twelve fantastic colored domes. It was begun in the reign of Ivan the Terrible, and there is a legend that he had the architects blinded when the work was done. It is now a Soviet museum.

"LITTLE MOTHER MOSCOW," as the city is sometimes called by Russians, is again the capital of Russia. It lies on both banks of the River Moskva. The outer city is called the White City, and is encircled by broad boulevards, intersected by wide thoroughfares radiating from the Kremlin which is seen in the distance. Moscow is one of the oldest cities of Russia.

PALATIAL ARCHED STAIRWAY OF THE METRO, MOSCOW'S SUBWAY

Polished marble walls, domed plaster ceilings, floral moldings and decorative wrought-metal chandeliers complete the picture of opulence in the Komsomolskaya-Koltsevaya Station.

IZMAILOVSKAYA STATION, A SHOW PIECE OF THE SOVIETS

Supplementing the surface means of transportation—streetcars and busses—the Metro branches out in four lines though it is not very long. It is meant for show.

SOVFOTO

THE SOVIET IDEA OF WHAT MODERN ARCHITECTURE SHOULD BE

A blend of the old and the new in a Smolensk Square, Moscow, building—an example of skyscraper art in the Soviet Union. Massive stone piers seem to brace the gigantic tower and sweep the eye upward to the timid, ornate spire. Symmetrical wings, some of them with pinnacles, others without, flank the tower. There are two thousand air-conditioned offices in all.

FROM THE IVAN VELIKY TOWER within the Kremlin, we can look down upon the vast city that has grown up around this inner fortress-city. The huge bell-tower was completed in 1600 and rises in five stories to a height of three hundred and eighteen feet. From it Napoleon is said to have watched the city burn in 1812. The Church of the Redeemer,

BECKETT

seen in the distance, with its golden domes and its marble walls, has been destroyed to make room for the Palace of Soviets. There were about four hundred and fifty churches in Moscow, many of them having golden cupolas, so that on sunny days, they caught the eye, no matter in what direction we looked. To Western eyes the city seemed unreal.

Volga; Letts, Estonians and Latvians; Caucasus tribesmen; Tatars from the Crimea; Russian intellectuals who failed to follow communist dictates. These groups have been sent to the most lonely, harsh areas of Siberia. Most of them live in little more than hovels. There are also "volunteer" settlers, young Russians given no real choice but to migrate—pawns in the Soviet Government's determined effort to develop Siberia regardless of the cost to individual human beings.

UNION OF SOVIET SOCIALIST REPUBLICS: FACTS AND FIGURES

THE COUNTRY

Occupies the eastern half of Europe and the northern part of Asia. On the north the boundary is the Arctic Ocean, on the east the Pacific Ocean, on the south is China, Afghanistan, Persia (Iran), Caspian Sea, Turkey and the Black Sea; on the west, Rumania, Hungary, Czechoslovakia, Poland, the Baltic Sea and Finland. The Soviet includes the Russian Soviet Federated Socialist Republic (area, 6,533,584 square miles), Ukrainian Soviet Socialist Republic (222,624), White Russian or Belorussian S.S.R. (80,154), Azerbaijan S.S.R. (33,088), Georgian S.S.R. (29,420), Armenian S.S.R. (11,545), Turkmen S.S.R. (187,200), Uzbek S.S.R. (157,335), Tadzhik S.S.R. (55,057), Kazakh S.S.R. (1,063,262), Kirghiz S.S.R. (76,023), Karelo-Finnish S.S.R. (68,918), Moldavian S.S.R. (13,050), Estonia S.S.R. (17,-413), Latvia S.S.R. (24,903), Lithuania S.S.R. (25,173). Total area, about 8,600,000 square miles; total population, about 210,000,000.

GOVERNMENT

By constitution of 1936, the U.S.S.R. is a "socialist state of peasants and workers." The highest organ is the Supreme Council made up of two chambers—the Council of Union, elected by proportional representation, and the Council of Nationalities consisting of representatives from each constituent republic, autonomous republic, autonomous province and autonomous district. Executive and administrative power is vested in the Council of People's Commissars, responsible to the Supreme Council.

Greater decentralization in the internal political structure was adopted in 1944 as a means of facilitating admission of new republics into the Soviet Union through the assurance of autonomy in foreign and military affairs. All citizens of either sex over 18 years of age are granted the franchise. A "dictatorship of the proletariat" is maintained through the agency of the Communist Party, which is the real governing class of the country.

COMMERCE AND INDUSTRIES

Formerly a strictly agricultural country Soviet Russia has become an industrial agrarian country, second only to the United States in its industrial output. Industrial production is organized under a planning system and conducted by state trusts and combines, operated under the supervision of appropriate governmental departments. There are great numbers of industrial establishments for the production of pig iron, steel, coal, oil, etc. Ninety-five per cent of the agricultural output, which includes wheat, rye, barley, oats, corn, cotton, sugar beets, flax, sunflower seeds, and tobacco, is produced on collective and state farms that have been highly mechanized. Mineral resources include coal, peat, oil, iron ore, manganese, copper, zinc and lead. The forests are important. Principal exports are sawn timber, furs, oil, cotton fabrics, pulpwood, grain, and manganese ore; the principal imports, industrial machinery and tools, sheet iron and steel, ferro-alloys, motor vehicles and parts.

COMMUNICATIONS

There are about 70,000 miles of railroads and 80,000 miles of navigable waterways, including the 63-mile canal that joins the Don and Volga rivers and so links the Baltic and White seas with the Caspian and Azov seas. There are some 2,550,000 miles of roads (highways and local roads). The number of telephones is about 1,500,000. The routes of major airlines cover about 138,000 miles.

RELIGION AND EDUCATION

Officially, according to the constitution, there is religious freedom in the U.S.S.R. However, the state is supreme in all things and even where a faith is tolerated (such as the Russian Orthodox Church, which was the largest denomination under the tsars), it is controlled rigidly by the Communist Government and, in fact, is far from free.

Education is compulsory and entirely state-controlled. There are special schools with emphasis on trade schools, classes and schools for adult education and various universities.

CHIEF TOWNS

All figures are approximate. Moscow, capital, population, 5,000,000; Leningrad, 3,000,000; Gorki, 1,000,000; Baku, 900,000; Kiev, 800,000; Kharkov, 800,000; Dnepropetrovsk, 700,000; Tashkent, 700,000; Odessa, 600,000; Rostov-on-Don, 500,000; Tbilisi, 500,000. In addition there are a number of new cities for which no reliable figures are available, among them: Magnitogorsk (in the Urals); Novoye Zaporozhie (Ukraine); Anjero-Sudjeansk, Stalingorsk, Prokopievsk (west Siberia); Cheremkhovo, Igarka (Krasnoyarsk Territory); Karaganda (Kazakhstan).

A GLIMPSE OF TURKESTAN

And Its Crumbling Cities of Old Renown

Once the home of barbaric conquerors and their fierce, savage hordes, Turkestan sprawled across the ancient trade routes from Europe to the fabulous East. Through the noisy, crowded marts of "Golden Samarkand" passed untold wealth in rich silks, brocades and jade. In their caravans, traders brought from Bokhara (or Bukhara) fine carpets, the likes of which had never been seen in medieval Europe. Turkestan was a land that stirred the imagination. Today the old glamour and feeling of romance have disappeared from Turkestan, but the inhabitants remain strange and picturesque, as our photographs show. As part of the Soviet Union, Western Turkestan is strategically important in the modern world, with its wealth of mineral resources, potential hydroelectric power and growing industrial expansion.

STRETCHING far away from the Caspian Sea and Persia on the west to the borders of China in the east is the vast country of Turkestan (or Turkistan). Eastern Turkestan is a part of the Chinese province of Sin-Kiang (Sinkiang) of which we speak elsewhere. Here we shall tell of the larger Western, or Russian, Turkestan.

It is a large slice of Asia with an area of over a million square miles, and with a history that goes back thousands of years before Christ. The Huns, centuries previous to the time we hear of them in Europe, had an empire in this territory. They were broken up and driven out by the Chinese who were in turn succeeded by a people later known as Tatars. The Arabs, converting to Islamism as they came, overran it, as also did the Turks and Mongol hordes.

Turkestan, like many another part of Asia, has been a fierce battleground for the wild tribesmen of that region. Emir and khan, one after another, rose in power and held sway until a stronger leader came to wrest supremacy from their hands. Jenghiz Khan was one of these Asiatic kings who became one of the greatest conquerors known to history but greater even than he was Tamerlane who led his plundering hordes from the Volga to the Persian Gulf, from the Hellespont to the Ganges, and was actually on his way to invade China with his victorious armies when death overtook him.

It was at Samarkand, the "Golden Samarkand" of the Oriental poet, that Tamerlane held his court. Magnificent though it had been before, the city attained greater fame and glory under this mighty ruler.

What have the changing centuries brought to this old Asiatic empire? As Tamerlane's kingdom crumbled away it was parceled out among lesser kings and khans. One race and then another won independence and set up a khanate, or kingdom, of its own. We find the Turcomans had gathered in the country between the great river, Amu Daria (the Oxus of the ancients), and the Caspian Sea, and elsewhere were established the petty kingdoms of Bokhara and Khiva.

The greater part of this western portion of Turkestan is desert, but here and there oases occur and the land has become extraordinarily fertile. At Merv, for instance, in the heart of the Turcoman's country, there is the largest area of cultivated land in the whole province. The climate is well suited for cotton-growing and many thousands of acres are given up to this industry.

Never a single nation, the name Turkestan means simply the place of Turkish peoples. In this strange land of Turkestan the surface of the earth is constantly changing, rivers are shifting their courses or wandering off to be swallowed up by the desert sands, lakes are drying up and earthquakes sometimes occur.

Uzbek is sprinkled with ancient and very famous cities planted centuries ago on the oases of this semi-desert land. The mere mention of the name—Bukhara—

D. CARRUTHERS

SAMARKAND, a city in the Uzbek Republic, is a most ancient town. We first hear of it 329 B.C., under the name of Marcanda, at which time it was destroyed by Alexander the Great. It lies by the Zarafshan River, about 160 miles north of the Afghan border. No other city has by its name alone so stirred the imaginations of men as has Samarkand ever since the days of its magnificence in the fourteenth century under Tamarlane. It has since been overshadowed by Bokhara. In 1868 it was taken by the Russians and a modern town was built beside the old one.

164

D. CARRUTHERS

BOKHARA, the province, bounds Samarkand on the south. The several native states over which Uzbek dynasties formerly ruled were founded in the fifteenth century upon the ruins of Tamerlane's empire. Bokhara, the famous capital, lies in the northwest. The ancient Eastern city is an expanse of flat, gray-brown roofs relieved by towers of mosques.

SOVFOTO

A COTTON PICKER IN THE UZBEK FIELDS

This smiling girl, dressed in the colorful costume of her district, holds an armful of freshly picked cotton.

brings memory of gorgeous oriental rugs which have been named after the cities where they have so long been marketed.

But Turkestan is known not only for its rugs but also for its eagles. For the Mohammedans love to train hawks and eagles for hunting. Their eagles will attack even wolves.

Across this country people have sifted through the centuries like sand over a desert. To understand modern Turkestan a brief historical sketch is necessary. The country has altered little since the time when Tatar, Turk and Mongol ranged over its mountains and plains, when "Sultan after Sultan, with his pomp, abode his hour or two and went his way." And in some respects the peoples themselves have undergone but little change. Large numbers of them live by raising horses, camels, cattle and sheep, by growing cotton and wheat and fruit, or by working the rich mineral deposits of the country.

Among the peoples in the western part

of this group of present-day Soviet Republics the Turcomans are the most important. Mohammedans by religion, they are akin to the Beduins in the nature of their life, for they have regular camping places and move from one pasturage to another according to the season. Turcomans were always nomads, and because of their fierceness they were always dreaded by their neighbors. They plundered ruthlessly, waylaying the rich caravans of the Persian traders and looting greedily. Out of this arose a great trade in slaves, but the Turcoman's activities in this direction have been checked by the Russians.

The Turcoman is rather a striking figure dressed in his baggy trousers and coarse shirt, which is mostly concealed by an outer garment of colored material somewhat like a dressing-gown. To complete his costume, he wears high-heeled boots, a shaggy high hat made of sheep's wool and a gaudy scarlet sash. This is the ordinary tribesman of the plains. In the case of the better class Turcomans, those who are counted wealthy in flocks and herds, the common garments give place to richly embroidered robes, while the trappings of their horses and camels are splendidly adorned with gold and silver and precious stones.

Their womenfolk like to wear quantities of jewelry and display many bracelets and anklets. In place of the sheepskin or felt hats of the men they cover their heads with cotton cloths, much in the form of a turban, and these headdresses, too, will be plentifully decorated with silver ornaments and coins. It is said that one judges the wealth of a Turcoman by the amount of silver worn by his wife. Like the Beduins to whom they have been compared, this people leave a great deal of manual work to the women for which reason the latter age quickly. The women go unveiled, like the Beduins again, but unlike the women of nearly all other Mohammedan countries.

There are Turcomans who settle in towns and villages, in which the houses are simply built of mud and stone. But the majority, true desert wanderers, live in tents—"kibitkas" they are called—which are made of braided willows and covered with felt. If we look into one of these tents we shall see that the furniture consists of a carpet on the floor and several brilliantly colored rugs hanging on the walls, together with cloaks, embroidered garments, saddlebags, bridles and other articles. In one corner is a wooden chest, which contains the women's clothing and other gear. During the winter time a fire burns in the middle of the tent, and as there is no chimney and the smoke has to find its way out as best it can, the atmosphere is none of the pleasantest.

Summer time on these western "steppes," or plains, is endurable, though often very hot. In the winter, especially when the weather is severe, the conditions of life are very hard. Terrible blizzards storm across the desert, often destroying flocks and herds and human beings as well. In January the temperature may go down to 40° below zero. We can get some idea of the intensity of the cold from the description given by Colonel Burnaby in his famous Ride to Khiva. The nostrils of the horses, he says, became blocked with ice, and cabbage soup froze solid when it was made. It had to be carried on camelback and broken off as it was wanted.

EWING GALLOWAY

TOWNSMEN AT EASE BEFORE A MOSQUE OF ANCIENT BUKHARA

A water seller sits behind his jugs; a melon peddler is at the foot of the steps to the mosque, a center of social as well as religious life in the Islamic city. Most of the people of Bukhara are Uzbeks, nomadic herdsmen of Turkestan who long ago drove the Persians and Turks from the Kyzyl Kum, the arid region between the Amu and Syr Darya (rivers).

LIEUT.-COL. P. J. ETHERTON

THE ROOF OF THE WORLD is the picturesque name man has given to that huge, bleak knot of mountains known as the Pamirs, lying in central Asia between Afghanistan, Turkestan and Sinkiang (Chinese Turkestan). From it run some of the earth's mightiest mountain chains, including the Himalayas, the Karakoram range and the Hindu Kush. "Pamir" means valley between two ridges. These valleys are nowhere less than 10,000 feet above the sea and the highest peak is over 26,000 above the sea. Through them roam the Kirghiz, the only dwellers in this inhospitable region.

It is desert country, this western region, as has been said, but it is made habitable by the presence of oases. A Turkestan oasis consists of wide fields of wheat, barley, cotton and grass, well watered by streams from a near-by river or by wells and irrigation ditches, and broken by groves of locust trees, with their sweet-smelling blossom, and orchards and vineyards. It is a paradise set in a stony wilderness. The soil here is usually very rich and it can be made to produce—as at Merv—fine crops of wheat and cotton. At one time Turkestan was quite a large wheat-growing country. Nowadays cotton is cultivated as yielding greater profit.

Peoples of Mongolian Origin

Two other peoples of the original Turki race go to make up the population of Turkestan. These are the Kirghiz and the Uzbegs. The first-named are themselves divided into the Kazaks, or Kirghiz-Kazaks, and the Kara-Kirghiz. Both tribes dwell in the eastern portion of Turkestan. Their features show plainly their Mongolian origin. They are a short people, with round, dark faces and small, keen, black eyes which look at one from beneath tightly drawn, slanting eyelids. The Kazaks are the lowlanders, the dwellers in the northern and eastern steppes, and are shepherds and herdsmen. The Kara-Kirghiz are the mountaineers, the highlanders, and their home is in the Pamirs and in the huge Tian Shan range, the Celestial Mountains.

By religion the Kirghiz, like other Turkestan peoples, are Mohammedans but shave their heads and allow their beards to grow. Their costume resembles that of the Turcomans, except that the baggy breeches are of leather. A coarsely made shirt with a wide-striped collar and an over-tunic of the dressing-gown pattern are worn, together with the usual tall hat of sheepskin.

The Persian name Kirghiz, it may be noted, means "forty daughters." In the tradition of the tribesmen, it was a son of Noah who settled in Turkestan after the Flood, and this son was the father of forty daughters. From these the Kirghiz believe themselves to be descended, and hence their name.

Turkestan's Fair-skinned Inhabitants

The Uzbegs, who, with a race known as Tajiks, are found in most parts of the country, are a people of light complexion. The men wear turbans of white linen, and their principal garment is the "khalet," a long flowing coat dyed in brilliant colors. With the Uzbegs, it is the custom for the women to wear a veil and no one but a husband, a son, or a very close relative is permitted to look upon their faces.

With a brief mention of the Tajiks, who lay claim to Arab descent, we may conclude this description of Turkestan's principal peoples. Actually they originally hailed from Persia; apart from physical characteristics and similarities in language, this is shown by their typical Persian aptitude for trade. They are the merchants of the province, and their reputation is one for cunning and greed. The intellectual superiors of the Uzbegs, the Tajiks congregate in the towns, while the majority of the former follow agriculture and kindred industries.

A Glimpse of Ancient Cities

And now, what of the cities of Turkestan, those strongholds of other days, which have witnessed such stirring events in the whirligig of time? First of all, let us take a peep at Tashkent. As a map shows, it lies on a branch of the River Syr Daria, with great mountains at its back. There are two cities actually—the old native city, inhabited by a people known as Sarts, a term used to designate the nomadic Uzbegs who have become settled, and there is the modern Russian quarter. Thanks to the care exercised by the Russian conquerors Tashkent has been beautified by many groves of trees and large gardens. One special feature of the capital is the market. The bazaars of Tashkent are declared to be the finest in the world, rivaling even those of Cairo. To its shops come all the treasures of the East, the beautiful carpets, the richly em-

BUKHARA STUDENTS TAKE TIME OUT FOR A JOKE IN THE SUN

The young men are Mohammedans who are studying the Koran. Their setting is appropriate
for the niche is in the Moslem style of architecture. Above the grill is a lovely mosaic.

170

EWING GALLOWAY

A SHOULDER MAKES A FINE PLACE TO DISPLAY A RUG

The fringed rug, in an interesting geometric design, is the product of a factory in Mary, Turkmenistan. Once called Merv, the city has long been a center of carpet manufacturing.

IN THE BROILING SUN OF THE DESERT, AT TEKKE OASIS, A CARAVAN PAUSES FOR REST AND WATER

So much of Russian Turkestan is desert that caravans of camels are still the chief means of transportation. Most caravans move on regular sched- ules, and there are inns (the Eastern word is "caravansary") at several oases for the convenience of travelers and their beasts of burden.

A KAZAKH TRIBESMAN, HIS FACE ETCHED BY TIME AND WEATHER

On his native plains he has endured withering heat in summertime and intense cold in the winter. For Kazakhstan is deep within Asia and has the extremes of a continental climate.

A UZBEK COBBLER GRINS CHEERFULLY OVER A WORN BOOT

The soles must be of tough leather for the boots of Uzbek horsemen get hard wear. Instead of settling down permanently in a shop, the shoemaker follows his roving customers.

UNIFORMED SCHOOL CHILDREN march beneath the statue of Lenin that dominates the town square of Ashkhabad, the commercially important capital of Turkmenistan.

SCHOOL DAYS IN THE FABLED CITY OF SAMARKAND

Books are a special delight to these boys for it is likely that they are the first members of their families to go to school. Samarkand is deep in central Asia, a region where people speak strange tongues. Even today some of these dialects have no written form. Tamerlane, the fierce fourteenth-century Mogul conqueror, made Samarkand his capital city.

broidered cloths and the delicate silver and brass ware of the skilled workers in metal. Among the frequenters of the bazaars a familiar figure is the sherbet-seller, who goes about in the crowd with a tank on his back and glasses in his hands. He makes his approach known by rattling the glasses together.

If Bokhara is not so large and important as Tashkent, it is, nevertheless, a great commercial centre. Into this old-world city pour the camel caravans from China, India, Afghanistan and Persia, loaded with their precious freights of tea, silk, furs, dyestuffs and other goods. These are the caravans which, in past years, were pounced upon by the rapacious Turcoman. From Bokhara they go out again with

cotton, ironmongery, sugar, coffee and other commodities, which have been mostly obtained from Russia.

As a leading trading centre Bokhara is noted for its carpets. The finest in the world are exhibited here. Another particular feature of its market is "caracul," a fur, which comes from the prepared skin of the Persian lamb, or sometimes kid. We are also familiar with it under the name of astrakhan.

But Bokhara has another claim to distinction besides that of commerce. It is a university town, a home of learning, and has been so for more than a thousand years. At one time the city could boast of 197 mosques and 167 "madrasahs," or Moslem theological colleges, most of which have fallen into decay. There are, however, many state controlled educational buildings in Bukhara that are still in use.

The most famous mosque is the Masjid Kalian, dating back to the tenth century. It was into this mosque that Jenghiz Khan, the great Asiatic conqueror, rode in defiance of the mullahs, or priests. He dismounted, went up into the pulpit, and threw the Koran on the floor, shouting to his followers as he did so: "The hay is cut! Give your horses fodder!" This was the signal for the savage Mongolian soldiery to begin a dreadful massacre and to loot the city.

The Mir Arab is another noted mosque, an ancient seat of Moslem learning.

The architecture of Bukhara, with its domes and minarets, tells the story of the city's past religious and cultural grandeur. Bukhara was once so important a center of Islam that it rivaled even the holy city of Mecca as a place to which young men came to study for the priesthood and to which scholars journeyed from great distances. It is still deeply Eastern in flavor, with its labyrinthine streets and outdoor bazaars.

As has been told, Khiva has been joined up with Bukhara to form a Soviet Republican State. It is an ancient province of Turkestan, for it dates back to the first and second Persian empires and to the days of Alexander the Great whose armies were in the country more than two thousand years ago.

In the town of Khiva are several "madrasahs," for so important a place cannot be without its colleges. Khiva was the capital of the province of Khiva, a distinction which previously belonged to Urgenj, in the markets of which were sold the corn, cotton, rice, tobacco and other products of the rich province, as well as the spendid breed of horses for which it was famed.

Ferghana is another province of Turkestan, and its chief town is Khokan. It

SOVFOTO

A STURDY TILLER OF THE SOIL IN UZBEKISTAN

As a Uzbek, he belongs to a group of people who are Mohammedans and whose way of life was influenced by Persia for centuries. Their language, however, is related to Turkish.

POLO ON THE ROOF OF THE WORLD

The Pamir Plateau is a lofty tableland north of the Hindu Kush range. Much of it is mountainous, but there are flat areas that make good pasture land. The region is sometimes known as "the roof of the world," for its average elevation is about 13,000 feet. Polo is a favorite sport among the Kirghiz who live there and who raise fleet, intelligent ponies.

lies in a fork of the great Tian Shan mountain range and is a very fertile and fair country. Of all places in Turkestan, there is none that appeals more to the imagination than does Samarkand. The town of this name was in olden time the capital of Asia, and its splendors were unsurpassed and were extolled by historian and poet alike.

"Golden Samarkand" could not attain to such a height of glory without paying the usual penalty of those times. It was attacked, destroyed and rebuilt over and over again, and in the course of years much of its beauty and greatness passed. Today it is a city of considerable size, with a trade in horses and asses; but, except for a few open squares, it is composed of narrow, ill-kept streets. Prominent among its buildings are the three "madrasahs," seats of learning, which are still famous throughout the province.

Apart from these survivals of the past, the "madrasahs" and mosques, Samar-kand has scarcely anything to show of its former splendor. In the city where Alexander the Great and Tamerlane in turn held sway are mean-looking houses, some of mud, and the rich trains of merchandise that once found their way thither by horse, mule and camel have long since turned their steps to Bokhara, to Tashkent and to the other newer cities.

These interesting cities with such a long and colorful past are all within the limits of the Uzbek Soviet Republic. In the Turcoman Republic, Merv, situated in an oasis renowned for its fertility, is considered in Hindu, Parsi and Arab tradition as the ancient Paradise. Like Samarkand and Bokhara, it became a rich and splendid city and at one time was the center of learning, but all its glory has passed away and in the nineteenth century, the old town was abandoned for a new site on the Transcaspian railway on which its carpets, long famous, and its agricultural products may be exported.

Ashkhabad, the capital, owes its growing importance as a commercial center to its situation on the Transcaspian railway, the western terminus of which is Krasnovodsk, on the Caspian Sea. Krasnovodsk is the port for the Republic. Cotton and dried fruits are the chief exports.

The people of Ashkhabad cannot look back on the glorious past of their city, for it has none, but they are already taking steps to insure for it a prosperous future. We should not be surprised, indeed, to find that they have a gardening school with a model garden and mulberry plantation, and that for years they have been reforesting the surrounding land.

One last feature of Turkestan—not the least notable—remains to be mentioned. This is the great mountain range known as the Pamirs, or "the Roof of the World."

From this bleak, craggy tableland run some of the mightiest mountain chains on earth, such as the Himalayas, the Hindu Kush, the Karakoram, the Tian Shan and the Trans-Altai.

It is as wild a region as can be found anywhere, and the fascination of it has drawn many famous travelers thither since Marco Polo crossed it on his way to the court of Kublai Khan. Here is to be found the great-horned mountain sheep, the "Ovis Poli," whose head is reckoned as one of the finest of sportsmen's trophies. And on these mountain slopes and in the valleys the Kirghiz hillmen pasture their flocks. For many years past the Pamirs have been occupied by Russia, and the present borders of Russia and Afghanistan have been settled to run across "the Roof of the World."

EWING GALLOWAY

MELON VENDOR IN THE ANCIENT CITY OF SAMARKAND, UZBEKISTAN

From the days when Samarkand was a stronghold of Tamerlane, the people of the dry area in which the city is situated have prized melons with their refreshing juice. Today the desert is being transformed. Irrigation is bringing water to the parched earth and it is beginning to yield bountiful crops. Two-thirds of Russia's cotton production is grown in Uzbekistan.

NOMADS OF THE DESERT IN RUSSIAN (OR WESTERN) TURKESTAN

Crossing the hot, shifting desert sands would be well-nigh impossible but for camels, those ships of the desert, which can do without water for long periods as well as detect it from afar.

TURKESTAN: FACTS AND FIGURES

THE COUNTRY

The territory east of the Caspian Sea, known as Western, or Russian, Turkestan, is divided into five Soviet Socialist Republics:—Turkmenistan, Uzbekistan, Tadzhikistan, Kazakhstan, Kirghizstan, and one autonomous republic.

TURKMENISTAN (Turkmen Soviet Socialist Republic)

Became a Soviet Republic in 1925. The area is 189,370 square miles and the population, 1,254,000, mostly Sunni Mohammedan. Agriculture is the main occupation of the people. Products include cotton, wool, and astrakhan fur. The region is famous for its carpets and special breed of horses. There are rich mineral deposits. A railway, air line and motor communication serve the country. The chief towns are Ashkhabad, the capital, Mary, Krasnovodsk, Kerki and Tashauz.

UZBEKISTAN (Uzbek Soviet Socialist Republic)

Became a Soviet Republic in May, 1925. The area is 159,170 square miles and the population 6,300,000, mostly Sunni Mohammedans. Agriculture, based on artificial irrigation, is the chief occupation, cotton the main product. There is a railway and air service. The chief towns are Tashkent, the capital, population, 585,000, Samarkand, Bokhara, Khiva and Andijan.

TADZHIKISTAN (Tadzhik Soviet Socialist Republic)

Became a Soviet Republic in October, 1929. The area is 55,545 square miles and the population, 1,500,000. Principal occuaption is farming and cattle-breeding, and there are rich mineral deposits. Capital, Stalinabad.

KAZAKHSTAN (Kazakh Soviet Socialist Republic)

Became a Soviet Republic in December, 1936. The area is 1,072,797 square miles and the population, 6,200,000. There are rich mineral deposits but the majority of the people farm and breed cattle. Capital, Alma-Ata.

KIRGHIZSTAN (Kirghiz Soviet Socialist Republic)

Became a Soviet Republic in December, 1936. The area is 76,042 square miles, population, 1,500,000. Capital, Frunze.

RUSSIA'S REPUBLICS IN THE CAUCASUS

Ancient Countries of Armenia, Georgia and Azerbaijan

Armenia, Georgia and Azerbaijan lie among the Caucasus Mountains between the Black and Caspian seas. At various times each has struggled for independence but such efforts have rarely been successful. For the region is in the unfortunate position of being a land bridge between Russia proper and Iran and Turkey, nations often in rivalry with one another and sometimes at war. Under the Soviet Government many of the people of these sensitive borders, distrusted because of their freedom-loving traditions, have been forced to move far into the interior of Russian territory in Asia.

ARAB invaders converted the people of both Georgia and Azerbaijan to Islam in the seventh century. Armenia is generally regarded as the oldest Christian country. Intolerant of one another's religious beliefs, the two Mohammedan nations and Armenia have often been at war with each other. Massacre and destruction of property, encouraged and often begun by neighbors for political reasons, and foreign invasions long kept these three countries from making any material progress.

In 1922, however, they laid aside their differences and formed the Republic of Transcaucasia. Fourteen years later they separated again and each became a republic in the Union of Soviet Socialist Republics. They are now clothed in secrecy behind the iron curtain.

A glance at the map will show us that these three little countries occupy a bridge of territory which connects Russia, in the north, with Iran (Persia) in the south. It is separated from Asia, on the east, by the Caspian Sea and from Europe, on the west, by the Black Sea. Forming a natural frontier on the north are the snow-topped Caucasus Mountains, the scenery of which rivals even that of the Alps, a fact not generally known, for it is not so easy to travel in this country as in Switzerland. Although the land is almost treeless and presents a bleak, rugged appearance travelers are usually fascinated by its wild aspect and by the ever-changing color of the mountains, and are loath to leave. Highest of the mountain peaks are Mount Elburz and Mount Kazbek. On the latter, according to mythology, Prometheus was chained as a punishment for giving fire to mankind.

Just over the border to the southeast, completely isolated from the Caucasus range, is the lofty and inspiring Mount Ararat, which rises from the surrounding plains to a height of 16,916 feet. On Mount Ararat, Noah is supposed to have landed after the Deluge, and the inhabitants claim to be able to show evidence that this is true. They will point out the site of the burial place of Noah's wife and the location of his vineyard, and they will even show you pieces of the Ark itself.

It was on Mount Ararat also that the donkey learned to bray, so it is said. The story goes that Noah, when assembling his companions for a sojourn in the Ark, issued an invitation to a donkey. The donkey was very stubborn, however, and refused Noah's kindness. Then the flood came and the water began to rise; the donkey kept going higher and higher to avoid it. Finally he reached the summit of Mount Ararat but still the waters rose, until they reached the neck of the poor animal. Thoroughly frightened, then, he raised his head toward the heavens and bawled, "No-ah-h-h! No-ah-h-h!" Noah went to his aid and donkeys from that time on have always called the name of their benefactor.

Mount Ararat was formerly in Armenia, which occupies the southwestern portion of Transcaucasia, while Azerbaijan occupies the southeast and Georgia the north. Travel here we should find very difficult indeed, for there are few railroads, and those connect only the largest cities and ports. Horseback and motor are the favor-

YEREVAN, AT THE FOOT OF MOUNT ARARAT

From Yerevan (or Erivan), capital of Armenia, you can look up to glacier-crowned Mount Ararat, the mountain that tradition makes the resting place of Noah's ark. Yerevan is an industrial city of 200,000 inhabitants, and the cultural center of Armenia. It has a university, an opera, a number of scientific institutes and a branch of the Academy of Sciences of the U.S.S.R.

The northern part of the Caucasus and the divisions marked 1, 2, 3, 4, 5, 6, 7, are included in the R.S.F.S.R. (Russia Proper). Georgian S.S.R. includes the Abkhazian (8), the Adzharian (9) Autonomous Republics and the South" Ossetian Autonomous Region (10). Armenian S.S.R. has no divisions. Azerbaijan S.S.R. included Nakhichevan Autonomous Republic (12) and the Nagorno-Karabakh Autonomous Province (11).

ite methods of getting about, but some of the districts are almost impossible to reach, so much so that the people living there are politically semi-independent.

Armenia, oldest of these countries historically, was once a great kingdom with territories to the south. Today it is divided between Turkey and the Soviet Union. In the Turkish section is Mount Ararat, highest point in modern Turkey and the traditional landing place of Noah's Ark. Russian Armenia is the Armenian Soviet Socialist Republic.

Like most countries, it was first inhabited by tribes who are thought to have come from the east and settled around the foot of Mount Ararat. These nomadic peoples were conquered about the sixth century before Christ by the Medes and Persians and then the territory was divided into two satrapies, or provinces, of the great Persian Empire. Eastern and Western Armenia, as they were known, became powerful in time and overthrew their overlord. This was accomplished mainly

by Tigranes the Great who welded Armenia into one strong kingdom. Although it did not last long, it brought the Armenian people together and gave them a feeling of unity which has lasted through the ages.

Armenia has had an unfortunate situation. From its beginning, it has been a buffer state between more powerful and warring nations, between Asia and Europe, between the East and the West. In addition it has been a lone Christian nation among states of other religions whose followers sought to convert their neighbors by force.

The Armenians were converted to Christianity early in the fourth century under Gregory the Illuminator, and became most ardent in their faith. When Persia, their overlord, tried to make them adopt fire worship, they replied: "No one can move us from our belief, neither angels nor men, fire nor sword." So they have felt always even though it has meant massacre and the scattering of their people. Their faith

183

SOVFOTO

GRAPE-PICKING TIME IN ARMENIA

Irrigation has made nearly half a million acres of soil in Armenia suitable for agriculture. All but 2 per cent of the agricultural workers belong to collective farms that produce cotton (long-fibered variety), grapes and other fruit.

and again. Now and then they had a brief period of independence, as that which began in 571, under the leadership of Vartan, but which lasted only seven years. Since then Vartan has been a favored Christian name for Armenian boys and Vartan's Day is celebrated even now as a national holiday.

The Turkish conquest was completed about 1514, when Selim I set out toward the East on a campaign against Persia. Turkey was then at the zenith of her power but she was in time to be checked in the north by a nation whose strength in Europe had been greatly increasing. That was Russia. In the wars between them, during the nineteenth century, Russia advanced her Caucasus boundary well into Armenia, and since then Armenia, divided, has belonged partly to Russia and partly to Turkey.

Russia found her Armenian subjects intelligent and industrious, and able to help in the development of the country. She therefore encouraged emigration from Turkish Armenia into the provinces she owned. The Armenians on their part felt better protected in Russia. They accumulated property, became more progressive, and the land itself was noticeably better cultivated than on the other side of the line. Except for feuds with their Moslem neighbors the people were better off than they had been in centuries.

During the struggle between Russia and Turkey, there had been growing secretly a party called the Dashnacks, who sought to secure the independence of Armenia. Although it represented only the more

has withstood invasions of the Persians, Arabs, Seljuks, Mongols and Turks, but their territory has been conquered time

MOUNTAIN CLIMBING AMONG THE PEAKS OF RUSSIAN ARMENIA

The ancient country of Armenia, divided today among Iran, Russia and Turkey, is on the southern edge of the breath-takingly beautiful Caucasus Mountains. They mark a land boundary between Europe and Asia. In the Russian part, there are many peaks above 10,000 feet; the highest, Alagöz, is 13,435 feet. These climbers are ascending the summits of the Aragats range.

radical element of the people, it brought about local warfare which served to arouse the Turks and as a result, during the years 1895 and 1896, thousands of the Christian inhabitants were exterminated in a series of massacres so atrocious that the story is almost unbelievable. Foreign nations were horrified and attempted to interfere, but as they could not agree to go to war with Turkey, their concern did little to help.

When World War I broke out the Turks again took occasion to rid themselves of their Christian subjects. Claiming that the Armenians were taking up arms against them, they slaughtered men, women and children with savage brutality and forced others toward Mesopotamia and the Syrian deserts to almost certain death. American and British missionaries helped to relieve the suffering by giving

185

MUSICIANS ENTERTAIN COLLECTIVE FARMERS AT HARVEST TIME

Armenia has undergone many changes since it became a Soviet Socialist Republic in 1920. A State Song and Dance Ensemble is the official musical group of the country. Some of its performers are shown here on a collective farm. Part of the Soviet program to encourage greater agricultural production is to supply on-the-spot entertainment for the workers at harvest time.

out food and first aid treatments, but in spite of their aid many thousands perished.

Russian Armenia quite naturally allied herself with Russia at the beginning of World War I, but the Russian Revolution three years later left her only partially able to protect herself. Caught between the advancing Turkish armies and the unorganized armies of the Bolsheviki who had control of Russia, she had a most difficult time. In addition the country became flooded with starving and disease-stricken refugees who had been able to escape from Turkey, and had trekked across Northwestern Persia to what seemed to be their only refuge. Unable to retain the independence which the Dashnacks had hastened to declare, Armenia finally decided to cast her lot with the Soviet Government which had succeeded the Bolshevists, and in 1920 became a republic of the Soviet Union under Russia. About 85 per cent of the people in the territory are Armenians.

The question of the Armenian people and Armenia was considered by the League of Nations. It was hoped that in time a national home could be es-

tablished in Armenia where those refugees who had reached other lands in safety might be repatriated. Armenians were especially interested in the plan as they had long desired a land of their own where they could live by themselves and could develop it into one of great prosperity.

Until the Soviet Government took the land over, it had been badly in need of development. In most of the region it was hard indeed for the peasant to make even a meager living. In the valley of the Araxes River, which girds Mount Ararat, there is rich and fertile soil, and tobacco, rice and cotton are grown as well as many varieties of fruits and vegetables. There are vineyards, but the vines must be buried during winter frosts. In the hilly districts, forestry is important and cattle are raised.

Agriculture is the main occupation of the people, and, as one might suspect, their methods have been quite primitive. Home-made wooden plows, drawn by oxen or water buffaloes, still serve some Armenian farmers. However, several large canals have been completed for irrigation purposes, and more than half the land is in large collective farms worked by modern machinery. Much of the irrigated land is devoted to the cultivation of cotton.

The houses of the peasants are usually built against the side of a hill or a mountain which saves the material necessary to make a back wall. Then, too, it gives protection from the wintry winds and thus saves fuel which is a very scarce article in this unforested region. The roofs are flat and are sometimes covered with earth, so that grass will grow and serve as pasture for the family cow or sheep. Inside the houses are almost bare of furniture—a few simple chairs and possibly a fireplace where the cooking is done. In the winter the cow and sheep are given a place in the house, for their body heat is needed to bring the temperature of the room a bit higher.

Accustomed to living in this mountainous region where the winters are long and severe, the Armenians are strong and energetic and not unused to hard work. They are usually dark and the women are noted for their beauty. Many Persians, Kurds and Turks have fallen under the spell of the beautiful black eyes of Armenian maidens, and have taken them back to their own countries as their wives. The women have won a reputation too for their beautiful handwork, which they do at home in order to help out the family income. Fine Armenian lace, lovely embroidery and Oriental rugs are made with painstaking effort, often at the cost of their eyesight

The Armenian farmer gets his real enjoyment out of a trip to market, for he likes to talk and argue, and the sale of a cow or sheep will give him a great opportunity. Like all buying and selling in Near Eastern countries, it will take hours, perhaps all day, to arrive at a price which each knew at first would have been perfectly satisfactory.

A birth or wedding also gives cause for a celebration. In the olden days a wedding in a prosperous Armenian home was a gala event. It would probably last all night and from start to finish, the tables would be piled with food and drink while the guests made speeches and danced, sometimes singly, sometimes together. The bride would be decked with jewelry—a headdress draped with coins, bracelets and necklaces, for, aside from their liking for decoration, the Armenians thought it safer to have their wealth in a form which would be easy to carry.

Suppose we had been invited to the home of a well-to-do Armenian and were pressed to stay to dinner. What interesting food we should have had! There would have been a meat dish consisting of tender bits of lamb combined with vegetables, in some appetizing way; there would have been pilaf, which is rice cooked in oil, and eggplant, probably, for the Armenians know many ways of preparing that vegetable—ways of which Western people have never heard. Then for dessert there would have been paklava, for that is, indeed, a delectable sweet—a light crusty pastry with nuts and honey. Of course, we should have wines to drink and small cups of sweet Turkish coffee, and we should all have agreed that we had had a delicious meal most bountifully served.

Armenians who have migrated to Europe or America have proved to be

SOVFOTO

A FISHERWOMAN of Azerbaijan brings her fine catch of sturgeon to a local fishery.

TECHNICAL SCHOOLS prepare future workers for Azerbaijan's expanding oil industry. Here students listen to a lecture in the chemistry laboratory of an industrial institute.

valuable citizens. They are shrewd and energetic, qualities that make them successful in business.

Most of the cities of Armenia are small, in fact hardly more than towns. However, Yerevan (or Erivan), the capital and largest city, has a population of about 200,000. It was almost completely rebuilt during the 1920's and made quite modern in appearance. The city reflects the communist emphasis on education—though *what* is taught, of course, must follow the dictates of the state. The Armenian State University is here, as well as several colleges, a library and a Tropical Institute. There is also a branch of the Academy of Sciences of the U.S.S.R. Imposing buildings house the government offices and the state theater of opera and ballet. One of the most interesting old structures remaining is the Blue Mosque.

Yerevan is on the Zanga River. Since a hydroelectric station was built here in 1926, the city has developed numerous industries. Machinery, furniture, brick, leather goods, silk, glycerin, wine and brandy are among the many products.

A few miles west of Yerevan is the ancient monastery of Echmiadzin, the seat of the Armenian, or Gregorian, Church. The monastery is the residence of the Catholicus, or head of the church. Reports indicate that the Soviet Union has not attacked the church directly, knowing how deeply the Armenians are attached to it. Instead, it has been made an instrument of the state. Armenians outside of Russia consider the Catholicus a communist puppet.

At Leninakan (once called Aleksandropol), which is on a branch of the Araks River, is another hydroelectric station. The waters of Lake Sevan have also been harnessed. Altogether there are more than fifty hydroelectric stations in Soviet Armenia, for both power and irrigation purposes. Under the Soviets, the region has become an important industrial center. More than 80 per cent of its products are manufactured goods.

Mining has kept equal pace. Armenia has rich stores of copper, zinc, aluminum, molybdenum and other metals. These are

NEAR EAST RELIEF

LIBRARY OF ARMENIAN LITERATURE

The monastery, Echmiadzin, includes the ancient and valuable library shown above. Though not beautiful architecturally, it contains a large collection of Armenian literature.

essential raw materials for heavy industry, which is one of the chief concerns of the communist planners. There is also a wealth of building materials.

Georgia is almost as old historically as Armenia and has suffered almost as many invasions. The Georgians, however, after their country had been devastated for nearly two centuries by the Arabs, finally succumbed to Mohammedanism and since then have not suffered persecution.

Tradition has it that the inhabitants of Georgia are descended from Japheth, son of Noah, but we cannot trace their history from that early time. We know of them first in the fourth century before Christ when Alexander the Great sent one of his generals to annex the territory then known as Iberia. The people were able to free themselves from the Macedonians after the death of Alexander and then enjoyed independence for over a hundred years. However, Georgia was not to be left alone. The great Persian Empire, always eager for more territory, was to the East what the Turks and the Byzantine Greeks later were to the West. Georgia had some friendly connection with the Byzantine Empire, for Constantine, the first Byzantine emperor, had sent Christian missionaries who had converted the Georgians. Therefore, when Persia's strength had somewhat weakened, Georgia took the opportunity to appeal to the Byzantine

CHURCH OF ST. HRIPSIME, AN EARLY CHRISTIAN MARTYR

Legend tells us that Hripsime, a beautiful Christian nun, who lived in Rome, fled to Armenia to escape the attentions of Emperor Diocletian, a pagan. The Armenian king, Tiridates, on beholding her beauty, fell in love with her, too, and because she repulsed him ordered her slain. Her body is said to have been placed in a vault buried deep beneath this church.

Empire for a king. She was granted a viceroy, and the Bagratid dynasty which was then founded ruled from 571 to 1803.

In the seventh century came the Arabs and for 180 years the country was overrun until the people finally accepted Islam. Georgia then enjoyed a period of relief during which the boundaries were extended from the Black to the Caspian Sea and at one time included part of Armenia. She had successfully repulsed the Seljuks and the Persians, but was not able to withstand the Mongol hordes who came west led by Jenghiz Khan. Again the land was overrun by the Mongols under Tamerlane who set fire to the entire country. Wars between the Persians and the Turks during the seventeenth century caused Georgia to seek the help of Russia and in 1801 she became a Russian province.

Since then Georgia has been independent for two short periods—from 1904 to 1906, when Russia was at war with Japan, and from 1918 to 1921. The latter period of freedom came immediately following the Russian Revolution, when Georgia felt she had an opportunity to break off, but she was finally forced to join the Soviets and to become a republic.

Like Armenia, Georgia is an agricultural country, but it is much more fertile owing to the fact that the melting snow from its many mountains and an irrigation system provides water in plenty for those who live in the valleys. However, those living in the mountains are wretchedly poor and have a hard time making a living from the barren soil. Rye bread, cattle and sheep is their principal diet, and a traveler will sometimes find that the village inn or rest-house cannot provide a speck of food.

In the valleys, one may see fruit of many varieties, both tropical and subtropical, corn, grown for food by nearly every valley peasant, wheat, barley, cotton, tobacco, tea and rice. A great variety indeed! Mulberry trees are seen, too, for silkworm culture is one of the oldest occupations of the people. Grapes grow in great luxuriance, sometimes wild, and so the making of wine has become the industry for which Georgia is most noted.

In a few areas, the workers still use a primitive press for squeezing the grapes, and when the wine is ready it is put into tarred buffalo skins and then piled on wooden carts which joggle along the rough mountain roads until they reach the city. In 1930, the Soviet Union made plans for a great expansion of the industry. One of the most important points in the plan was for the development of champagne!

Because of the mountains, Georgia has rich mineral deposits, chief of which is a fine quality of manganese, but there is also copper and iron and there are numerous mineral springs, both hot and cold, containing sulphur, iron and radium.

So much for Georgia's products. Let us now see what the people are like. The majority are Georgians, although there are a goodly number of Armenians, Tatars and Russians. The Georgians speak a language that is supposed to have been connected with the Sumerian-Babylonian and so difficult has it proved that very little has been translated into other languages.

The Georgians are fine looking people and very intelligent and they delight in colorful costumes. The women, even though poorly dressed, usually seem gay with many colors. The well-to-do women wear a long coatlike garment of silk covering loose trousers which are caught at the ankles. On their heads they wear scarlet velvet caps decorated with pearls. The men usually wear a tall cap made of astrakhan which is called a papahk, and a shaggy wool coat. Part of the male costume is a dagger or sword for Daghestan.

Near East Relief

ANCIENT CHRISTIAN CHURCH OF ECHMIADZIN

The monastery of Echmiadzin, west of Erivan, was the seat of the Catholicus or primate of the Armenian church. Among the buildings is an ancient Christian church which is thought to have been founded by St. Gregory the Illuminator in 302, and is said to be the oldest Christian church. The Church of the Nativity in Bethlehem also claims this distinction.

A SHEPHERD AND HIS FLOCKS IN THE GRASSLANDS OF GEORGIA

A shepherd watches over his sheep as they graze on the rolling Shiraki Steppe of southern Georgia. In the summer the flocks trek more than a hundred miles to mountain pasture.

that province of Georgia which borders on the Caspian, is famous for its fine artistry in silver and steel.

In the mountainous districts, the houses are built on terraces, but in the more prosperous places they are made of rough stone or baked mud and often have large wooden balconies around the first floor, and roofs of undulating red tiles. The houses of the rich are often very beautiful, especially those which are decorated with colored glazed tiles, indicating the Persian influence.

Now and then there is a neat, orderly village inhabited by German people. Early in the tenth century, the founders of these villages started toward the Holy Land because they thought the end of the world was near. They made their way slowly until agents sent in advance returned to report that all was not as they believed in Jerusalem and so they stayed where they were. They farmed as they had done in Germany, built villages on the German plan and retained their German language until recently. Since World War II, German place names have been changed to Russian, and the people speak Russian.

One may see also villages where the Molokans reside. These people belong to a sect of the Russian Church comparable to our Quakers. They derive their name from the custom of living on milk (*moloko,* in Russian) on fast days. The Molokans have no organized priesthood.

Tbilisi (Tiflis, in Russian) is the capital. It is the largest and one of the oldest cities in Georgia. The old section has an Asiatic air. A tangle of narrow, crooked alleys and primitive architecture, it is in the center of the city. To the north and to the south extend modern industrial and residential areas where the buildings are European in style. Tbilisi has many scientific and technical institutions, among them the Georgian Academy of Science.

The people of Azerbaijan are mostly

A DANGEROUS CURVE ON A MOUNTAIN HIGHWAY IN GEORGIA

A gigantic cliff leans menacingly over the road from the right, and on the left is the deep Kheva Gorge. The narrow highway through the mountains is a masterpiece of engineering skill.

Tatars, or Tartars, a people related to both the Turks and the Mongols. The Tatars (also called Azerbaijanians) follow the Mohammedan faith, but just how this religion has fared under the Soviet Government is hard to determine.

A Divided Land

Since 1920 the ancient country of Azerbaijan has been divided between Russia and Iran, with Russia holding the smaller but richer part to the north. In 1936, this was organized into the Azerbaidzhan Soviet Socialist Republic (A.S.S.R.). The republic also includes two other sections—with jawbreaking names—the Nakhichevan Autonomous Soviet Socialist Republic and the Nagorno-Karabakh Autonomous Region. Nakhichevan is a high plateau, on the Iranian border, separated from the rest of the A.S.S.R. by a narrow strip of Soviet Armenia. The forest-clad mountains of Nagorno-Karabakh, also on the Iranian border, form a continuous part of the A.S.S.R.

Only about three-fifths of the population of Soviet Azerbaijan is now of Tatar stock. The balance is made up of Armenians, Georgians and Russians. Too, national groups such as the Tatars have been disappearing. In 1949 a mass deportation, probably to somewhere deep in the interior of the Soviet Union, was carried out, mainly against people of the Caucasus border. At the time, Soviet officials said that this was necessary to guard against "enemy agents, diversionists, spies, saboteurs and all doubtful and suspicious people." All of which would seem to indicate that the Tatars, among other minority groups in the Caucasus, have never been completely reconciled to communist rule.

The central part of the A.S.S.R. is a plain, naturally arid, through which the Kura River and its tributaries flow to the Caspian and empty into that vast inland sea south of Baku. North of the plain are the moist, cool slopes of the eastern end of the Caucasus Mountains, and to the south are the eastern peaks of the mountains of Armenia.

In former years, Azerbaijan was a pastoral country, remote from the world's bustle, where the Tatars wandered with their flocks of sheep. Like many other people who live in mountainous lands, they were proud and independent. They could also be fierce fighters on occasion. Indeed, to English-speaking people the name of "Tartar" calls up a fellow with a violent temper—whether or not the Tatars really deserved this reputation. Hospitable to a fault, they would kill a sheep in a stranger's honor. After it was cooked whole in a huge pot, the host would fish out delectable morsels and pop them, willy-nilly, into his guest's mouth. The mutton would be washed down with kumiss—fermented mare's or camel's milk—poured into a bowl from which all drank.

Where the shepherds once roved there now are vast state farms with irrigated fields and numbers of drab little workers' settlements. The greatest change of all is represented by the oil derricks that bristle the land along the coast of the Caspian Sea. Here is one of the world's largest petroleum fields, which supplies the Soviet Union with about 75 per cent of its oil. Baku—center of the industry, seaport and capital of the A.S.S.R.—commands a bay on the south shore of the Apsheron Peninsula, which juts out on the southwest coast of the Caspian. There are oil wells on the peninsula, on off-shore islands and even in the bed of the sea itself, near the shore.

Baku, the Petroleum City

Baku is one of the largest cities in the Soviet Union, with a population of around 800,000. The old part of the city, to the west, dates back to at least the ninth century A.D. Here the streets are narrow and crooked, with a decidedly Oriental atmosphere. In their midst a medieval mosque still stands. Most of Baku, however, which has grown with the oil industry, is modern, with tall buildings and boulevards. It has a university and technical schools. Baku is connected with the Black Sea by two railroads; and it handles more tonnage—mostly oil, as one would expect—than any other port in the Soviet Union. Much of the crude oil is treated on the spot, and there are large refineries. The

SOVFOTO

A FOUR-HUNDRED-ACRE TEA PLANTATION, PART OF A COLLECTIVE

In Georgia, on the subtropical coast of the Black Sea, tea is one of the most important crops of the collective farms. The worker is removing the ripest leaves from the shrubs.

city also has chemical plants for processing fertilizer and rubber. This rubber is made from kok-sagyz—the Russian dandelion—which is being cultivated extensively in southern Russia.

From very ancient times it was known that the area around Baku was rich in oil, but it was not until 1871 that the first scientifically drilled wells were sunk. In 1901, Baku supplied half the world output of oil, although, of course, the total was quite small in comparison with production today. Development of this tremendous resource leaped forward after the U.S.S.R. came into existence. Some of the wells have now been drilled to a depth of more than 8,500 feet.

Pipe Lines and Tankers

Nevertheless, the Baku field is only part of a great petroleum area that spreads north beyond the boundary of Azerbaijan. Grozny, to the northwest, is second only to Baku in Russian oil production; and the Maikop field, still farther west, is almost equally important. From Baku to Batum, on the Black Sea just north of the Turkish border, there is a double pipe line, one pipe for crude oil and one for refined. However, much of the Baku oil is shipped by Caspian tankers to the Volga River—which empties into the Caspian some distance north of Baku—and thence distributed throughout the Soviet Union. Other pipe lines carry the "black gold" from the Grozny and Maikop fields to Tuapse, also on the Black Sea, or to Trudovanya, in the eastern Ukraine. All of the oil fields are electrified and connected with Baku. Altogether they yield at least 175,000,000 barrels of petroleum a year.

As we indicated earlier, Azerbaijan has also been transformed by means of irrigation, large-scale machine-farming methods and hydroelectric power. Three huge pumping stations alone on the Kura River, powered by hydroelectric installations, are said to irrigate about 75,000 acres. In fact, the A.S.S.R. has become a center of subtropical agriculture. Excellent Egyptian and Sea-Island cottons (long-fibered) are being grown in the one-time semi-desert of the central plain. Too, at vari-

ous seasons of the year, the irrigated tracts may be golden with ripe wheat, grayish green with alfalfa or show the pale jade of rice seedlings.

In the mountain valleys, in addition to walnut orchards and vineyards, silk culture has become important. It is claimed that Soviet scientists have bred a new kind of silkworm, one which gives twice as much silk as the older Bagdad variety. For the silkworms, mulberries are raised in the north.

On the Caspian coast, where malaria used to be rife, the marshlands are being drained, and there are thriving tea and tobacco plantations and groves of tangerines pomegranates and figs.

Few travelers from the West have ever visited this Caucasian region, even before it was organized into three Soviet republics. Until the days of the airplane, Caucasia was a long journey from Western centers of civilization, although those who made the difficult trip were rewarded by some of the most magnificent rugged mountain scenery to be found anywhere.

Today, the Caucasian republics are of critical importance to the Soviet Union. They contribute a large share to the state's wealth. Soviet economy and industry—not to speak of Russia's fighting forces—are at least partly dependent on the petroleum of this region.

Caucasia—Question Mark

Even more important, perhaps, is the fact that this is a border region where the Soviet Union has no buffer satellite countries to take the brunt in the event of war. Across the mountains lie a strong Turkey, closely allied with the Western community of nations, and an unpredictable Iran. The oil wells of Baku are only a brief flying distance from either of these countries. From another point of view, it is through Caucasia that Russia could reach the fabulous petroleum wealth of all the Middle East and the long-coveted water route of the Persian Gulf. One may be certain that all these possibilities have entered into the calculations of the councils both of the Western powers and of the Soviet Politburo.

SHOTA RUST'HAVELI, AN IMPRESSIVE THOROUGHFARE IN TBILISI

Cutting a broad, decorative swath through the center of the capital city is the impressive boulevard that has been named for the greatest of Georgian poets, Shota Rust'haveli.

PHOTOS, SOVFOTO

A CHORUS AND FIVE KHORUMI DANCERS IN THE ADZHAR REPUBLIC

Adzhar stalwarts kick out fiercely in the spirited Khorumi to the accompaniment of a folk song. The Adzhar Republic is a political subdivision on the Black Sea coast of Georgia.

RICH OIL FIELD IN BAKU

In the seventies of the last century, Baku, on the Caspian Sea, was a sleepy village of some 1,500 inhabitants. Today it has a population of more than 800,000. The increase has been due to the discovery of rich oil deposits in the neighborhood. The forest of derricks photographed here from offshore is in the Ilyich oil field. Baku is in the Azerbaidzhan Republic.

TRANSCAUCASIA: FACTS AND FIGURES

THE COUNTRY

Region south of the Caucasus Mountains and north of Iran and Turkey between the Black and Caspian seas; was known as the Transcaucasian Federation. Armenia, Azerbaijan and Georgia, the members of the federation, have, since 1936, been administered as separate republics within the Union of Soviet Socialist Republics.

ARMENIA

In southern Transcaucasia; area, 11,500 square miles, and population, 1,345,000. Soil is fertile and major industry is agriculture. Chief crops are grain, cotton, tobacco, sugar beets, grapes and other fruits. Irrigation and hydroelectric works and projects have been built. Livestock, 1,600,000 head. Mining of copper, zinc, aluminum and molybdenum is important. Other industries include production of synthetic rubber, fertilizers, building materials and textiles. In 1950 there were 300,000 pupils in primary and secondary schools, technical and special colleges and the Armenian branch of the Soviet Academy of Science. Population of chief cities: Yerevan (capital), 255,000; Leninakan, 75,000.

AZERBAIJAN

In eastern Transcaucasia, it includes Nakhichevan Autonomous Republic, an enclave within Armenia, and Nagorno-Karabakh Autonomous Region, within Azerbaijanian borders. Total area, 33,100 square miles, and population, 3,100,000. Oil production, centered on the Caspian coast around Baku, and agriculture are the leading industries. Chief farm products are grain, cotton, rice, fruits, vegetables, tobacco and silk. Other products include copper, chemicals, building materials, food, timber, salt, textiles and fish. Over 500,000 pupils in primary and secondary schools; also technical and special colleges, Baku University and a branch of the Academy of Science. Population of chief cities: Baku (capital), 800,000; Kirovabad, 110,000.

GEORGIA

In northwest Transcaucasia, it includes Abkhazian and Adzhar autonomous republics and South Ossetian Autonomous Region. Total area, 29,400 square miles; population, 3,555,000. Chief crops are tea; citrus fruits; tung, eucalyptus and bamboo trees; tobacco, and grapes. Livestock, 4,100,000 head. Mountain streams afford immense electrical power. Chief minerals are manganese and coal. There are large iron and steel works and auto plants. Batumi is the terminus of an oil pipe line from Baku. Nearly 750,000 pupils attend about 4,800 primary and secondary schools; also technical schools and colleges, a branch of the Academy of Science and 80 research institutes. Population of chief cities: Tbilisi (capital), 540,000; Kutaisi, 90,000; Batumi, 75,000.

A LAND OF ANCIENT GRANDEUR

The Iranians and Their Rugged Home

Under Cyrus the Great and his immediate successors, the Persian Empire became a powerful state but was conquered by the Greeks. Again, it rose to power under the Sassanians who were finally overthrown by the Arabs and, although it has retained its independence, it never regained its former position. In the early part of the twentieth century, it could have been called a land of the Middle Ages ruled by an official class that was both lazy and dishonest. Government appointments were bought and the purchasers in order to get their money back extorted large sums from the people. In 1925, the Shah Ahmed was deposed and a man of humble birth, Riza Khan, who was possessed of energy and enlightened ideas, ascended the Peacock Throne. This man of the people did much to restore law and order in Persia, now called Iran. In 1941, however, he was forced to abdicate and his son, Muhammed Riza Pahlevi came to the throne.

PERSIA, one of the most interesting and historical countries of the Middle East, consists mainly of a vast plateau between Afghanistan and Pakistan on the east and Iraq, or Mesopotamia, on the west. To the north lies the Caspian Sea and on each side of this stretch of water the Persian frontier adjoins that of Russia; to the south lies the torrid Persian Gulf.

The Persians call their country Iran and themselves Irani (a form of the word Aryan). Their beginning is legendary, but it is thought that as nomadic tribes they wandered from parts further east and, attracted by the Caspian Sea, settled near its shores. In about 550 B.C. Cyrus the Great made himself known to history for he conquered all the neighboring tribes and formed the Persian Empire, the first great Aryan empire. His successors extended the boundaries from the Punjab in India to beyond the desert in Egypt and sought to conquer Greece, but were defeated by Alexander the Great, who in 334 B.C. made it a Greek province.

The next great period in Persian history began about six hundred years later under Sassanian rulers, who again brought to Persia the glory and splendor of her earlier period. This empire endured until it was overrun by the Arabs in the seventh century A.D.

Up to the time of the Arab invasion, the Persians were followers of Zoroaster and worshiped the sun and fire, but after the Arab conquest, they were converted to Mohammedanism, which is their religion still, although they belong to a division known as Shiite or Separatist.

Arab rule, however, fell before the warring Mongols under Jenghis Khan, which in turn gave way to Tamerlane the Tatar and his hordes who swept over the country on their way westward. In the sixteenth century, a strong leader, Ismail, came to power and founded the Safavid Dynasty. Under the first Safavid rulers, the boundaries were extended and Persian art, especially miniature painting and hand-woven carpets, reached a height of perfection that has never been surpassed.

Weak rulers followed, and the next centuries saw the territory reduced to its present boundaries. In the twentieth century, the country fell into a sad state of political corruption under the Kajars who were ousted in 1925 by a man of the people, Riza Khan, who became Shah.

The climate of Persia is one of extremes, for while frost is common enough in the winter season, the heat in the summer months is intense, especially in the low-lying provinces bordering on the Persian Gulf. As a rule the heat is a dry one and the climate on the plateau is delightful, but the storms are terrible.

The present population of Persia is about fifteen millions, and, as the area of the country is about three times that of France, it is very widely scattered. Owing to the scanty rainfall, there is a lack of water except in the Caspian provinces and there are huge uninhabit-

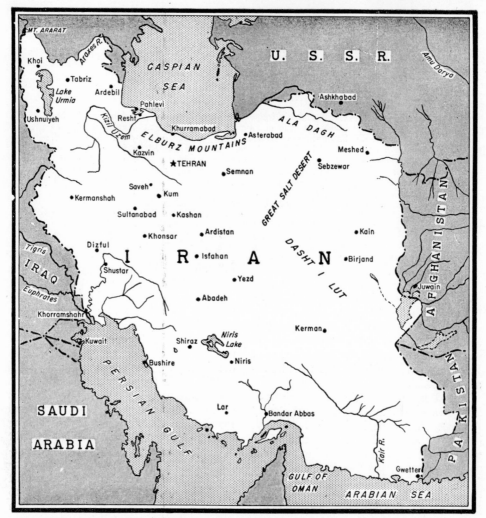

THE ANCIENT LAND BETWEEN THE CASPIAN AND ARABIAN SEAS

able areas. The country may be described as a desert with a few towns and villages dotted about in it, wherever water happens to be available.

The Elburz Mountains run across the north of Persia, south of the Caspian Sea, and contain the superb cone of Demavend, which rises to a height of 19,400 feet—the loftiest mountain of Asia west of the Himalayas.

Elsewhere in Persia the ranges generally run from southeast to northwest, a fact that has made the country difficult of access, especially from the Persian Gulf and from Iraq. If we look at a map we shall see that the chief cities, such as

Teheran (or Tehran), Meshed, the sacred city of Persia, and Tabriz, its chief trade centre, are situated close to the mountains. It might be said that the size of a city mainly depends on the height of the neighboring ranges and the amount of water obtained from them. The country relies for its water on the snow on the mountains which melts in the spring and fills the irrigation channels.

The most important feature of Persia, which has impressed itself forcibly on the life and character of the people and on its government, is the Great Desert. This desert occupies the centre of the country and separates one province from another more effectually than any mountain barrier.

The southern part of this vast area was described by Marco Polo, the great Venetian traveler of the thirteenth century, as "a desert of surpassing aridity . . .; here are neither fruits nor trees to be seen and what water there is, is bitter and bad, so that you have to carry both food and water." Government and trade are both rendered very difficult by this desert, which is a refuge for rebels and brigands who can only be caught with extreme difficulty.

Owing to the meagre rainfall and the high ranges surrounding the plateau, there is not a single river of importance in the many hundreds of miles of coast which lie between the mouths of the Indus and the Shat-el-Arab. One of the tributaries of the latter river is the Karun, which flows through what was, in ancient times, the kingdom of Elam. Its modern importance consists mainly in its being the only navigable river in the whole of the huge Persian Empire.

The Persian Gulf, which washes the southwest and south coasts of Iran, is an almost completely land-locked body of water 700 miles in length, with an average width of about 120 miles. It is shallow and receives the waters of the Tigris and Euphrates, which are united in the broad stream of the Shat-el-Arab. If we are fortunate, we shall pass into the gulf through the Straits of Hormuz by moonlight, with the black cliffs of Cape Musandam rising to the south.

People of southwestern United States can well imagine a country so dry that

THE DUSTY HIGHWAY that crosses the Iranian plateau in the west and connects the cities of Shiraz and Isfahan. In the background dry, gray mountains rise, without even a touch of green.

PIX

WANDERING TRIBESMEN OF LURISTAN

About a fifth of the inhabitants of Iran are nomads, wandering tribesmen who drive their flocks and herds from place to place seeking fresh pasture. They set up rough, temporary shelters as they go. On crude looms the women weave tent cloth, blankets and other textiles. The tribesmen in this picture are Luris, of Luristan, in the west-central part of Iran.

THREE LIONS

BATHHOUSES, NOT IGLOOS

In the towns of northern Iran, the village bathhouses are the cleanest structures in the section. Their mortar surfaces are painstakingly scrubbed to a dazzling perfection. Elsewhere cleanliness is less evident. Bad sewage, inadequate medical facilities and the lack of pure water are responsible for the prevalence of diseases that thrive in unsanitary surroundings.

trees and crops can be grown only where the land is well irrigated. The vegetation consists of bushes, generally of a thorny nature and only two or three feet high, with a little grass which shows green for a month in the spring and then disappears.

Where there is water, crops of wheat and barley (which is the staple horse food), millet, cotton, opium, lucerne (known here as alfalfa), clover and tobacco are grown. Rice and corn flourish in the moist Caspian provinces. Persia is rich in fruits, which grow well in spite of the lack of scientific cultivation. Pears, apples, quinces, apricots, black and yellow

plums, peaches, nectarines and cherries are produced in great abundance. Figs, pomegranates and the famous almonds and pistachio nuts grow best in the warmer districts, and the date-palm, orange and lime are confined to the low-lying "Hot Country." The grapes and melons of Persia are famous. We owe to Persia the peach, the pistachio nut, spinach, the narcissus and lilac, all of which have retained their Persian names.

Persia has long been famous also for her carpets and rugs, and a trip to the rug dealer's shop is a very interesting experience for the proprietor will probably

203

serve coffee and cigarettes while lengthy discussion takes place. Bargaining is quite the order of the day, and one must never seem in haste for then the dealer will surely get the better of it. Among the Persians themselves, it sometimes takes days to conclude a transaction satisfactorily.

Persia's Industries

With the exception of rug-weaving and the manufacture of silk and cotton textiles, pottery and some leather goods, Persia has few industries. Most of the manufactured goods used by the Persians must be imported.

Persia's chief wealth is in her oil fields, which cover about five-sixths of the country. The richest single oil field in the world is in the southern region. At Abadan, a town near the head of the Persian Gulf, is the world's largest oil refinery.

Oil and the British

For many years the fields were operated by a British company. Persia could not run them herself, at least partly because there were few Persians with the necessary technical training. This arrangement began in 1901, when Persia granted a monopoly in the exploitation of the oil fields to an Englishman, William Knox D'Arcy. His venture eventually became the Anglo-Iranian Oil Company—53 per cent British-owned. Then in 1919 Persia agreed to a convention by which British advisers were placed in various departments of the Persian Government, military as well as civil. This made Persia practically a British protectorate.

As the years went by, resentment against British domination grew more open and bitter in Iran (Persia changed its name to Iran in 1935). After World War II, the unrest came to a boil, particularly over the oil situation. It was heated still further by a growing spirit of nationalism—Iran for the Iranians—the same spirit that has been emerging in so many other parts of Asia since the war.

The climax came in the spring of 1951. Under the leadership of Mohammed Mossadegh, who was Prime Minister of Iran at the time, Iran suddenly nationalized the oil industry. This meant the end of British control. It also brought the industry, Iran's chief source of income, to a standstill. The British technicians departed and there were few trained Iranians to take their places. Regardless of Iranian feelings, it was obvious that the industry could not be operated without outside help of some kind.

An International Problem

The Western world was alarmed. Here was one of its chief sources of oil idle. What is more, there was a threat that communism might gain headway in Iran just as it has thrived on turmoil elsewhere. The specific dispute between Britain and Iran was carried all the way to the UN Security Council, but that body failed to settle it.

When the oil industry came to a halt, its Iranian labor force of about 65,000 was thrown out of work. These men received unemployment compensation, a drain on the Iranian treasury. On the whole, however, the stoppage affected the great mass of the Iranians much less than one might expect. Actually, very little of the wealth from the oil fields had ever trickled down to them. Their standard of living had always been low.

Oil Begins to Flow Again

In 1953 popular backing of the Shah led to an uprising and overthrow of Premier Mossadegh. The new premier, Fazlollah Zahedi, reopened the oil issue. In the following year an agreement was reached with eight British, United States, Dutch and French companies to get Iran's frozen oil industry humming again. Under a twenty-five year plan, the companies began to extract, refine and market the products of Iranian oil fields.

With the resumption of earnings from the petroleum industry, plus borrowed money, Iran embarked on an ambitious five-year development program to increase agricultural and mineral production, to improve transportation and communication facilities, and to develop a huge hydroelectric project in Karaj.

In ancient times, the Iranians obtained valuable pearls from the Persian Gulf and even now pearl fishing is carried on to some extent. The principal export is oil, followed by rugs, dried fruits and some medicinal plants. The exports are brought overland or down the Tigris River to the ports on the gulf and the Caspian Sea.

For centuries, the only means of land communication were the caravan routes. In the last few decades, however, under an ambitious government program, new roads have been constructed and old ones improved. Many hundreds of miles of railways have been opened with more under way. Telegraph, telephone and radio systems have been installed. Airplanes fly regularly from the capital, Teheran, and Kermanshah to Bagdad, where there are scheduled flights to Western countries.

Iran has awakened to her need for improvements, but many obstacles stand in the way. The greatest, perhaps, is the mutual distrust that exists among the different groups within the country. The lawmakers fear one another and are all jealous of the Shah. Whatever money is made is not reinvested in Iran, but banked outside the country.

EWING GALLOWAY

SHAH ABBAS I built the Ali Kapu in the early seventeenth century. It is a gateway structure in Isfahan.

The peasant is the backbone of the nation. His village is sometimes enclosed within a high mud wall, in which case the houses are small and dark. The open space in the center of the village, where the cattle are driven at night, is usually dirty. When the houses are scattered about, each occupies a good deal of space, having one courtyard around which the living rooms are grouped and a second courtyard for the cattle. Adjoining many of the houses are orchards, surrounded by mud walls. The peasants are still practically serfs under a real feudal system and they are the people who are most eager for improvements to be made. The land is sparsely settled and labor is scarce. The most primitive methods of agriculture are still in use. A few model farming communities exist, but they have been built with outside aid. The ruling classes may be divided into the landowners, who have a great deal of wealth, and the prosperous merchants of the towns and cities who own their own shops or cafés. The peasant has little voice in the Government.

Besides these, Iran has many nomadic tribes, who live in tents of goats' hair and

A BAS-RELIEF FROM THE DAYS OF THE SASSANIAN KINGS

At Taq-i-Bustan, near Kermanshah, there are arched recesses cut into the rocks containing bas-reliefs. In this one King Ardashir II appears to be presenting a trophy to the victor of a battle. The sculptures date from the Sassanidae, a dynasty of Persian kings who ruled from the third century A.D. and were finally overthrown by the Arabs in the seventh century.

TRIBUTE-BEARERS ON THEIR WAY TO A PERSIAN CONQUEROR

The sculpture is from a building wall still standing among the ruins of Persepolis, the dazzling capital founded by Darius the Great around 500 B.C. Under Darius and his successor, Xerxes, the Persian Empire was at the height of its power. The story of its vanished glory may still be read from the sculptures at Persepolis, though the city has long been dust.

CHILD WORKERS IN IRAN

Children are shown weaving carpets in Hamadan, a district where famed Persian rugs are produced. Rug-making ranks among the top native industries in Iran, and in normal times about $3,000,000 worth of carpets are exported to the United States alone. The law of 1943 calling for the gradual establishment of compulsory education has lagged in enforcement.

PEACE WITHIN THE SHELTERED GARDEN OF A MOSQUE IN TEHERAN

Students reflect on the Koran by a serene pool, where their eyes may rest on exquisite mosaic
tile. The teeming, noisy city just outside their retreat seems far away.

STREAMLINED MODERN ARCHITECTURE FOR THE SHAH OF IRAN

The Shah's palace in Teheran is in vivid contrast to the delicate design of the guarded gateway. The appearance of Iran's capital has been undergoing rapid changes in recent years.

A YOUNG IRANIAN PRACTICES AN OLD ART WITH A SKILLED HAND

The boy is painting a graceful design on the kind of pottery for which Qum is well known. The shelf above is stacked with bowls, and there are lids in the hole behind him.

move about with their flocks and herds in search of fresh grazing-grounds. They spend the summer months in the mountains and move down to the plains at the approach of winter. They follow the same route year after year. Physically, they are splendid people, but they are very fond of raiding villages and of plundering caravans. When they are on the march the old men, the women and children look after the sheep, goats, cattle, camels and donkeys, while the fighting men act as scouts and try to rob any villages that may be in the vicinity.

In Persia the position of the men is far better than that of the women. When a boy is born the father receives congratulations, whereas the birth of a girl passes almost without notice. The baby will have amulets to avert the evil eye hung around its neck; no glass may be brought into the room lest its rays might cause the child to squint and indeed the very word glass may not be mentioned. Moreover, no one wearing black clothes is permitted to enter.

The baby is swaddled tightly and, when taken out for an airing, is dressed in coarse clothes—this again being to avert the evil eye. Friends may admire the child without causing him ill-luck provided they exclaim "Mashallah!" (that which Allah wished).

In former times, upon reaching the age of eight, the boy was placed in charge of a manservant, and a mullah, or priest, undertook his education, which consisted mainly of learning to read and write. The textbook was the Koran (the Moslem scriptures) and the unfortunate pupil was forced to learn sentence after sentence in the original Arabic with its meaning in Persian. He repeated it exactly as a parrot so he learned neither Arabic nor Persian. Little else was studied under private instruction or in the numerous religious schools.

WOMEN THRESHING GRAIN BY A CENTURIES-OLD METHOD

When the sieve is shaken vigorously, the grain falls through to the rug spread to catch it and the chaff is left behind. It is a tedious method that yields little in proportion to the effort.

COURTHOUSE OF BANDAR SHAH VIEWED ACROSS A PUBLIC GARDEN

The attractive building is one of many modern structures in the port on the southeast coast of the Caspian Sea. Bandar Shah is the northern terminus of the Trans-Iranian Railway.

THE SIMPLEST OF SCALES SUFFICES THIS MERCHANT

The stones in one pan determine the weight as the scales are held aloft and filled with raisins or nuts. The technique is old, but no one questions its accuracy.

MASJED-I-SHAH (SHAH'S MOSQUE) ON THE ROYAL COURT IN ISFAHAN

Covered with glazed tiles and ornamented with gold and silver, the Masjed-i-Shah is a dazzling sight. The court—the Maidan-i-Shah—is an enormous rectangle 1,680 feet by 522 feet.

If a boy was idle, his feet were tied to a pole and beaten by canes. This punishment of the bastinado is known as "eating the sticks." All exhibitions of high spirits were discouraged and it was impressed on the young pupil that it was undignified to run or to jump.

The result was that a boy soon became a miniature man. He wore a long coat much kilted at the waist and the same kind of "kulla" or astrakhan headdress as his father. His manners, too, tended to become artificial and when greeted by a friend, he would reply, "May your nose be fat," "May your shadow never grow less," and other similar compliments that formed an important part of Persian etiquette.

When a boy reached the age of sixteen, his mother arranged a marriage with a cousin, whom, perhaps, the boy had not seen since he was a child, for women were kept strictly secluded and were always veiled in public.

The bride and bridegroom then met and gazed intently at one another's faces which were reflected in a mirror at which they both looked together. Finally the bride was taken, with rejoicings, to her future home, where the young couple par-took of bread, cheese and salt that had been brought by the bride, and were left by their relatives to settle down.

This plan of selecting a wife and the marriage customs are still practiced in some parts of Persia, but as girls are now admitted to the public schools, this, as well as other old customs, is dying out in the face of rapid Westernization.

Great progress has been made in education. Modern schools have been established, which, in the lower grades, are attended by boys and girls together. Hundreds of students have been sent abroad to study so that they may return to teach in the schools or become leaders. A university in Teheran gives higher education in all branches of sciences and arts.

We have said that the position of women is lower than that of men. This is true in any Mohammedan country. The Koran, by which the followers of Mohammed model their lives, makes no provision for the education of women and puts many restrictions on them. Nevertheless, the number of both women and men who cannot read or write is decreasing, and women without veils are seen more and more. In wealthy families, women are given

A BRASS BOWL TAKES SHAPE BETWEEN ANVIL AND HAMMER

The clang of the worker in brass is an ever present sound in cities and villages. Almost every kind of household utensil is made of the bright metal. Articles may be polished smooth or they may be left with the marks of the hammer showing—beaten brass. A great advantage of brass, especially in warm countries, is that it will not rust, as iron utensils would.

ABADAN, OIL-FAMOUS HARBOR

From the harbor of Abadan, oil refineries may be seen in the background. The tanker at the right rides high in the water as she awaits her cargo of the flowing wealth of Iran. In the foreground is a native sailing craft. Abadan became a familiar name overnight as a result of the nationalization of the oil industry and the expulsion of the Anglo-Iranian Oil Company in 1951.

special quarters, called in Persia the anderun, in which no man except a relative may enter. Turkey was the first to throw off these customs and Persia is following slowly. To-day, Persian women may attend the theater and movies unveiled and are encouraged by the government to adopt the dress and the manners of Western women.

The new order which is gradually taking the place of the old in Persia is due to a large extent to the efforts of Riza Khan, who was Shah from 1925 to 1941. His story is a fascinating one. A man of humble birth, he began his career as a trooper in the Persian Cossack Brigade. He gradually rose in rank through sheer energy and ability and at last assumed command of the brigade. In February, 1921, being then in command of more than 2,000 Cossacks, he overthrew the Persian Cabinet. He became Minister of War in the new cabinet formed by the Shah.

In this Middle East land of Omar Khayyam the Allies had a land bridge. In Iran's capital, Tehran, was held the historic conference of November, 1943, at which the leaders of the United States, Great Britain and the Union of Soviet Socialist Republics, among other statements of policy, pledged the independence of Iran.

Iran presents a medley of East and West, ancient ways and modern magic of the machine age. The single-track Trans-Iranian Railway streaks by baked-mud villages whose outlines were old a thousand years ago. On its way it ducks into more than 200 tunnels, crosses thousands of bridges, and in some places winds so sharply it can be seen at three different levels. Yet Iran still holds the flavor of the old East, from the lonely shepherd on the mountainside to the crowded, covered bazaars where bearded merchants bargain over products of Oriental handicraft. As planes fly over, a nomad with a hawk on his wrist looks up respectfully. Strange to us are many Iranian customs—the still sheltered lives of women, the Moslem taboo against drinks and dogs; their particular rituals of prayer and fasting.

IRAN (PERSIA): FACTS AND FIGURES

THE COUNTRY

An independent kingdom which occupies the western and larger half of the Iranian plateau. It is bounded on the north by Transcaucasia, the Caspian Sea and Turkestan, on the east by Afghanistan and the Dominion of Pakistan, on the south by the Arabian Sea and the Persian Gulf, and on the west by Iraq and Turkey. The total area is about 628,000 square miles, and the population is about 20,000,000, of whom about 3,000,000 are nomads.

GOVERNMENT

Legislative government consists of a National Assembly called Majlis, elected every two years. The shah, or king, appoints a prime minister who selects a Cabinet agreeable to the Majlis.

COMMERCE AND INDUSTRIES

Food products include wheat, barley, rice and fruits. The production of gums, tobacco, cotton, silk, wool and opium is important. Sheep-raising is carried on to some extent. The minerals, though numerous, are, except in the case of oil, undeveloped. They include deposits of iron ore, coal, copper, lead and manganese; there are turquoise mines in Khorasan worked by primitive methods. Weaving of rugs and carpets is by far the most important

industry. Chief exports include petroleum, carpets, raw cotton, and wool, and the imports are cotton piece goods, sugar, tea, machinery and automobiles.

COMMUNICATIONS

About 1181 miles of railway. Much of the country's commerce is carried on over the great trade routes. There are over 11,436 miles of telegraph line. There is a regular air service.

RELIGION AND EDUCATION

Bulk of population belong to the Shiite sect of Mohammedanism, and there is a large minority of adherents to the Sunni persuasion. Besides these Mohammedans, there are about 10,000 Parsees, 50,000 Armenians, and 40,000 Jews. By Government order the foreign schools have been liquidated by the Ministry of Education. Primary education compulsory since 1943. There are 8,381 schools with 457,236 pupils. Primary school for children of Soviet nationality is run by the Soviet Government. Religious schools maintained from endowments.

CHIEF TOWNS

Teheran, capital, has a population of 1,000,000; Tabriz, 250,000; Isfahan, 225,000; Meshed, 185,000; Shiraz, 140,000; Hamadan, 120,000; Resht, 115,000; and Kermanshah, 100,000.

In the Garden of Eden

Modern Iraq, Cradle of Ancient Empires

Some believe that the site of the Garden of Eden lay between the Tigris and Euphrates rivers in the land once called Mesopotamia, and known today as Iraq. Certainly the land is very ancient, and the earliest civilizations may have risen there. There is little in modern Iraq, however, that resembles a paradise, although in the days of the Sumerian, Babylonian and Assyrian empires it was one of the world's most fertile regions. Decay had set in before it came under Turkish rule in the sixteenth century, and it became a desolate tract. Iraq's present rulers are attempting to restore the country's rich soil to its fertile state so that it can once again be cultivated. Because Iraq is one of the world's great oil-producing countries it holds a position of great strategic importance in the struggle between free nations and the communist powers. Its vital oil has more than once in recent years been the cause of serious international disagreements.

MESOPOTAMIA, now known as Iraq, has been called the "cradle of civilization" because here the human race is thought to have had its beginning and it has also been termed the "dust heap of the nations," because the ruins of mighty empires of ancient times are buried under its sun-baked soil. This tract of country, which was before World War I the Turkish provinces of Mosul, Bagdad and Basra, stretches in a southeasterly direction from Kurdistan to the Persian Gulf. Two mighty rivers, the Euphrates and Tigris, flow through the land and finally unite to form the Shatt-al-Arab, which discharges its waters into the Persian Gulf over one hundred miles farther to the south.

Tradition says that the Garden of Eden lay somewhere in this land, and modern excavation has shown that there once existed here what is believed to be one of the oldest civilizations on earth—the Sumerian. The Sumerians, who were probably of Indo-European origin, were the first known astronomers. It was they who divided the day into twelve double hours and who gave us the first writing. They had laws and learning and they practiced medicine. After long years, they were overrun by the Semite invaders, nomadic peoples of Arabic origin, who adopted the writing, laws and customs of the Sumerians.

From this fusion of Sumerians and Semites rose the Babylonians and Assyr-

ians. The first Babylonian Empire was founded about 2100 B.C. Its chief city was the Biblical Babylon. Centuries later the Assyrian nation arose in the north and there was a long struggle for supremacy between the two kindred nations. Babylon and Lower Egypt, for a time, fell under the sway of the bold Assyrian conquerors, and then Nineveh, its capital

PHILIP GENDREAU

AN AGED SHEPHERD OF IRAQ

An Iraqi's face, furrowed and wrinkled, tells of lifetime toil against desert wind and sun.

RODD

THE **TOMB OF EZRA**, blue-domed and surrounded by palm trees, stands on a bend of the Tigris near Kurna. It is known that Ezra was buried on the banks of the Tigris many centuries ago, so this cannot really be his burial place, as the river has changed its course since that time. However, bands of pilgrims pause here as they do at other Biblical sites of Mesopotamia although, like this one, they are probably legendary. On the Euphrates below Baghdad is the supposed tomb of the great Jewish prophet, Ezekiel, revered as a shrine by both Jews and Christians.

218

SAMARRA, with its gold-domed mosque and minarets of richly colored tiles, is considered a very holy place by the Shiah Mohammedans. They believe that the Mahdi, the savior who is expected by all Mohammedans, actually appeared long ago, and vanished in a cave near Samarra. Here, they think, he will reappear at the end of the world.

BLACK S.AR

THE GATE OF ISHTAR, THE BABYLONIAN GODDESS OF LOVE

Bulls and goats molded from glazed bricks decorate the Ishtar Gate in Babylon. Nearby is E-Sagila, the great temple of the god Marduk and the site of the Biblical Tower of Babel.

—the ruins of which are found on the bank of the Tigris opposite Mosul—was the premier city of the world. With the destruction of Nineveh in the seventh century B.C., Babylon again rose to power. Nebuchadnezzar rebuilt the city, enclosing it with mighty walls which, with the "hanging gardens," formed one of the Seven Wonders of the World. The ruins of Babylon lie to the south of Bagdad (Baghdad).

But Babylon, as recorded in the Bible, was taken by Cyrus, king of the Medes and Persians. The Persians in turn fell before the Greeks under Alexander the Great. The Greeks were followed by Parthians, Romans and then Persians again. After the death of Mohammed in 632 A.D. his Arab followers overran the Persian Empire. At Ctesiphon, the Parthian and Persian capital, they found great treasure and the materials of its wonderful buildings were used for the construction of Bagdad in 762. Under the famous Harun-al-Rashid, Bagdad became the centre of the wit, learning and art of Islam. Then in 1516 A.D. the country finally passed to the Turks, under whose misrule it remained for about four hundred years.

And so, during the centuries, the greatness of Babylon and Assyria passed away. Their magnificent cities were used to supply the bricks for succeeding towns and villages, and such ruins as the barbarians left fell into decay until they became shapeless mounds whose very names were forgotten. The peoples of these cities had used a curious writing called "cuneiform," which they had developed from the script of their Sumerian ancestors. They scratched figures with a triangular pointed instrument on soft tablets of clay which

KEYSTONE

A WINGED GUARD OF KHORSABAD

A minister to a sacred winged bull flanks a gate to the palace of King Sargon II of Assyria.

they afterward baked. The knowledge of this writing also passed away.

That old phrase "the changeless East" is obsolete. Change is resistless. Following the expulsion of the Turks, Mesopotamia was left under British control. In 1921 Emir Feisal was crowned King of Iraq under a British Mandate. Then Iraq became independent in 1932. Governmental shifts, plus oil, speeded up far-reaching changes.

The "Mosul question," involving rich oil areas, caused international rivalry and dispute. Mosul, city of northern Iraq,

221

AN ARAB WOMAN loves jewelry. This one is adorned with rings, bangles, necklaces, brooches and a pendant from her head-dress. Although her head is amply covered, her feet are quite unaccustomed to shoes or stockings. Arab people are of marked character and intelligence and usually are possessed of self-confident manners and a great sense of dignity.

CLIMBING A DATE PALM is no great difficulty to this Arab. He first girds the tree with a rope which he fastens to his sash so that when leaning back, he is held securely. He is further aided by the leaf-scarred trunk which makes a good foothold. Dates fresh from the tree are much different from the dried fruit we know.

OPEN-AIR FERRY ON THE TIGRIS

The glorified raft, or kelek, as it is called, is made of alternating layers of planks and logs supported on the inflated skins of sheep or goats. This one is ready to float its load of passengers comfortably down the Tigris from Diarbekr, Turkey, to Mosul, Iraq. Keleks are as familiar on the Tigris as ferryboats are on the Hudson River and the St. Lawrence.

ROOFS OF REED BY THE EUPHRATES

An old-time Arab village by the Euphrates, of a type rarely seen nowadays. The houses, or huts, are made of reeds and are roofed with reed matting. The Tigris and Euphrates once emptied into the Persian Gulf through separate mouths. Now they meet, on land which they themselves have laid down bit by bit through long centuries, and flow into the gulf as one.

OUTSIDE THE WALLS OF OLD BAGDAD—THE TOMB OF ZOBEIDE

Herdsmen lead their flocks near the base of the strange building outside Bagdad where Zobeide, wife of Harun-al-Rashid, is buried. He was the great caliph who ruled over Bagdad at the height of the city's power, when it dominated most of the Arabian world. The roof of the tomb, a pyramid of small overlapping domes, surmounts a bold octagonal base.

225

MOSUL, the chief town in an oil-bearing province, stands on the Tigris River opposite Nineveh, the ruined capital of ancient Assyria. A tree-less city, Mosul's skyline is relieved by towers, domes and minarets. The Great Mosque, formerly dedicated to St. Paul, has leaning minarets.

Here the Tigris is crossed by a floating bridge, a span that rests on boats placed side by side and is similar to a pontoon bridge. Mosul was once known for its fine cotton goods, which fact has given us the word "muslin" for a kind of sheer cotton fabric, though muslin may also be heavy.

RODD

THE ARCH OF CTESIPHON was once a part of the royal palace in Ctesiphon, the capital of the great Persian Empire when it extended over Mesopotamia, or Iraq as it is called at present. It became an important city and in 550 A. D., Chosroes I built this magnificent palace there. Beneath the arch, which was the roof of the audience chamber, there was once a blue ceiling set with gold stars to imitate the sky. The ruins are very important from an architectural standpoint for they are among the few existing examples of construction in the Sassanid or Persian period.

THE ROUND BARGES OF THE TIGRIS, LADEN WITH WATERMELONS

On the Tigris at Bagdad, Iraqi boatmen guard their striped, delicious cargo. For perhaps as long as man has been transporting goods on the waterways of Mesopotamia, the unwieldy, almost unsinkable gufa has been bounding its useful way from farm to market. The gufa is made of reeds, covered with hides and plastered inside and out with pitch for waterproofing.

is on the west bank of the Tigris. Each large house is built round an open courtyard. The houses are of burnt brick faced with slabs of a kind of gray marble, quarried nearby. The same marble serves for paving and for wall panels in the interiors. There is a fine mosque, the cupolas and minarets of which are of turquoise blue tiles. The summers are very hot, and for three or four months the inhabitants are glad to sleep on the flat roofs. The winters are rainy, and frost is sometimes experienced.

Although there is a railway line, considerable trade on the upper Tigris is by means of native craft. As some parts of the river are very shallow, use is made of rafts of saplings lashed together and packed underneath with inflated goatskins. These are floated and paddled down the river, but the return journey has to be made by road for at Bagdad the raft is pulled to pieces and sold.

Iraq is not a well wooded country. Much of the north is undulating pasture land, but wheat, barley, linseed and flax are grown and, if the rainfall be sufficient,

yield good crops. A little distance to the north of Bagdad we find an alluvial plain formed of the mud which the two rivers have deposited. This was once the most fertile and thickly populated spot on earth. Here we meet the first palm trees in the narrow strips of cultivated land beside the rivers. Wherever the land is irrigated it responds readily to cultivation. The growing of wheat is increasing and the cotton crop shows a yearly gain. But the land under cultivation is only a small proportion of the entire country, and that is the reason why Iraq is so sparsely settled.

The clay of the plain, mixed with chopped reeds and grass, can be baked into a hard substance by the sun alone, and of this the single-storied dwellings of the villages are built. We find also huts made of reeds, which in some of the swamps grow to a height of 20 feet. The larger canes, placed side by side, are bent over in a half loop for the framework and are then covered with mats made of rushes. The end walls are of reed straw bound together, and the entrance is covered with a hanging mat. These huts can be put up in a day and can be taken down and moved elsewhere whenever the owner wishes.

The nomadic tribes who wander about with their flocks and herds use tents made of goat hair. The houses in the towns are mainly strong, two-story buildings. In order to lessen the terrific summer heat, screens made either of camel thorn or of licorice twigs, are hung before the windows and kept moist by having water thrown over them.

The Tigris is navigable by steamers as far as Bagdad, and though the passage of "the Narrows," just beyond Ezra's Tomb,

is difficult for large craft, the river is crowded with boats of all descriptions, carrying passengers and merchandise. The famous round basket which is known as the "gufa" was in use in the days of Nineveh's glory. Below Sheikh Saad the gufa gives place to the canoe-shaped "bellum."

The Euphrates, which is navigated by native craft only, is much better wooded than the Tigris. In its lower reaches it passes through marsh land which by draining is becoming rich and fertile. At Kurna the rivers unite and form the Shatt-al-Arab, and the cultivated land near this

SAWDERS FROM CUSHING

LINES OF DRYING WOOL ON FLAT ROOFTOPS

The nomadic tribes of the Middle East depend upon their flocks for their living. They wander with their herds of sheep and goats looking for suitable pasturage. Shearing time is a big event in their lives, for cropping the wool means that they will soon have money. Then the nomads halt to cut and dry the wool, often using rooftops as a drying place.

RUDD

KERBELA is a very holy city to the Shiah Mohammedans, or Shiites, since here is the tomb of Hussein, grandson of the prophet Mohammed. Hussein was killed at Kerbela, and is regarded as a martyr. Thousands of pilgrims visit his tomb every year, and seem so grief-stricken by Hussein's death that it would be easy to imagine that he had died recently and not years ago.

RODD

THE PORT OF BASRA is Iraq's chief outlet for world trade. Situated on the Shatt-al-Arab, seventy-five miles upstream from the Persian Gulf, the port is open to ocean-going vessels. Basra is also connected by rail with Bagdad, Iran and Kuwait. There is a busy commerce in various cereals, and the city is also an important livestock market.

IRAQI FARMERS AND THEIR CRUDE HORSE-DRAWN THRESHING SLED

The sled-like contraption separates the grain from the stalks. It is by no means the crudest of implements in a land where tractors and other farm machines are seldom seen. In fact, the design of the contraption, rough as it is, shows a considerable amount of ingenuity.

estuary is one of the largest date-producing centers of the world. Nearly 200 varieties of dates are grown, and they are a staple article of food and a big item of export.

In the midst of this fertile strip, and 70 miles from the Persian Gulf, stands Basra, the principal port of the country. During World War II, Basra's trade and importance greatly increased. The modern city has up-to-date shipping facilities and is a road, rail and air terminal. Basra has been called the Venice of the East for all through and about the city are numberless waterways and creeks.

The majority of the population of Iraq is Arab. There are Arabs of all types and ranks with a large admixture of Persians. These people are Mohammedans and are divided mainly into the Shiah and Sunni sects. In this country are some of the most famous places of pilgrimage in the Moslem world.

The holy city of Nejef, which lies to the west of the Euphrates, stands on a cliff overlooking the desert. The golden dome of the mosque which covers the tomb of Ali, the murdered saint, makes a most conspicuous landmark. The city is walled, and consists of very narrow streets where tall houses shut out most of the light and air. Some of these houses stand on as many as three, four or even five floors of cellars hewn out of the rock, which form a cool retreat from the stifling heat of the crowded city above. A broad bazaar, a quarter of a mile long, leads up to the mosque. This small city of devout citizens during certain feasts has as many as 120,000 pilgrims pass through its gates.

Everything required in the city has to be brought from without and water has to be carried in skins a distance of three-quarters of a mile.

The Jews, who today number only a few thousand—we remember the captivity of their race in Babylon and the fact that Abraham their founder came from Ur of the Chaldees, which was near the junction of the canal Shat-el-Hai with the

BUYING POLISHED COPPERWARE AT A SIDEWALK SHOP IN BAGDAD

The robes might have been worn in Harun-al-Rashid's day, but the merchandise comes from modern factories in the capital. Present-day Bagdad is a manufacturing and trading city.

EWING GALLOWAY

COOLING OFF IN THE WATERS OF THE TIGRIS RIVER, NEAR MOSUL

There is very little rainfall in Iraq, and river water is doubly precious. Iraqis wash and bathe
in the Tigris, finding surcease from the heat when the sun is high.

Euphrates—have also their holy places
of pilgrimage here. The Jews are chiefly
men of the towns, traders, shopkeepers
and sometimes bankers.

The Christians, who are more in number than the Jews, are found around Mosul
and are mainly Assyrians. Being better
educated than the rest of the natives they
form for the most part the professional
class. In addition to these people there
are wild Kurds from the north, nominally
Mohammedans, and representatives of
many other nationalities and religions.
Among the latter are two communities
that call for notice, the Sabæans and the
Yezidis.

The Sabæans, or Subbis, get their name
of Star-Worshipers from the fact that

they turn to the polar star when praying,
under the belief that the supreme deity
has his residence beyond that star. Sunday is their holy day, they practice baptism
once a week and they have a ceremony in
which bread and wine are used. They are
not Christians, but they have great venera-
tion for John the Baptist. They are a
very handsome people. Living among the
marshlands in the south, their chief industry was the making of canoes until the
war made their wonderful inlaid silver
work known to the British troops. When
the latter captured Amara the Sabæans
migrated thither, and their silver work has
brought them increasing prosperity.

The Yezidis are often called Devil-Worshipers. Although they believe in God the

234

SCREENED WINDOWS THROUGH WHICH SECLUDED WOMEN MAY PEER

In many places in Iraq, such as Mosul where this picture was taken, the Mohammedan way of life is still followed strictly. Women have little freedom; on the street they must wear veils.

A CROWDED CANAL JOINS BASRA WITH THE SHATT-AL-ARAB RIVER

Mosques and their minarets rise above simple dwellings and the activity of the canal. Basra is only seventy miles from the Persian Gulf, whence the Shatt-al-Arab (Tigris and Euphrates) flows.

235

Creator, they hold that the devil is very powerful and treat him with deference.

Although the red fez, formerly worn in Turkey, is much in evidence, the characteristic headgear of Iraq is the shafiyah. This is a piece of material, usually cotton, which covers the head and falls down over the shoulders, and is often crowned by a thick loop of wool. Worn with the flowing robes it is always associated with the Arabs. There is a great variety of costume here. We meet the poorer classes of the country and the desert dressed in a single long shirt and a shafiyah. Then we see the costume so frequently affected by the wealthy young Arab of Bagdad or Basra—that of a European gentleman save for the hat, which is replaced as a rule by the red fez.

The women when they appear out of doors are usually enveloped in a shawl-like outer garment, and even when they adopt European clothes they generally wear a shawl over the head to protect them from unwelcome glances.

All classes rise early, and rest during the afternoon heat. Coffee is taken many times a day, and much of the leisure time is spent in the coffee-shop, which is the meeting place for recreation and social intercourse so far as the men are concerned. The women, especially those of the upper classes, usually follow the custom of the East and lead secluded lives.

Within recent years there has been truly a marvelous change in many respects. A great deal of money has been expended, and the results are to be seen in all directions. Education—elementary, secondary and technical—is advancing; sanitation, to which no attention was ever paid before, has been introduced, and the streets of the cities have been paved and lighted with electricity.

Hospitals and dispensaries have been established, railways extended and motor roads constructed; bridges have been built over rivers where only rickety bridges of boats existed before, and, strange to say, taxicabs are to be seen in the streets of Bagdad. The traffic is controlled by an efficient police force and aeroplanes are to be seen flying all over the country. Two miles outside the old city of Bagdad a new town has sprung up where the Europeans and officials reside—for Bagdad is the capital and seat of government. The story of this city of Harun-al-Rashid and the Arabian Nights is reserved for another chapter.

The future of the new Iraq is full of promise, but its realization will depend on the way in which its people adapt themselves to the new conditions.

IRAQ: FACTS AND FIGURES

THE COUNTRY

Consists of the former Turkish vilayets of Baghdad, Basra and Mosul, which are bounded on the north by Turkey, on the east by Iran, on the south by the Persian Gulf and Kuweit, on the southwest by Arabia and on the west by Jordan and Syria. The total area is 116,600 square miles and the population is more than 5,100,000.

GOVERNMENT

A limited monarchy ruled by a king and Cabinet. Legislative body consists of a Senate of 29 elder statesmen, nominated for 8 years, and a Lower House made up of 138 deputies, who are elected.

COMMERCE AND INDUSTRIES

Chief product is oil. The rich soil is now being developed by irrigation. Cotton, wheat, barley, oats, linseed and flax are produced though mostly in the experimental stage. Dates are grown. Principal exports are barley, wheat, wool and dates, and the imports are textiles, sugar, carpets and tea.

COMMUNICATIONS

Railway length is 1,027 miles, and the telegraph line mileage, 6,493; telephone line, 73,876 miles. There is a regular air service.

RELIGION AND EDUCATION

Bulk of the population is Mohammedan of both Shiah and Sunni sects. There are primary schools, secondary schools and several colleges and technical schools.

CHIEF TOWNS

Bagdad, the capital, has a population of about 550,000; Mosul, 230,000; Basra, 110,000; Kirkuk, 80,000; and Amara, 60,000.

THE CITY OF THE ARABIAN NIGHTS

Bagdad (or Baghdad) the Historic City

Bagdad! At the mention of this magic word our thoughts turn to the wonderful stories of the Thousand and One Nights, to the great Caliph Harun-al-Rashid, during whose reign the city reached the zenith of its splendor. It was then the capital of the Saracenic Empire, a vast centre for the trade of all Asia, a home of romance, of mystery and of learning. Unfortunately the Bagdad of to-day is not the Bagdad of the Arabian Nights. The palaces, gardens and courtiers have gone with most of the splendid buildings of the vanished city, on the site of which is a suburb—a collection of mud hovels—of the modern Bagdad. Bagdad, as we shall read in this chapter, is gradually being transformed into a city of the West and in due time it may regain some of its bygone splendor and commercial importance.

WHEN speaking of Bagdad we conjure up visions of the genii and of the Forty Thieves, for the glamour of romance hangs over this city from its associations with the Caliph Harun-al-Rashid and the Arabian Nights. We think of the palms, the splendid cities, wealthy merchants, mighty princes and beautiful princesses—all the glory of the East, as pictured in the greatest story-book of all times.

Not much is known of the town of Bagdad previous to the period of Islam. In 762 A.D., Caliph Mansur decided to transfer his residence from Damascus, which was then the seat of the Caliphate, and was looking about for a place for the new seat of government. The Arabs themselves say that a Christian monastery stood on the site and that a Christian monk very obligingly pointed out to Mansur the great advantages of its position. However that may be, Mansur built a mosque and a palace as the centre, and the city was laid out around them in concentric circles with three strong walls. The townspeople and the bazaars occupied the space between the first and second walls but, for purposes of defense, the space between the second and the third was left entirely empty.

In the days of Harun-al-Rashid about twenty-five years later, Bagdad was the capital of a large empire. It comprised not only Mesopotamia and Arabia, but also Persia, Egypt, Syria, North Africa and all the Caucasian countries such as Georgia and Circassia near the Black Sea.

The court of the Caliph was the most magnificent the world has ever seen; more than eighty thousand servants lived within the palace. There were ornaments of gold and silver and in the Hall of Audience stood the famous golden tree upon which, so tradition says, birds of gold and silver, studded with precious stones, fluttered mechanical wings and poured forth delightful songs. Everything was agleam with precious gems and some say that one street was even paved with silver.

Under Harun-al-Rashid, it became also the golden age of commerce, of science, of literature and of art. It was no wonder then that its fame reached far and wide and that it was coveted by ambitious nations. Constant warfare followed the death of Harun-al-Rashid, and it was not many years before the fine buildings were all destroyed. Although it was rebuilt, it never regained its former splendor.

The city changed hands many times—Turks, Mongols, Persians fought for it and held it for a time until finally the Turks conquered it again in 1638 and retained it until World War I. But the Bagdad of to-day is not that of long ago as we shall soon see.

From the south we approach it by the River Tigris, sailing through a flat and desolate country of sand, upon which we may see an occasional encampment of wandering Arab tribes. Within a few miles of Bagdad the land begins to assume a different aspect. Native boats are plying along the river, and the paddle-steamer

RADISHES GROW AS BIG AS PARSNIPS IN THE WARM SUN OF IRAQ

A bumper crop of the edible root is being washed in a trench before being taken to market. Radishes are thought to be native to Asia, but they can no longer be found in the wild state.

that has brought us from the Persian Gulf threads its way through a maze of craft of all descriptions, and berths at one of the rough wooden jetties. We are in the center of the land of the Caliphs, of Sindbad the Sailor, and the peris and genii of which we have read in the Thousand and One Nights.

We shall be disappointed to learn that the present site of Bagdad is not the one of the Caliphs. They had their city on the west bank and now almost all that remains of their glory are some of the royal tombs and the shrine of Zobeide, the favorite wife of Harun-al-Rashid. We see a group of mud hovels, a new railway station, trim bungalows with English gardens where the railway people live, and we turn away disturbed indeed by the fact that we cannot see Bagdad as it was.

Two pontoon bridges connect the old city with the present city which is situated on the east bank of the Tigris. Here the buildings straggle along about two miles of the shore and each end is marked by the North and South Gates which were used formerly when the city was protected by a wall. Bright-colored domes and minarets greet our eyes, for Bagdad is still one of the centers of the Shiite sect of Mohammedans and the Faithful come from afar to worship at its holy places. Of the difference between the Shiite and the Sunni sects, we shall read in the article on Arabia.

Connecting North and South Gates, a distance of about three miles, is a broad thoroughfare called New Street. This was started by the Turks in 1916 for transporting artillery and many buildings were torn down to make way for it. When the British captured the city in March, 1917, they continued the building of the street.

Bagdad is now the capital of Iraq which

TENDING THE VALUABLE SKINS OF KARAKUL LAMBS NEAR BAGDAD

The karakul is a hardy breed of broadtail sheep that thrives in dry regions. Newborn lambs have a tightly curled, glossy fur, sometimes called astrakhan, that is widely used in clothing.

PHOTOS, PHILIP GENDREAU

HOW COTTON IS SPUN IN THE LAND OF DATE PALMS AND TURBANS

The climate of Bagdad is so dry that some kinds of factories may be rigged up out-of-doors in a shady spot. Cotton is an important crop in Iraq, and its production employs many people.

THE BAGDAD RAILWAY, the most important route of overland transportation between Europe and the Middle East, has been made famous by adventure stories of international intrigue.

BARGES ARE LOADED at Bagdad with goods for export. The small boats will steam down the Tigris River to Basra where their cargoes will be transferred to ocean-going vessels.

was formerly under British mandate. In 1932 the mandate ended and Iraq became independent. Iraq took an active part in founding the Arab League and has been a member of the United Nations since the signing of the UN Charter in 1945. British influence in Iraq, as in most Middle East countries, declined after World War II, though British and American firms still held large interests in Iraqi oil.

New Street Becomes Arab

Toward North Gate the city becomes Arab in character and just beyond the Gate is the residence occupied by King Feisal whom the British selected as the native ruler of Iraq. He died in 1933, and was succeeded by his son Ghazi. He died in 1939, and his infant son succeeded as Feisal II.

We must go through the narrow cross streets, which lead from New Street to the river, to find the real atmosphere of Bagdad. Here are the bazaars and the coffee-houses and the many types of people that form an interesting part of the city.

A large number of the population is Arab but as we go wandering about we shall see also Syrians, Armenians, Indians, Persians, Turks—members of all the tribes and races of the Near and Middle East. The languages used mostly are Arabic and Turkish, and the principal religion is, of course, Mohammedanism.

Let us take a walk through the bazaars, where we shall see the life of Bagdad. On market days they are crowded with town and country-folk who come in from the surrounding districts laden with the produce of the field and looms and with various articles made at their homes. All classes are represented, from the rich merchant to the beggar who clamors for alms amidst the din of bargainings.

Importance of the Letter-writer

Here and there in the narrow streets, we may see a fortune-teller who for a small sum promises life-long prosperity to his patrons; and the professional letter-writer is also a common sight. He sits cross-legged with paper spread out upon his lap. Clients gather round him and recite documents and letters and the scribe writes it all down. Education is not so universal as in the West, so the professional letter-writer is kept very busy on market day, when the terms of the bargains have to be recorded and deeds of sale drawn up.

The medical profession is often popular amongst Orientals, since it affords a ready means of acquiring wealth and influence, for among these simple people anyone may pose as a healer of all the ills to which flesh is heir. I remember once discharging a groom for inefficiency who shortly afterward set up as a medical man. As I passed through the market place one day, I saw my former groom presiding over a stall, which was well stocked with herbs and potions. Quite a crowd was assembled at his consulting room, and before dealing out the medicines he felt the patient's pulse and looked at his tongue, as he had probably seen European doctors do. Then he glanced through a book in his hand, following this up by selecting some medicines, as if in accordance with the instructions in the book. I was curious to see that book, and on inspection it proved to be a copy of a novel that had formerly been in my library!

Houses Built for Extremes of Climate

The houses in Bagdad are interesting because they are built to meet extremes of climate. From the end of April until the beginning of October the heat is excessive, so the houses are constructed partly underground with windows high enough to admit light and air. The occupants sleep on the roof in summer, retiring to the cellar at sunrise for soon after that time the temperature will rise to as much as 110° Fahrenheit in the shade. During the winter the weather is cold and there are often ice and snow.

Primary and secondary education is free and compulsory. However, there are less than a thousand elementary schools. Iraq has no university, but there are a number of vocational and technical schools, and about twelve colleges for training teachers, doctors, lawyers, engineers and so on.

MONUMENT TO A KING

King Feisal I Bridge spans the colorful Tigris at Bagdad. Feisal was chosen King of Iraq by a referendum in 1921, receiving 96 per cent of the votes cast. He remained on the throne until his death in 1933. His grandson, Feisal II, who has ruled through his uncle, the prince-regent, since 1939, will take over in his own right in 1953 on his eighteenth birthday.

KING FEISAL SQUARE

This view of still another monument to a beloved monarch is taken from a department store roof. The buildings under construction and the state-owned Iraqi Airways office add a modern touch. In contrast, the domes of some ancient mosques may be seen in the background. These, together with other buildings of historic importance, make Bagdad a tourists' paradise.

THE ICE-CREAM VENDOR IS A POPULAR FELLOW, EAST AND WEST

Arab children in a street in Bagdad gather eagerly to clamor for a portion of the cooling sweet. Hundreds of years ago ice cream was such a rare delicacy that only kings and emperors could enjoy it, but today it is for everyone. These youngsters would probably enjoy it in cones. Instead, they are eating it from little flat dishes, and the hot sun says, "Hurry."

The schools tend to be nationalistic, that is, they teach the rich history of Iraq's past and try to stimulate the pupils to think about the future of their country. In the campaign against illiteracy nearly 150 tribal schools have been opened and free books are distributed to those students who cannot afford to buy texts.

Many children do not attend the more progressive government schools, but are taught by comparatively ignorant teachers in badly organized, primitive classes. The pupils in such poor schools must sit on the ground at desks made of rough-hewn logs. Some sing their lessons aloud, in an ancient Oriental belief that the mind

A PAUSE AND A POSE ON THE WAY TO MARKET IN BAGDAD

With airy nonchalance, the farmers appear quite willing to have their picture taken, while their laden donkey waits patiently. Harun al-Rashid may have walked this byway long ago.

absorbs knowledge through the ears rather than by the eyes.

There is one thing that we do not meet with in Bagdad, that is caste—the distinction between the different classes which is such a handicap to the people of India. Here any means of livelihood may be adopted, and no one will sneer at a man because of his trade.

Market day reveals the national costumes in all their many colors. The under-garment is usually a long shirt, over which is a close-fitting coat of colored cloth fastened at the waist by a girdle. Above this is a cloak of camel's hair, often with black-and-white stripes. Perhaps the most practical part of the costume for this hot climate is the scarf which is arranged over the head in a form of turban so that the long ends hang from the shoulders and can be used as a protection against the rays of the sun.

The food of the people consists of wheat, barley, corn and mutton, and the date is also an important article of diet. It is, in fact, the staff of life of the Arab, and the Prophet Mohammed directed all his followers to honor it as they would their parents. Coffee is another thing of which the people are very fond, and the first thing an Arab does in the morning, after he has said the early prayers ordered by his religion, is to take a cup. It is said that coffee was first discovered by an Arab near Bagdad, who one day lighted a fire beneath a wild shrub. A most uncommon and pleasing smell resulted which led to the discovery of the famous beverage. At first it was considered an intoxicant and was forbidden by the Mohammedan religion but its popularity was so great that it seemed impossible to prevent it and so it became the favorite drink of Near Eastern people.

KEYSTONE

A BAGDAD STREETCAR TRAVELS LEISURELY

The car may not move faster than a boy can walk, but it offers some shade on the way. The roof is a popular spot since it affords the best view of the passing scene.

Music of a kind peculiar to the Orient is played in the bazaars and at entertainments, but the tunes are a monotonous repetition and mainly of a dull and plaintive character. Indeed, there is no accounting for taste in that direction. Some years ago a party of desert tribesmen were taken to Leningrad, in Russia, where they witnessed a performance at the Opera House. At the fall of the curtain they unanimously agreed that the finest part of the entertainment had been the tuning-up of the violins!

The coffee-house, a form of open-air café, is a feature of Bagdad. There the gossips congregate to discuss the news of the day and a great deal of business is accomplished over the cups. As the Bagdadis are strict Mohammedans they observe the fast of the Ramadan, the foremost religious observance of the Moslem faith, and it is then that the coffee-shops are most crowded.

The Ramadan is chosen as the period of fasting, because the Koran is believed by the Mohammedans to have been revealed to Mohammed during this month. While the fast lasts no food whatever may be taken between dawn and nightfall; there can be no eating, drinking, nor any form of material pleasure, and the fast is considered to have been broken if perfumes are smelled.

During the hours of complete darkness eating is permitted, and so the coffeeshops remain open all night and are gay with lights and other attractions until the coming of dawn, when the fast begins again. While the rich may lessen the severity of the ordeal by turning night into day, its hardships fall heavily upon the poor and industrial classes, who must continue their daily labors.

All through Bagdad we shall find evidence of the historic past, and, with the advance of civilization and under the great influence of Western ideas it is being gradually developed into a great and prosperous city. Vast distances in this land are now covered by aeroplane in a few hours, where formerly all transport was by camels, which averaged but fifty miles per day. Now double as much is done in an hour, and soon this once magnificent city, with its quaint streets, its cafés, mosques and market places, will be within reach of the traveler, who can, if he has the imagination, then feel himself really in touch with the Orient.

KEYSTONE

WISE CARE FOR PERISHABLES WHERE REFRIGERATORS ARE SCARCE

The Arab woman is carrying milk straight home from the cow. The man walking on the left holds a squawking chicken, which will not be killed until it is time to cook it.

THE CHANGING FACE OF TURKEY

The Turks in Europe and in Asia Minor

The mental outlook and the customs of the Turkish people have undergone great changes since the 1920's. Traces of some old Eastern ways still linger; but on the whole, modern Turkey bears a close resemblance to a progressive European nation. Since 1923, when the country became a republic with a democratic constitution, Turkey's industry has expanded in many directions, agricultural programs have increased the output of the soil, and foreign trade has shown great gains. Today Turkey is the strongest and most advanced of any nation in the Middle East and is a member of the United Nations and also of the North Atlantic Treaty Organization.

BEFORE it began to crumble late in the seventeenth century, the Ottoman Empire, with Turkey at its heart, was one of the greatest powers in all history. Under its conqueror-sultans, it reached out to embrace all of North Africa, the Balkans east of Vienna, Arabia and many other parts of Asia. Turkey today cannot compare in area with the vast holdings of the Ottomans. However, it has gained in progress and internal stability much of what it has lost in size. From a declining Oriental despotism, it has been transformed into a dynamic nation governed as a democratic republic.

The ancestors of the Ottoman Turks, a handful of nomads from central Asia, entered Anatolia (Asia Minor) in the thirteenth century and settled there under their chief, Ertogrul Bey. Anatolia was then in the hands of the Byzantine Greeks and the Seljuk Turks, who had overrun Asia Minor in the eleventh century. By the time Ertogrul and his tribesmen appeared, the once-mighty Byzantine, or Eastern Roman, Empire had shrunk in size and power and was at the mercy of the Seljuks. Its capital, Constantinople,

TURKISH INFORMATION OFFICE

TWENTIETH-CENTURY ARCHITECTURE is typical of Ankara, one of the most modern cities of the Middle East. A wide overhang shields the first story of this building from the sun.

TURKEY

on the European continent, was threatened by Slavs pressing across Thrace (northern Greece). Also by this time, the Seljuk Empire had broken up into many jealous factions which were constantly at war with one another or with the fading Byzantine Empire. Ertogrul's nomads made their home between these two fast-decaying powers. Since they were a hardy, energetic people, unspoiled by the wealth and luxury that had weakened their neighbors, they at once began to make the best of their opportunities.

First Sultan of the Ottomans

Ertogrul's son Osman expanded his holdings and was proclaimed the first sultan of the newly arrived Turks. It is from him that the Turks derived their name of Osmanli or Ottoman Turks, which distinguished them from their Seljuk cousins. It was by that name that the world was to know them until the sultanate was abolished and the new republic came into being.

Many of the Seljuk princes rallied under Osman, and soon a small new nation took root in the soil of Anatolia. After Osman's death, his son Orkhan, banking on the growing strength of his country, led his warriors across the peninsula of Gallipoli. There they gained a foothold in Europe, which proved to be a fateful

event for both Turks and Europeans.

The Turkish soldiers who helped to extend the boundaries of the Ottoman Empire were called janizaries. At that time they constituted the best-disciplined fighting force in the world. At first they were recruited by force from among the young sons of Christian subjects. These youths were taught the Moslem religion and, in fact, became Turks. Later, children of well-to-do Turkish families were enrolled, for it was an honor to be admitted to the *Ojak* (hearthstone) of the janizaries. The young boys were subjected to rigorous training in the art of warfare. Each soldier was physically strong as well as an expert in the arms of the day. With these fearless troops, the Ottoman sultans overran the Balkans. Finally, in 1453, Sultan Mehmet (Mohammed) the Second, called Faith or the Conqueror, captured Constantinople and put an end to the Byzantine Empire.

The Spread of Turkish Power

Thus, in less than two centuries after they had settled in Anatolia, the Ottoman Turks not only crushed the Eastern Roman Empire but built an empire of their own. As for the Seljuks, they had long ago been absorbed by the Ottomans. Only one power remained in Asia Minor —the Ottoman Empire, with its new cap-

248

ital Constantinople, or Istanbul as the Turks called it.

Successive sultans pushed the empire's frontiers westward and eastward. Under Suleiman the Magnificent, whom the Turks called the Lawgiver, the Ottoman Empire reached the height of its power. It included Hungary, Transylvania and other areas in the Balkans, the Caucasus, Azerbaijan, Mesopotamia and the Arab peninsula. The Sudan and Egypt were also under Turkish dominion, and the Turkish banner had been carried into Ethiopia and Libya. Suleiman's janizaries marched to the gates of Vienna and threatened the city. But Vienna did not fall, and from that time the Turkish tide began to recede.

After the reign of Suleiman the Mag-

nificent, the rising might of Russia and the Austrian Empire threatened the power of the Ottomans. Jealousy and corruption began to undermine the Turkish government. The janizaries became so unruly that Mahmud the Second, in the nineteenth century, had to crush them and disband the corps. The Moslem clergy opposed all reforms that might have saved the empire and sided with the ignorant to keep Turkish lands backward. This happened at a time when the Western world was taking enormous strides in political and social reforms and in the sciences.

Several attempts were made at Westernization, but they could not check the downfall of the Ottoman Empire. The most important period of reform was in the middle of the nineteenth century.

BLACK STAR

DRY AND WARM in his embroidered felt cape, a Turkish shepherd takes his sheep up from the Mediterranean plains to the plateau of the Taurus Mountains for spring pasturage.

HOUSES OF PUMICE are dug from the lava plateau of Cappadocia. The cone in the background is one of many left by erosion of deposits of an extinct volcano in central Turkey.

Then a constitutional government was established under a liberal sultan. But when the tyrant Abdul Hamid came to the throne in 1876, there began one of the most despotic periods in the empire's history. For a short while, Abdul Hamid allowed a constitutional government, but tyranny soon returned and lasted until 1908, when the parliamentary constitution was restored. From then until its collapse, the empire was under a form of constitutional monarchy.

The Ottoman Empire allied itself with Germany in World War I and was defeated. In 1918 the Allied armies of occupation moved into Turkish territory to enforce the terms of the armistice. Two years later the victorious powers imposed on the Ottoman Empire the Treaty of Sèvres. It took from the Turks not only the territories they had possessed as an empire but also lands that were purely Turkish in population. These areas were to be divided among Great Britain, France, Italy and Greece. Under the leadership of Mustafa Kemal, the Turks unfurled the banner of independence and, after a grim struggle, ousted the foreign troops of occupation.

Like the people of the United States, the Turks call their struggle for freedom the War of Independence. It began in 1920 and officially ended on July 24, 1923, when the Treaty of Lausanne was signed and the world recognized the new Turkish state. When, on October 29, 1923, Turkey became a republic, Kemal was elected its first president.

As a first step toward Westernizing his country, Kemal accomplished the seemingly impossible—the separation of church and state in a Moslem country. The sultanate and the caliphate were abolished, and so were the veil and the traditional

BLACK STAR

YOUNG GIRLS in some sections of southern Turkey wear an elaborate braided hair-do and take pride in the length of their tresses. After marriage, a scarf covers the braids.

POURING OUT YOGHURT, prepared from ewe's milk. Yoghurt may be thick or thin and is something like cottage cheese. It is delicious served, say, with fruit or sliced cucumbers.

headgear, the fez. The schools were taken out of the hands of the religious authorities, and a program of free, compulsory education was set up. The Turkish language was partially purged of Persian and Arabic words. The Latin alphabet was adopted instead of Arabic script, and adult Turks were taught to read and write the new letters. International calendar, clock and metric systems were also introduced; and various European civil, penal and commercial codes replaced the old Moslem law. Women were freed, given the right to vote and permitted election to the Grand National Assembly. Everyone acquired a family name. Kemal's was Atatürk, which means "father of the Turks." The Constitution of the Turkish Republic summarizes the change from the feudal estate: "Every Turk is born free and free he lives."

Atatürk realized that, in order to enjoy equal standing with European nations, Turkey must become an industrial country. He initiated a program of economic and technological development which attempted to rush through centuries of Western evolution within a few decades. Turkey, straddling East and West, definitely stepped into the Western world.

Turkey in Europe and Asia

Turkey is divided into two parts by the small Sea of Marmara and the narrow straits of the Bosporus and the Dardanelles. The smaller European part is bounded by Greece and Bulgaria. The larger part occupies the Anatolian Peninsula in Asia. It is bordered by the Black Sea on the north, the Soviet Union and Iran on the east, the Mediterranean Sea, Syria and Iraq on the south, and the Aegean Sea on the west. Turkey is about 1,000 miles long and 350 miles wide and covers 296,185 square miles—an area larger than the state of Texas.

Turkey lies in about the same latitude as Spain. Along the Black Sea, the Pontic Mountains rise steeply to heights of 7,000 feet in the west and 12,000 feet in the east. On the south, the Taurus and Anti-Taurus ranges are just about as high. Between the mountains lies the interior plateau, parts of which are desert. For the inhabitants of this plateau, life is a ceaseless struggle against the forces of nature. The land yields good hard grain and provides pasture for the goats that produce the soft Ankara wool (Angora mohair), which derives its name from Ankara Province. But long, cold winters, with snow lingering into May, and dry summers, with frequent droughts, are a constant menace to man and beast as well as to the land and its yield.

Ancient City with a Modern Air

Ankara, the capital of Turkey since 1923, is about two hundred miles southeast of Istanbul on the interior plateau. Although it is a very ancient city, its appearance today is that of a modern metropolis, with broad boulevards, fine new buildings and spacious parks.

It is only near the coastline of the peninsula that the land and climate of Turkey become more kindly. The mountains that fringe the central plateau are, in turn, fringed by a narrow strip of green and fertile plain, where there is a variety of climates and products. On the Black Sea coast, there is rain and dense vegetation through all the four seasons. Istanbul, which sits astride the cross currents of the Black Sea in the north and the Mediterranean in the south, often becomes as cold in winter as Toronto or New York, but in summer it enjoys dry and breezy days.

Mild Climate, Fertile Soil

South of Istanbul, on the Aegean Sea coast, is the part of Turkey that faces Greece, and the climate is much like that of Italy and Spain. The winters are mild and the summers hot and dry. It is a fertile land of olive trees, figs and grapes. Here are the remains of ancient cities, such as Pergamum and Ephesus. This is one of the country's main export regions, in the midst of which stands modern Izmir—ancient Smyrna—the second largest city of Turkey and one of the important cities of both contemporary Mediterranean civilization and the early world.

Farther south, in the region of Adana, around the town of Tarsus where St. Paul

TURKISH TOBACCO, collected in great baskets, begins its journey to world markets.

key are varied and rich in quality rather than quantity. Despite its rough climate, the central plateau throughout the course of history has been renowned for its wheat. Nine out of ten cultivated acres in Turkey are devoted to cereals, and wheat forms about half of the total grain production. It is an important item in Turkish domestic economy because wheat bread is the most important staple food of both the village and town folk. Barley, rye and oats are other cereals grown in the central plateau. All of these play a large part in the domestic economy, but in Turkey's foreign trade other products are more important.

Crops Raised for Export

In the regions around Izmir on the Aegean coast and in the Samsun and Trebizond areas on the Black Sea, one finds the crops that, from the standpoint of quality, enjoy the highest reputation in the markets of the world.

Tobacco ranks first among these choice products. The United States, the largest cigarette producer in the world, is also the greatest purchaser of Turkish tobacco, which is the country's leading export. This tobacco is used for blending purposes to lighten the color, to add flavor and aroma, and to increase the burning qualities of cigarettes. Almost all cigarettes made in the United States contain from 4 to 8 per cent Turkish tobacco.

Raisins and figs—particularly dried figs—are the next most important of Turkey's high quality agricultural products for export. Opium-poppy seed, olives, olive oil, flax, hemp, sesame, spices and attar of roses are also valuable export items.

With over 40 per cent of the land available for grazing, livestock raising is an important aspect of Turkish rural life. Some 60,000,000 sheep, mohair-producing goats, cattle, horses and donkeys are raised; sheep account for about half that number.

The principal minerals are coal, lignite, chrome, iron, salt and copper. Other minerals being mined include manganese, mercury, antimony, asbestos, sulfur and

was reared, the coastal strip broadens into the Plains of Cilicia, an area of large-scale agriculture. Here, in a subtropical climate, cotton, sugar cane, oranges and bananas flourish.

The vast majority of Turks are producers of food and other agricultural products. The agricultural resources of Tur-

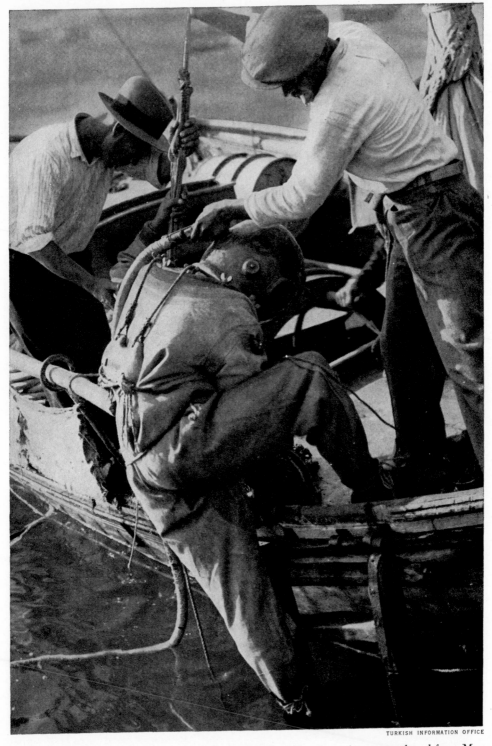

HIGH-QUALITY SPONGES are found in Turkish waters, where they are gathered from May until about October. Many Mediterranean sponge divers today use modern equipment.

SLENDER MINARETS of mosques lift their white spires above Bursa (or Brusa), near the Sea of Marmara. The garden city was the residence of many Turkish sultans.

emery. Turkey has a virtual monopoly on meerschaum, the white or cream-colored mineral used in making fine tobacco pipes. Oil fields in the southeastern part of the country are considered promising and are being developed by domestic and foreign private capital.

In consumer goods, textiles, sugar, paper, leather, shoes, food processing and alcoholic beverages rank highest. Major heavy industries include iron and steel, metalwork, cement, building materials and chemicals. Practically all of these industries have been established within the last two decades.

Education in Turkey is compulsory and free in the government-operated schools between the ages of seven and sixteen. The average citizen of today is interested in learning. In 1923, when the Republic was founded, only one out of every ten

people knew how to read and write. Today five out of every ten are literate. There are many primary schools as well as universities in Istanbul and in the capital city of Ankara. Students from poor families are given scholarships which enable them to attend both high schools and colleges. Hundreds of foreign students attend Turkish universities, and many Turkish students are enrolled in North American educational institutions. Technical and vocational schools are well attended. A great many students in Turkey's universities are women, and throughout modern Turkey one finds an increasing number of women doctors, lawyers and judges.

A person who has never been within Turkish boundaries probably pictures the Turks as wearing baggy trousers and red fezzes. To him, Turkish women may still

THE BEST SMYRNA FIGS are grown about sixty miles inland from Turkey's Aegean coast. The figs, ripened and partially dried on the tree, are gathered after they have fallen.

257

KUTAHYA in western Turkey is noted for its decorative ceramics and tiles. These vessels are being made by hand on a potter's wheel. Notice the beautifully fluted rims.

be hiding themselves behind a mysterious veil. But the minute he steps on Turkish soil, he learns that the picturesque costumes and customs he expected to find disappeared with the Ottoman Empire. The fez and the veil are no more. He will find blondes and brunettes and even freckled redheads. Turkey has not been the bridge between East and West for thousands of years without showing it. People of all races, creeds and cultures have intermingled there, but the dark-haired, swarthy Mediterranean type is predominant.

The same person who expected to see costumes of an earlier day may be surprised to learn that Turkey has adopted such Western sports as football and base-

BLACK STAR

AN OLD COVERED WAGON serves for a holiday ride into the countryside near Istanbul. There are many picturesque spots along both shores of the Bosporus north to the Black Sea.

AN EARLIER DAY'S GRANDEUR. Among the older structures remaining in Ankara is a former palace, set among formal gardens. The building now houses a government department.

ball. Horse racing has long been one of the national pastimes. Every year a field day is held in which Turkish youths participate in various sports and exercises.

Turkey's main aim in her foreign policy is to preserve her independence and territorial integrity. Since the foundation of the Republic, she has constantly cultivated the friendship of all countries touching her borders. With the majority of them, such as Greece, Iraq and Iran, she has succeeded in basing her relations on sound principles of co-operation and understanding.

Since the fall of 1939, following the outbreak of World War II, Turkey has had a treaty of mutual friendship with Great Britain and France. The war also cemented friendly ties with the United States, and in 1947 the Truman Doctrine of military aid to nations threatened by the spread of communism resulted in a great strengthening of Turkish defenses. Relations have been developed with Italy during the postwar period; in 1950 Tur-

key and Italy signed a treaty of friendship. Turkey is taking active part in the military planning of the North Atlantic Treaty Organization for the defense of the Mediterranean. She signed the defensive alliance with Greece and Yugoslavia in 1953.

Turkey is a member of the United Nations and of all its auxiliary organizations, such as the World Health Organization, the International Labor Organization and the Food and Agricultural Organization. In July 1950, she responded to the United Nations' appeal for troops to resist aggression in Korea. In the Korean conflict, the Turkish brigade quickly won the respect and admiration of its allies.

Ties with the Western World

Geographically, historically, politically, economically and culturally, Turkey today is a European country. Her geographical status in Europe is determined not so much by her European territory as by the fact that the Turkish Peninsula has turned its back on the Asiatic continent. The mountains that rise on the eastern borders of the country increasingly open up toward the Mediterranean and southeastern Europe as they fan out into fertile western valleys. Historically Turkey has been a part of Europe since the conquest of Istanbul in 1453. It would be very hard to name any event in the last five hundred years of European history that has not influenced Turkey or that has not been directly influenced by her. Since the founding of the Republic in 1923, Turkish political thought and institutions have been based on Western European political philosophy. Turkey's place in the Organization for European Economic Cooperation shows that her trade and commerce are part and parcel of European economy. Her social reforms since the 1920's have united Turkish everyday life with that of Western Europe.

By SENIHA TASKIRANEL

A TULIP PATTERN flows from an artist's clever fingers, in a tile factory in Kutahya.

GOLDEN SULTANA RAISINS (small and seedless) being washed. They are gathered from vineyards that thrive on the rich, sunny plain of Manisa, known long ago as Magnesia.

A MODEL VILLAGE near Antalya, in southern Anatolia. The dwellings have a tidy look with their whitewashed walls and tiled roofs. Each one is home for a low-income family.

TURKEY: FACTS AND FIGURES

THE COUNTRY

In the eastern Mediterranean, between Europe and Asia, it occupies the greater portion of Asia Minor and is a small part of the Balkan Peninsula. It is bounded on the northwest by Greece and Bulgaria, on the north by the Black Sea, and on the northeast by the U.S.S.R.; on the east by Iran; on the south by Iraq, Syria and the Mediterranean; on the west by the Aegean Sea. The climate is temperate on the Aegean and Black Sea coasts. There are extremes of summer heat and winter cold in the inland plateau regions. Land area, 296,185 square miles; population, 20,935,000.

GOVERNMENT

In 1921 the Grand National Assembly at Ankara drew up a constitution which declared that all sovereignty belonged to the people and that the legislative and executive power was vested in the hands of this Assembly representing the people. The term "Ottoman Empire" was abolished and the country officially designated Turkey. A republic was proclaimed in 1923, and Mustafa Kemal became first president. In 1924 a new constitution provided for election of the Assembly every four years. All citizens over 22, including women, may vote. Executive power is exercised by the president and a Council of Ministers appointed by him. In 1937 the Assembly agreed to recognize only one party and established a form of state socialism. Other parties have since been allowed.

COMMERCE AND INDUSTRIES

Agriculture is the main occupation of the people. A Land Reform Bill, passed in 1945, distributed large tracts of agricultural land among peasants who had none. Despite the fact that two-thirds of the population is rural, only about 20 per cent of the fertile land is under cultivation and irrigation is underdeveloped. The rich mineral deposits of Turkey are worked to a very slight degree. Its main products are wheat and other grains, tobacco, cotton, figs and raisins, mohair, filbert nuts, olives and olive oil, coal, copper, iron and chrome. Principal exports include tobacco, grains, chrome, ore, copper, dried fruits, nuts, opium and skins. It imports chiefly machinery, textiles, vehicles, iron and steel products, mineral oils and chemicals.

RELIGION AND EDUCATION

Most of the people are Mohammedans, though Mohammedanism has been abolished as a state religion. Primary education is compulsory. State schools, which include primary, secondary and preparatory schools are free and are all under the Ministry of Public Instruction. Many non-Mohammedan communities maintain their own private schools that are, however, subject to the Ministry of Education. Religious instruction, which is optional, has been permitted since 1948. There are teachers' colleges and other advanced schools as well as the universities of Istanbul and Ankara.

COMMUNICATIONS

Turkey is making every effort to improve its transportation system. It has about 4,800 miles of railroad. Its merchant marine is under government control. Airlines now link the main centers, and the Orient Express connects Turkey with southern and western Europe. The Baghdad Railway links Turkey with Syria, Iraq, Lebanon, Israel and Egypt.

CHIEF TOWNS

Ankara (Angora), capital, 286,800; Istanbul (Constantinople), 1,018,500; Izmir (Smyrna), 230,500; Seyhan (Adana), 117,800; Bursa (Brusa), 100,000.

ISTANBUL

City of Two Continents

Istanbul, at the crossroads of Europe and Asia, is one of the oldest and busiest cities in the world. From the most ancient times it has been an extremely important center of commercial and political life. Straddling the historic waterway known as the Bosporus, it offers both a short passage between Europe and Asia and a maritime route between the Black Sea and the Mediterranean. So it was that Istanbul (once Constantinople) advanced rapidly in importance in the ancient world and has always played a star role in the drama of history. Though it is no longer a capital city, it remains one of the world's great metropolises.

THE oldest part of Istanbul lies on a triangular peninsula, washed on the south by the waters of the Sea of Marmara, on the east by the strait of the Bosporus and on the north by the Golden Horn, an inlet of the Bosporus.

Because of its peculiar situation, its climate in several respects recalls not only that of the Mediterranean but also that of central Europe and of the Black Sea. There are marked changes of temperature according to the season and the year. The prevailing winds of this zone are from the north. When they blow from the northwest in winter, they bring frigid weather and snow. Winter is a short season, however, and spring comes in abruptly. In spring and autumn the wind usually blows from the south and is often followed by rain. In summer the sky is clear and the climate mild owing to northeasterly breezes. From every point of view, the best season in Istanbul is the autumn, which is long and beautiful.

The Golden Horn is a narrow fiord that cuts European Istanbul in two—Galata and Pera on the north and old Istanbul on the south. From Saray Point, at the entrance to the Bosporus, the inlet is about five miles long. The broadest part is between the districts of Kasimpasa and Cibali, where it is 770 yards wide. It is said to owe its ancient name, Chrysokeras, meaning "golden horn," to the resemblance of its outline to a bull's horn. But others hold that it owes its name to its great wealth in fish. It is a unique natural harbor, almost made to order for shipping. The waterway is unaffected by

tides and can take vessels of deep draught.

Pouring through the Bosporus, which is seventeen miles long, the waters of the Black Sea divide the great continents of Asia and Europe from each other. These waters also divide the whole of Istanbul in another way. Like a river, they flow between the European and Asiatic parts of modern Istanbul. About halfway along the rushing Bosporus there is a mile and a quarter stretch of water called the Kanal. At either side of the narrowest part of the Kanal, 605 yards, where Europe and Asia come closest, there are medieval fortifications: Rumeli Hisari (Castle of Europe) and Anadolu Hisari (Castle of Anatolia, or Asia).

For the Byzantines, the Bosporus had only military importance and was neglected. But under Turkish rule the natural beauty of both shores was more appreciated. Villas, gardens and castles were laid out along the sparkling waters of the strait. Among the most picturesque of the old structures still remaining are the palace of Beylerbey on the Anatolian (Asiatic) shore and the fortresses of Rumeli and Anadolu mentioned earlier.

A ride of only ten minutes on a ferryboat takes you from old Istanbul to the Anatolian coast and its lovely summer resorts. Here, also, is the Istanbul district of Uskudar (Scutari). Once it, too, was a summer resort, and its aging houses and cobbled streets still have much of their old charm. The section is rich in Turkish monuments, and the Karaca Ahmet cemetery with its cypress trees is a lovely spot.

Within a short distance of Istanbul,

scattered like jewels on the Sea of Marmara are the Adalar (the Islands, or the Princes Islands). There are nine islands in all; the most important are Kinali (Proti), Burgaz (Antigoni), Heybeli (Halki) and Büyukada (Prinkipo). The last one is especially lovely, with its dreamlike villas nestling mid pine groves, and its elaborate gardens. All the Islands still have traces of the Byzantine period.

No one knows exactly when Istanbul was founded. The Roman historian Pliny, however, wrote that in the ninth century B.C. a small settlement named Lygos existed on what is now Sarayburnu, or Seraglio Point.

Advice from the Delphic Oracle

A more certain date is 658 B.C. That year the Megarians (Greeks of the city of Megara), wishing to found a colony, followed the advice of the Delphic oracle and built a city on Sarayburnu. They called it Byzantium, supposedly from the name of their leader, Byzas. The city flourished and expanded, and became the object of numerous attacks and invasions as its location increased in importance.

In 513 B.C., the Persian King Darius crossed the strait and occupied Byzantium, as part of his campaign against the Scythians. Persian domination ended in 479 B.C., when the Spartans under Pausanias colonized the city. Later Athens and Sparta disputed possession of Byzantium. Philip of Macedonia besieged the city in 340 B.C. It fell into the hands of Alexander the Great, Philip's son. On Alexander's death, the small states founded by his generals, Byzantium among them, fought among themselves. At length it became a self-governing city under Roman rule.

Because the city had taken sides against him, the Emperor Septimius Severus razed it to the ground in A.D. 193–95 but rebuilt it shortly afterward.

There were now many conflicts within the Roman Empire, partly in regard to religion. The city of Rome was still largely pagan. This is one reason why the Emperor Constantine, after he was converted to Christianity, made Byzantium his capital, on May 11, 330. Under him the city was enlarged and renamed Constantinople (City of Constantine). In 395 the Empire was permanently divided into Eastern and Western parts; and Constantinople became the capital of the Eastern, or Byzantine, Empire.

For several centuries thereafter, it was besieged in turn by Huns, Goths, Ostrogoths, Bulgarians, Slavs and, in the seventh and eighth centuries, by Muslim Arabs. However, the rapidly expanding city was strongly fortified by Theodosius II (408–450); and in 507–12 the Emperor Anastasius built the Long Walls extending from Silivri (about 40 miles from the city) to the Black Sea coast. Justinian (483–565) built further fortifications in Thrace to safeguard the city.

Ebu Eyyib Halid Ibn-i Zeyd, at whose house the prophet Mohammed stayed following his flight from Mecca to Medina, took part in one of the Arab sieges and was killed before the walls of the city in 668. For centuries his grave was venerated by the Byzantine people and became famous as a place where they went to pray for rain. After the capture of Constantinople by the Turks, in 1453, a big tomb was built over the grave—a tomb that today is the heart of the locality known as Eyüp.

Early in the thirteenth century, Constantinople was in the hands of the Crusaders, who set up various Latin kingdoms on Byzantine soil. At the same time there was large-scale destruction of the city and many landmarks vanished.

The Historic Siege of 1453

Meanwhile, a new Greek empire formed at nearby Iznik developed with great speed. After prolonged and fierce battles, its ruler succeeded, on August 15, 1261, in capturing Constantinople. The city failed, however, to regain its former magnificence. It now became subject to pressure from the Ottoman Turks. Finally, on May 29, 1453, after a siege that lasted fifty-three days, Sultan Fatih Mehmet (Fatih the Conqueror)—or Mohammed II—captured Constantinople.

ISTANBUL UNIVERSITY is on the edge of Beyazit Meydan. This inviting square, with its fountains, is in the Latin Quarter, a part of the most ancient section of the city.

265

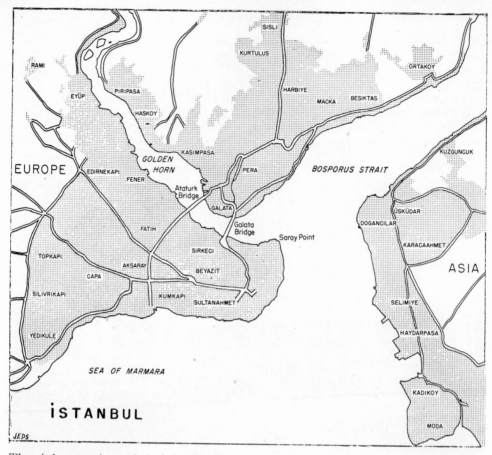

ISTANBUL

JEDS

Thus it became the capital of the Ottoman Empire. Fatih the Conqueror's conquest was an amazing feat. He hauled seventy-two ships of his fleet from the Bosporus overland down to Kasimpasa on the Golden Horn, thus outflanking the chains that had been strung across the narrow Bosporus to keep the Turkish vessels out. When the news of this feat came, despair fell upon the people of the doomed city, yet they resisted stubbornly for four more weeks. But after the general assault of May 29, the city was forced to yield.

The capture of Constantinople (now to be known by its Turkish name of Istanbul) by the Ottoman Turks is generally regarded as a climax in history. With it the Renaissance, or rebirth of learning, that had slowly been developing now took on a swifter pace. When Constantinople fell, scholarly Greeks fled, with many tokens of a bygone culture, to Italy. Besides this, the situation of the city had made it a key point on the old trade routes between the Orient and the Occident. Consequently, the Italian states, since their trade was now in danger, supported those seeking other routes to the Far East and thus opened the way to the discovery of America.

As the Turkish capital, a new life opened for Istanbul. The culture of Islam, including the beautiful works of Muslim craftsmen, began to appear. Libraries were established. Scholars and artists of all races were encouraged. Even at this early date, there was concern for the needy, and free kitchens were opened for them.

After the Egyptian campaign of Sultan Selim in 1517, the already great importance of Istanbul was enhanced by the fact that it became the seat of the Caliphate. Also, as the Ottoman Empire rose, so did Istanbul grow and prosper, becoming the greatest center of learning and the arts

266

and commerce in the Islamic world. Graced with numerous masterpieces of Turkish architecture, such as monuments, palaces, mosques, public baths, madrasahs (theological colleges), villas and so on, Istanbul expanded far beyond the boundaries of the old Byzantine city. However, Byzantine monuments and works of art were preserved with meticulous care.

After the first World War, the Turkish people won freedom for themselves and complete independence of any foreign power, under the leadership of Atatürk. When the Turkish Republic was proclaimed in 1923, Ankara (in Anatolia) became the capital. But Istanbul was in no way neglected by the republican government.

Istanbul, which for 467 years was the center of the Ottoman Empire, is today a vilayet (province) of the Turkish Republic. However, its historic riches, its culture, trade, taxable value, attraction for foreign visitors, its industries—all remain of great importance.

In regard to architecture and archaeology, Istanbul is unique. For 1,600 years it was in turn the capital of Roman, Byzantine and Ottoman empires, so almost everywhere there are historic structures. Exhibits that display the old civilizations as well as the magnificence of the Ottoman Empire are to be seen in the Istanbul museums. Their collections are priceless.

Although life in modern Istanbul is quite different from what it was in the past, the city is still evocative of the

PIX

HOTELS, STORES and other buildings in the modern part of Istanbul are often built with pillared arcades at street level. The thoroughfare is nonetheless quite Western-looking.

267

THE BLUE MOSQUE is the only one in the world with six minarets. It was built in the seventeenth century, and the interior is adorned with exquisite tiles in soft shades of blue.

HAGIA SOPHIA, architectural gem erected under Byzantine emperors. The name means "holy wisdom." Originally a church, today it is a museum, filled with priceless treasures.

EARLY MORNING HAUL. The waters that flow past Istanbul teem with finny creatures. This is particularly true of the Golden Horn, perhaps so named because of its wealth in fish.

legendary East. At every step, one is confronted by history. Yet old and new stand side by side in delightful and harmonious contrast.

Hagia Sophia, the glory of Byzantine art, was first a Christian church, then a mosque and in recent times has become a museum. (Hagia Sophia means "holy wisdom"; to the Turks it is Aya Sophia.)

It is one of the noblest buildings inspired by religious faith in the world. As architecture, it is on a par with St. Peter's, in Rome, or St. Paul's, in London.

Originally built by Constantine, in the year 347, Hagia Sophia was destroyed by fire in 404. Justinian the Great had the present structure built on the old site between 532 and 552.

AN ANCIENT FIRE TOWER overlooks the courtyard of Bayezit Mosque, in the heart of old Istanbul. There are several such towers; fire must have been a threat from very early times.

BLACK STAR

THE GORGEOUS INTERIOR of the Blue, or Sultan Ahmet, Mosque. As one looks up toward the great dome, the eye is enthralled by the intricate, flowing designs worked out in blue tiles.

THE MEDIEVAL TOWERS of Rumeli Hisari (Castle of Europe) are on the European side of
the narrowest part of the Bosporus. In the historic siege of 1453, the city's defenders strung

chains across the racing waters from this castle to Anadolu Hisari (Castle of Anatolia) on the Asiatic shore. The Turks, however, outflanked the chains by dragging ships overland.

FRESH FRUIT AND VEGETABLES for sale along a cobbled alleyway. The produce is an enticing blend of colors and fragrances—figs and dates, oranges, lemons and succulent greens.

The magnificent pile of Hagia Sophia covers an area of about 75,000 square feet. Within it gives the impression of being one vast domed space, though the details are actually intricate. At ground level there are 40 great columns and on the raised gallery section 67 more. Some of these columns are of dark green marble, and others are of dark red porphyry. The massive central dome, which seems to float without visible support, is 180 feet above the ground. The buttresses that keep the structures erect today were built by the Turkish architect Sinan the Great. Among the building's priceless treasures are the exquisite mosaics, dating from the fourth to the fourteenth centuries, on the floor, vaults and domes. Since 1935, when Hagia Sophia became a museum, extensive work has been done to uncover and restore its masterpieces of Byzantine art to their original beauty.

Rumeli Hisari, the famous fortifications on the European shore of the Bosporus, was constructed in 1452 in the amazingly short time of three months, by order of Sultan Mehmet the Conqueror. He was then getting ready to lay siege to Constaninople. It was from Rumeli Hisari that the chain meant to thwart him was stretched across the strait to Asia. From far back in the mists of time, the place where Europe and Asia almost touch has been called the most beautiful on earth. As the light is caught in the sparkling waters of the Bosporus, there is an ever changing interplay of color.

Istanbul is famous for its ancient cisterns, or reservoirs, for the supply of water. They are enormous underground structures, their roofs upheld by countless columns. The Sunken Cistern is also known as the Yerebatan Sarayi, or Sunken Palace, or the Basilica Cistern. It was constructed by that great builder, the Emperor Justinian, in the sixth century. One of the largest of the Byzantine cisterns, it is 154 yards long by 77 yards wide. It has 336 columns, each about 26.5 feet high. It is the only one of the old Byzantine cisterns that still contains water, which is brought from reservoirs in the forest of Belgrade to the northwest. Electric lights have been installed in this cistern, and it is possible to ride through in a rowboat.

The Cistern of a Thousand and One Columns is said to have been constructed by a great Roman dignitary named Philoxenus, one of the senators who followed Constantine to his new capital, though some historians give Justinian the credit. This is the biggest cistern of all, designed to contain more than 7,000,000,-000 gallons of water. Inside, it is 220 feet long and 184 feet wide. Actually there are not a thousand and one columns, but only 224—2 feet in diameter, arranged in 15 rows, and all identical. Light is admitted to this cistern through 11 air holes. There is a small entrance.

Though the ancient Hippodrome has vanished, it was once one of the city's most impressive structures. It was first laid out by the Emperor Septimius Severus in 196. Here the people wit-

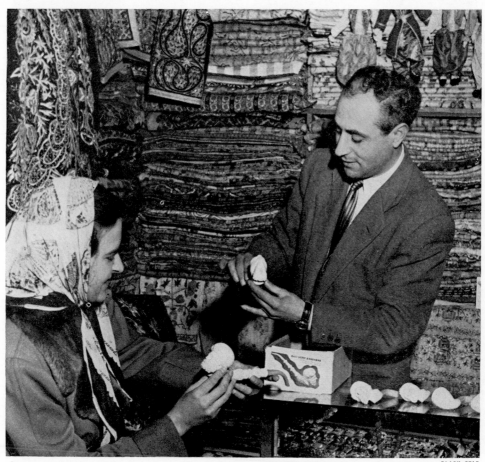

BLACK STAR

MEERSCHAUM PIPES, brocades, tapestries—all at a single shop in the Covered Bazaar. Most of the world's meerschaum—a fine claylike mineral—is mined in Turkey, near Eskisehir.

ANCIENT GRAVES are scattered all over Istanbul. Long ago, noted men were buried beside the institutions they had founded. Today such graves may be in the midst of busy markets.

THE GOLDEN HORN, looking toward the north shore. An arm of the Bosporus, the Horn cuts through the European part of Istanbul. Right center is the fifth-century Galata Tower. The area around it had foreign colonies at an early date and is still the city's most cosmopolitan section.

THE GALATA BRIDGE sweeps across the Golden Horn just above its entrance into the Bosporus. Connecting the ancient and modern areas of the city, the span carries heavy traffic.

EXHIBITION HALL, built to display the great variety of Turkish products and to attract foreign trade. Since World War II, Turkey's commerce with Western Europe has increased.

278

ON THE FERRY across the Bosporus between European and Asiatic Istanbul. The ride takes only twenty minutes. Turkish newspapers are printed in Roman rather than Arabic letters.

279

DOROTHY LOUISE NORRIS

MILES OF SHORE along the Golden Horn and the Bosporus provide delightful settings for homes. In some places the houses are built right at the water's edge with only a narrow footpath in front. Dwellings atop the cliffs offer the added charm of long views.

nessed games, including the chariot races that were their favorite pastime. The noble Hippodrome, with all the astonishing wealth of decoration lavished upon it, saw its best days in the reigns of Constantine the Great and Theodosius II. On the site today are the German Fountain (the gift of Kaiser Wilhelm II, in 1895), the Mosque of Sultan Ahmet, the Cadastral Office and the School of Economics and Commerce.

The Serene Blue Mosque

The Sultan Ahmet Mosque, a seventeenth-century masterpiece of Turkish religious architecture, is also known as the Blue Mosque. Its serene, lovely interior is adorned with azure tilework. It was completed in 1617, after eight years of work under architect Sedefkâr Mehmet Agha. The Blue Mosque is near the site of the ancient Hippodrome, facing Hagia Sophia, from which it is separated by a landscaped square. The mosque covers an area 208 by 235 feet. Surmounting it is a central dome 110 feet in diameter, 8 feet more than the diameter of the great dome of Hagia Sophia. The outline of this fine mosque, with its 6 slim minarets —it is the only mosque in the world that has 6—is a specially wonderful sight from the sea. Attached to the mosque are a madrasah (theological school), imaret (free kitchen) and other social and cultural institutions which were founded by Sultan Ahmet.

Towering over the third of the seven hills on which Istanbul is built, the Süleymaniye Mosque is one of the most magnificent works of Sinan, greatest of all Turkish architects. It is considered one of the five noblest religious edifices in the world. The mosque was completed in 1557, and its great central dome stands at a height of 174 feet and has a diameter of 105 feet. There is a series of smaller domes, each of which is 75 feet in diameter, at a height of 131 feet above the ground. The interior (207 by 226 feet) is illuminated by 138 windows. Matchless marble paves the courtyard of the Süleymaniye, which is circled by 24 pink-and-white marble columns. Con-

sidered the most glorious of any building in Istanbul, Süleymaniye has a symmetrical beauty on the outside as well as within. When it was finished the Sultan handed a golden key to Sinan so that the architect himself might open the mosque, a gracious tribute to the genius of the architect.

The Yeni (New) Mosque is a masterpiece of Turkish architecture of the seventeenth century. Situated on the old Istanbul side of the Galata Bridge, which spans the Golden Horn, its tier upon rising tier of domes dominates the skyline. These domes are supported by long galleries of marble columns. The interior is a treasure house of priceless tilework in every imaginable shade of green and blue. Seen in the soft light that sifts through the picturesque windows, the soothing colors help to create an atmosphere of unequalled peace and serenity.

The Mosque of Bayezit, in the middle of the square of the same name, is the oldest and least changed of any Istanbul mosque since its construction. It was completed in 1506 by the architect Hayrettin Aga, and the work took five years. In this mosque the great dome is supported by four stout columns and has four great arches, each of which supports two half-domes. Two of the arches are filled in with sculptured walls.

Into the Covered Bazaar

The Covered Bazaar is one of Istanbul's most extraordinary landmarks, and its like can hardly be seen today even in any other Oriental city. Actually the bazaar itself is a vast roofed city, divided into districts. One such is the old Cloth Market, which was built by Mehmet the Conqueror in 1461. It was enlarged in the reign of Süleyman the Lawgiver, when much timberwork was added. Visitors enter the maze of twisting streets by way of thirteen enormous wrought-iron gates, which are locked at night. Even on the hottest day, the passageways are cooled by breezes and drafts. Unhappily, this fact adds to the danger of fire. In the sixteenth and seventeenth centuries, the bazaar was severely damaged by fires and earthquakes. On July

HAMMERED COPPERWARE for the bazaars, where such utensils are sold by the hundreds. There are skilled Turkish artisans in many fields. Some have a special gift for work in metal.

10, 1894, it was completely burned down after a violent earthquake. Four years later, however, it was rebuilt. One of the worst fires in the twentieth century (November 24, 1954) destroyed four thousand shops. In a little more than a year, however, they were restored.

The Topkapu (or Seraglio) Palace, the residence of the Ottoman Turkish sultans from 1472 to 1853, is today a museum. "Seraglio" refers to its former women's quarters. The treasures it holds cover nearly five centuries of Turkish culture. In its four vast wings there are oil portraits of the Ottoman Sultans, a fabulous collection of jewels, beautiful fabrics and hand embroideries from the sixteenth to the eighteenth century, Turkish tiles, the most remarkable collection of Chinese porcelains in the world (six thousand items dating from the ninth to the thirteenth century), Japanese porcelains, Turkish miniatures from the thirteenth to the eighteenth century, wall texts in exquisite Arabic script, antique Turkish and European watches and clocks, musical instruments, royal and state coaches and saddles ornamented with trappings in cloth of gold and silver, ancient royal kitchen utensils and silver table furnish-

BLACK STAR

CLAMBERING UP A HILL from the Golden Horn. The European part of Istanbul is built on seven hills. Climbing the steep streets is worth the effort for the views from the top.

283

ings—a dazzling repast for the eyes.

Standing like sentinels around the palace are four charming but widely different structures called kiosks—open pavilions. Taken in turn, they are the Tile Kiosk of the fifteenth century, built only nineteen years after the conquest of Istanbul in 1453; the Baghdat in 1638, erected by Sultan Mahmud the Fourth; the Mustapha Pasha Kiosk of the eighteenth century, which represents Turkish rococo (an ornate architectural style) at its best; and, finally, the so-called New Kiosk of the nineteenth century.

In the Military Museum is a unique collection of ancient weapons used by Saracens and Crusaders, including the sword of Mehmet the Conqueror. There is in the museum an armlet worn by Tamerlane, the Mogul conqueror. The gallery houses wax figures dressed in the colorful costumes worn by Turkish soldiers, starting with the famous Janizaries, who constituted the first regular army to be organized anywhere in the world. In the courtyard are tombs of Byzantine emperors.

As the name would suggest, the Museum of Antiquities houses superb examples of Hittite, Greek, Roman and Byzantine art and archaeology. There are also Egyptian, Sumerian, Babylonian

PIX

SOCCER, BASEBALL, whatever the game, the spectators in Istanbul's stadium are finding it thrilling. The Turks are a vigorous people and are keenly interested in all kinds of sports.

A PALATIAL HOTEL that caters to luxury-loving globe-trotters. From the roof garden one looks out over the old city, with its domes and minarets, to miles of sparkling blue water.

and Assyrian relics. In addition to sculptures, terra-cotta work, jewelry, pottery, coins and medals, there are some magnificent tombs. Prize of them all is the sarcophagus of Alexander the Great, in delicate pink marble.

The four main galleries of the "Evkaf" Museum of Turkish and Islamic Art contain ancient Turkish rugs and carpets dating from the thirteenth century, rich brocades, fifteenth-century illuminated manuscripts, costumes worn by sultans and princes of the Ottoman Empire, embroidered dresses, and mother-of-pearl

caskets studded with precious stones.

In the midst of all this ancient grandeur, life goes on much as it does in any other large cosmopolitan city. There are excellent restaurants, and Turkish food can hold its own with the best anywhere. Theaters and fine shops line Beyoglu Caddesi (Avenue), and for night life there is Taksim Meydan. From the nearby city park of Taksim there is a superb view of the Bosporus. For, above all, it is the surrounding waters that give Istanbul its greatest charm.

By Seniha Taskiranel

285

MINARET AND ROWS OF ARCHES—THE GREAT MOSQUE, DAMASCUS

One of the greatest examples of Mohammedan architecture, the mosque was built under the
Omayyad caliphs who reigned from 661 to 750, not long after the Prophet's own time.

THE TROUBLED LAND OF SYRIA

Trade Center of the Ancient World

Syria is a country that is rich in the remains of vanished empires. There are ruins of what were once splendid cities, such as Palmyra; and the strongholds of the Crusaders stand gaunt and crumbling on lonely crags. The land has echoed to the war cries of conquerors—Alexander the Great, the armies of Rome, Tamerlane and his Mongol hordes, the Turks and many others. Today, as we shall see, Syria is still a country of violent changes and its unsettled present makes its future unpredictable. In order to understand the problems of modern Syria, we must first understand the people who inhabit the land.

SYRIA is a land with a rich yet stormy history. The tapestry of its past is embroidered with scenes of bloodshed, upheaval and Eastern splendor. Like its past, the country's present is turbulent and unsettled. Even independence and home rule have not succeeded in bringing peace to the ancient land and its people.

Syria's boundaries once embraced not only the area of the present-day Republic but also Lebanon, most of Israel and Jordan and parts of Saudi Arabia. Since this area lies at the strategic crossroads of three continents, it formed the highway along which trading caravans and armies from Europe, Asia and Africa had to pass. As a result, Syria grew rich on the trade of the ancient world, but it also shook to the thunderous tread of many invading conquerors and existed under foreign rule for the better part of its history.

Modern Syria, formed out of the old, stretches from Turkey on the north to Jordan on the south. It is bordered on the west by the Mediterranean Sea, Lebanon and northern Israel. To the east and southeast lies Iraq.

In northwestern Syria, an extension of the Lebanon mountain chain parallels the country's short Mediterranean coastline. Its western slope dips gently to the sea. The eastern slope falls away sharply for some 3,000 feet to the marshy, malaria-infested Ghab Valley and the rich valley of the Orontes River. Farther to the east the land rises to a plateau. The well-watered and relatively productive valley of the Euphrates River lies in northeast-

ern Syria and forms part of the Fertile Crescent, which extends inland from the Mediterranean, along the mountains of southern Turkey and then down the Tigris-Euphrates basin to the Persian Gulf.

Along the Lebanese border are the main peaks of the Anti-Lebanon Mountains, which are arid and largely uninhabited. The chain is continued southward in the equally inhospitable and uninhabited Hermon range and reaches its high point of more than nine thousand feet at Mount Hermon.

Southern Syria, below Damascus, is a plateau region of long-extinct volcanoes. Some of the cones reach a height of three thousand feet. The lava-enriched soil of the Plain of Hauran in the southwest has long been cultivated. In ancient times this section was a main source of grain for the Roman Empire, but its modern output is on a much smaller scale. The volcanic plateau reaches its highest level in the Jebel Druse region of the southwest, where one cone rises almost five thousand feet above sea level. This area is unsuitable for cultivation and is a refuge for outlaws and bandits. The central and southeastern parts of Syria are the arid wastelands of the Syrian desert.

The country's climate ranges from the cold winters and very hot summers of the desert to the mild Mediterranean climate of the western coast. Sufficient rain falls only in the western mountains and droughts are frequent in steppe and desert regions. Strong winds, some of great force and violence, blow the hot, dust-filled air from the deserts across the face

SALT ENOUGH TO MAKE A HOST OF GIANTS THIRSTY

The mineral has been extracted from salty rivers and seas; and the usual beasts of burden in this part of the world are used to transport it. The "salt mountain" is near Aleppo.

of the country, leaving a parched path.

Because of the land's varied geography, the ancient Syrians, who were of Semitic stock, never developed a single, strong and politically united civilization such as those existing on the great river plains of Egypt and Mesopotamia. Instead, a group of small city-states sprang up, each one jealous of the others. As the early civilizations of Egypt and Mesopotamia grew and spread, their merchants established trading routes across Syria, and the city-states came to depend on the rich commerce of the larger empires. It was from the Lebanon Mountains, for instance, that Egypt obtained lumber and also the rare oils used in embalming its pharaohs. As the city-states grew in wealth, outsiders began to envy their prosperity.

The first known invaders came down from the north and included the Hyksos, or Shepherd Kings, the Kassites, the Mitanni and the Hittites, all vigorous and ingenious peoples. They brought with them the horse and the chariot, and the Hittites introduced their discovery of iron which was later to replace the bronze then in common use. Invaders also moved in from the southern desert regions and settled around some well-watered areas. In this way a number of communities grew up and gained in power and cultural influence. Prominent among them were communities of the Philistines, Canaanites, Israelites and Phoenicians.

Syria fell in turn under the rule of the Egyptians, Assyrians, Babylonians, Persians and Macedonians. The Persians, in their attempt to unite all the Middle East under a single ruler, spread a common language (Aramaic) throughout Syria and introduced the Semitic culture of the west to the great Indo-Aryan culture of the east. The Macedonians found that they could exercise their power in Syria more readily through the townspeople than through the farmers. Therefore they established a number of new cities, and Syria became a center of Greek life, with Antioch (now Antayka in Turkey) as its capital.

The legions of Rome conquered Syria in 64 B.C., and Roman engineers built a chain of fortifications along the old trade route across Syria to the East. The bases reached from the Hauran and Jebel Druse in the southwest, through Damascus, and then across the desert by way of Palmyra to the mountains near Nisibini in the extreme northeast. A Roman fleet occupied the country's coastal harbors.

Under Roman rule, Syria reached heights of prosperity probably not equalled since. The land was intensively cultivated for grain to supply the growing needs of the Roman homeland. New industries flourished, notably textile production, glass blowing, and metalworking. Antioch was the center of Rome's rule and was said to have had a population of three-quarters of a million people. Most Syrians, however, continued to live in the country.

When the Roman Empire was divided into two parts, East and West, Syria came under the domain of the Eastern, or Byzantine, Empire. In 636 the Arabs wrested the country from the weakened Empire, and ever since Syria has remained an important part of the Moslem world. In the eleventh century the Seljuk Turks overran the land.

For about a century, beginning in 1096, Crusaders from Europe established strongholds in Syria and tried to take the holy places from infidel hands. They were eventually driven out of the country by the brilliant Moslem warrior Saladin and his Saracen armies. It was about this time that savage Mongol hordes from the wilds of central Asia began to terrorize the Middle East. They ravaged the countryside and destroyed cities, massacring the inhabitants. Tamerlane (Timur), a Mongol leader, pushed on into Syria where his armies looted and burned the cities of Aleppo, Homs and Damascus.

The barbaric Mongols were finally checked by the Ottoman Turks who rose

EWING GALLOWAY

A WATER WHEEL NINETY FEET IN DIAMETER AT HAMA

Hama has breath-taking gardens, irrigated by means of huge water wheels. The water comes through aqueducts from the Orontes River. Outside of Hama, in western Syria, is a desert.

ALL THAT REMAINS OF THE BIBLICAL "CITY OF PALMS"

The Bible refers to this site as Tadmor, meaning the "city of palms." It is supposed that it was built by Solomon. The present-day village near these ruins is called Palmyra.

HITTITE SCULPTURES CARVED PERHAPS 3,500 YEARS AGO

Though the sculpture of the Hittites was crude, it had force and imagination. The Hittites were vigorous fighters, and these carvings represent archers and warriors armed with shields.

to power rapidly after they had captured Constantinople in 1453. These fanatical Moslems ruled all Syria by 1516. Their control was maintained through a highly trained military police force known as Janissaries. It was during the period of Turkish rule that Syria began to decline economically and politically.

The discovery in 1498 of a new overseas trade route around the Cape of Good Hope to the markets of the Orient spelled out doom for the affairs of Syria. The difficult overland trade route across the country fell into neglect and Syria's decline was rapid. From the sixteenth century until trade began to flow through the newly opened Suez Canal in 1869, Syria and other countries of the region held an unimportant place in world affairs.

The Era of French Control

The weakened Ottoman Empire controlled Syria until World War I. In 1920 the country was placed under French protection by a mandate from the League of Nations. A French-controlled government was set up, but internal unrest plagued Syria and several times disturbances had to be subdued by armed force.

With the outbreak of World War II, Syria was still a part of the French colonial empire. After France surrendered to Germany, the pro-Vichy government collaborated with the Germans in Syria. Consequently British and Free French forces, after some fighting, occupied the country in 1941. By the end of 1946 occupying troops were withdrawn, the French mandate was formally ended, and Syria was declared a sovereign republic.

The course of Syrian politics continued to be one of violent change. King Abdullah of Jordan was ambitious to unite under his rule a Greater Syria, to be made up of Syria, Lebanon, Iraq, Jordan and Palestine. His plan had the support of important political groups within Syria but was opposed by the military and by the Arab League nations of Egypt and Saudi Arabia. In a single year Syria was rocked by three military-led revolts to establish new governments, and plans for a Greater Syria were put aside.

BLACK STAR

ORCHARDS ON WALLED TERRACES

Apricots, figs, almonds and pomegranates grow on the narrow plots to the top of the hill.

291

A SYRIAN FARMER GLOWS WITH PRIDE OVER HIS NEW TRACTOR

Though few Syrians who work the land have such up-to-date equipment as this, modern agricultural methods are slowly making headway. There is good soil, which could give greater yields.

FREDERIC LEWIS

PRECARIOUS WORK—SPLITTING A LONG LOG LENGTHWISE

The saw is rigged to move up and down, and as the man wields it he must also keep his balance as he steps backward.   This ancient way of cutting logs seems awkward in the extreme.

FROWNING LANDMARK IN ALEPPO—THE ANCIENT CITADEL

Built in the late fourth century B.C., the Citadel has witnessed the rise and fall of empires. Aleppo
is on a plateau in northwest Syria, and the Citadel is on a still higher hill.

TROLLEY TRACKS GUIDE A COUNTRY FAMILY THROUGH THE CITY

Riding donkeys, this family has come from a remote district and it is probably their first sight of a
city. All their worldly goods are stowed on the backs of the patient animals.

WHO'LL BUY MY COFFEE—HOT, SWEET AND THICK?

Most people of the Middle East love coffee, and vendors are a common sight on city streets. The beverage is usually made in the Turkish way, so sweet and thick it is almost a sirup.

"THE STREET WHICH IS CALLED STRAIGHT" IN DAMASCUS

The famous byway, mentioned in the New Testament in connection with Paul's conversion, really crooked. It runs from the eastern to the western gate, flanked by bazaars.

The people of Syria are mostly of Arab origin. Arabic is the principal language although some Armenian, Turkish, Kurdish and Syriac is spoken. The large majority of the people are Moslems and most of them follow the Sunní branch of Islam. The rest of the population is divided between Christians and Jews.

Around the volcanic plateau of Hauran in the southwest live the Druses, a proud people famed for their fierce fighting qualities. More is told about them and their customs in the chapter on Lebanon.

Many tribes inhabit Syria, particularly the Bedouins of the desert region. In northwestern Syria dwells a group known as the Ismaili, or Assassins. They are the remainder of a once-powerful secret order of religious fanatics who flourished during the eleventh and twelfth centuries. From his stronghold in the wild Syrian mountains, Sheik el Jebel (the Old Man of the Mountain), leader of the sect, dispatched young men to assassinate enemies of the order. So that the killers would be unafraid, they were first drugged with hashish. Because of this practice, these religious murderers became known as *hashashin,* from which comes the English word "assassin." Today the production of hashish is a concession of the Syrian Government and is an important source of revenue.

Another group of the northwest is the Alawi who live in the Jebel Ansariyeh, a part of the Lebanon mountain range. Though they are considered Moslems, they have taken over the celebration of Christmas from the Christians and also practice certain ceremonies of pagan origin.

The Yezidi, a small group, live in northeast Syria. The largest body of them is in neighboring Iraq. These people still possess a strange pagan religion and believe that evil powers dominate the world. Their rites to ward off the evil spirits have led outsiders to call them devil-worshipers.

The life of the nomadic Bedouins has

EWING GALLOWAY

THE MODERN FACE OF PERHAPS THE WORLD'S OLDEST CITY
Twentieth-century shops and apartment houses line a street in a section rebuilt within the old walls of Damascus. Most other parts of the city, however, have an Oriental atmosphere.

A MODEL OF ISTANBUL'S HAGIA SOPHIA HIGH ON A PEDESTAL

The attractive square, laid out with formal flower beds, is in the center of Damascus. Its most curious feature is the replica of the celebrated Byzantine structure in Istanbul.

PIX

PICNICKING ALONG THE BANKS OF A RIVER IN DAMASCUS

In the cool of the evening families come to enjoy a meal beneath the trees. Two rivers flow through the city—the Barada and the A'waj—called the "waters of Damascus" in the Bible.

A CUP, A BOWL, A COFFEE URN—BRASS DAZZLING IN THE SUN

The Syrians have always excelled in metal work. In the days of chivalry a blade of Damascus steel was prized above all others. That craft has vanished but not the skill with metals.

A MARKET SQUARE—OPEN-AIR DEPARTMENT STORE AND GROCERY
Whatever a Syrian needs for his house or his person he is likely to find in the market square.
Bargaining is the order of the day, a game of wits that both buyer and seller relish.

changed but little down through the centuries. Their life and customs are described in detail in the chapter entitled The Desert Rangers. It has been said that if Abraham were to return today to a Bedouin encampment in the Syrian desert, he would feel quite at home, noting few changes since his time.

Bedouin tribes rarely combine with one another. If some strong leader does accomplish a union of a number of tribes, it proves to be a temporary arrangement that falls apart at his death. There is an almost perpetual state of warfare and feuding between tribes. Warfare is conducted according to strict rules. It is through warfare that a young Bedouin proves himself a worthy member of the tribe. Tribal territorial limits are carefully drawn. Some tribes remain in a relatively small area; others travel great distances in their search for pasture for their livestock.

Despite the numerical importance of the Bedouin and the farmer, or Hadhar, the dominant element of Syria's life centers about the cities. Here live the great landowners or feudal lords, owners of most of the nation's arable land. The landowners and traders or bazaar merchants guide the political career of the country. In recent years, however, as we have seen, the better-educated military class has begun to wield considerable political power.

The principal cities are all in the western part of the country and near the foothills of the mountains where there is an ample water supply. Damascus and Aleppo are the two main cities, followed by Homs, Hama and Latakia.

Damascus, the capital, is sometimes called the Pearl of the Desert because of the beauty of its surroundings. It is said to be the world's most ancient city, and it appears to have been a notable place as early as 1913 B.C. At one time Damascus was a thriving center for the trade between Europe and the Orient and its bazaars and markets overflowed with goods from the Eastern and Western worlds.

A PURCHASE OF FRUIT CALLS FOR SERIOUS CONSIDERATION

The vendor of the fruit appears indifferent to the outcome and ready for a nap alfresco. Meanwhile his unhurried customers examine the fruit and discuss its possible merits.

A HAWKER CRIES HIS WARES—HEAPS OF LUSCIOUS FRUIT

What passer-by would not be tempted by the fragrance and colors of downy apricots, pomegranates bursting with red pulp or ripe, purplish figs with the morning dew still on them?

The plain on which the capital is situated is watered by the Barada River and is rich with orchards of figs, apricots, almonds, pomegranates, lemons, oranges, plums, pears and apples.

The modern city is still very Oriental in character and has preserved most of its Eastern flavor. The Moslem section is considered the best and wealthiest quarter of Damascus and has wider streets, better houses and a more abundant water supply than other parts of the city. Elsewhere the streets are narrow and crooked and often extremely dirty. The house fronts are generally prisonlike in appearance, with a few small grated windows piercing their mud walls. Sometimes, however, a drab and forbidding front conceals a luxurious interior.

The trade and commercial life of a Middle Eastern city centers about the bazaar section, an area where the merchants buy and sell almost everything under the sun. In Damascus the bazaars and khans (inns housing men and pack animals) are very large affairs. To the noisy, bustling bazaars come the Bedouins to exchange wool, leather and other products for cereals and the few manufactured things they need. The varied products of field and orchard are brought there, and cargoes from overseas find their way to the bazaars. Although the city no longer makes and sells the famous Damascus steel, fine handmade metalwork can be bought in the bazaars. There are tea merchants, sellers of beautiful textiles, dealers in fine leatherwork and furniture, jewelers and merchants who handle imports from other countries. If you should wish to buy a radio or a typewriter, they, too, can be found in the colorful bazaars of Damascus.

Damascus is linked by railway with Amman, the capital of Jordan, and with Aleppo in the north. There is a connecting railway line with Beirut and Cairo, and a huge bus runs across the desert country to Bagdad. At the Damascus airfield one can board a plane for Bagdad and other Eastern cities, or for Cairo.

Aleppo, on the ancient main caravan

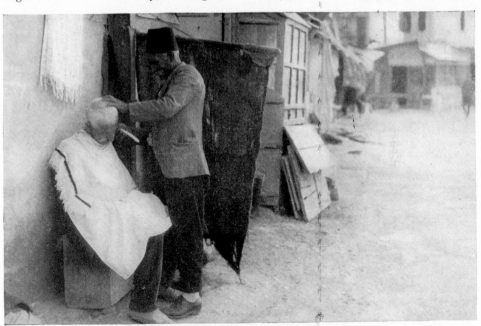

FREDERIC LEWIS

A SIDEWALK IS AS GOOD A PLACE AS ANY FOR A SHAVE

A Syrian barber is ready to set up shop wherever he finds a customer. Instead of a red-and-white pole, he hangs up a towel on the wall to mark the place as his for the time being.

route across Syria, is a typical Oriental city of darkened, narrow streets. Parts of it, however, are modern and possess great charm. Aleppo is the junction for railroads serving the upper Tigris-Euphrates valley, Hama, Homs, the Damascus region and the Mediterranean coastal plain. Rail lines meeting in Aleppo connect with Cairo, Ankara and Bagdad.

About two-thirds of Syria's people live in villages and depend upon agriculture for their livelihood. The mountain slopes and other arable areas are farmed to produce all kinds of cereals, fruits and vegetables. Cotton and tobacco are grown in the warmer regions, such as that about the Mediterranean port of Latakia. The villages themselves are parts of large estates of the landlords. The small farmers live in poverty, for the city-dwelling landlords contribute nothing to the development of the land, yet they claim up to half of all crops. When a harvest is made, an agent of the landlord is present to collect the landlord's share.

The life of the farmer, like that of the Bedouin, is a very hard one. He must always be on guard against Bedouin raids. His agricultural implements are primitive and he plows with wooden sticks that are pulled by long-horned oxen, camels, donkeys or by the farmer himself. He lives in a mud hut that consists of only one or two rooms which he shares with his animals. Landless laborers are even worse off than the farmers. They get enough to eat only at harvest time. In winter they subsist on grain, bread and grass.

Education is quite limited and the great bulk of Syria's people cannot read or write. Except for the small educated class, the people sign a document by inking their thumb and making an imprint on the paper. There are elementary schools, largely private, and a university in Damascus. Health standards are low.

Western nations have tried to bring about improvements in Syria, and there are many Syrian leaders who well understand the difficulties that must be overcome if their country is to have order and stability and democracy approaching that of Western lands.

By E. S. Ferguson

SYRIA: FACTS AND FIGURES

THE COUNTRY

Formerly a mandate of France and situated in Asia Minor, the Republic of Syria became a completely independent state in 1946. It is bounded on the west by the Mediterranean and the Lebanese Republic, Israel and Jordan on the south, Iraq on the east and by Turkey on the north. It is composed of nine administrative Sanjaks (districts): Aleppo, Damascus, Euphrates, Hama, Hauran, Homs, Jebel de Druz, Jezire and Latakia. Area, 66,046 square miles; population about 3,253,000.

GOVERNMENT AND CONSTITUTION

Since gaining her complete independence, Syria's government has changed hands several times through military coups. Normally, the government consists of a president, premier and a parliament, all popularly elected. However, Parliament was dissolved in 1951, and all political parties in 1952. Syria is a member of the UN and of the Arab League.

COMMERCE AND INDUSTRIES

Agriculture and cattle-raising are the leading occupations. About half of the cultivable land, some 7,000 square miles, is normally under crops; the chief crops are wheat, barley, oats, maize, sesame, hemp, sugar cane, lentils and chick-peas; fruit trees cultivated are banana, orange, lemon, olive and the white mulberry for feeding silkworms. Cotton cultivation has increased during recent years; cotton and its products, raw wool and silk are exported. Cereals and manufactured goods constitute the bulk of the imports. The mineral deposits, although largely undeveloped, include iron, lignite, gypsum, marble and building stone.

COMMUNICATIONS

The means of communication in Syria are being steadily improved. The total mileage of improved roads exceeds 3,000; the railway mileage is 890 miles. Steamers give regular service to ports and there are air services to Marseilles and Bagdad from Damascus.

RELIGION AND EDUCATION

Over half of the inhabitants of Syria are Moslems, chiefly of the Sunni sect. Over 1,612 public elementary schools have been established. The elementary schools are still largely private. There is a Syrian university in Damascus and an Arab academy. There are also two agricultural colleges.

CHIEF TOWNS

Damascus, the capital, has a population of 335,060; Aleppo, 362,541; Homs, 244,094; Hama, 146,564; and Latakia, 100,462.

NEW AND OLD LEBANON

From Snow-capped Peaks to Sunny Shores

As a separate state Lebanon is very young, but its story reaches far back into the mists of time. Tyre, on the coast, was the chief city of the daring Phoenician sailors and merchants; and in the Old Testament the prized cedars of Lebanon are mentioned time and again. Through the passes of the Lebanese Mountains strode conquerors and traders. There is a footway, between Beirut and Baalbek, that has been in existence since 1500 B.C. Modern Lebanon is on a bridge between old and new, weighed down on one end by customs that are centuries old, while at the other end twentieth-century ideas beckon.

AT the dawn of history a civilization already existed in Lebanon. Archaeologists have established that at Gebal, or Jebeil—today a village of about a thousand people, about twenty miles north of Beirut—there existed a city named Byblos around 3000 B.C. Because of its export of papyrus for making books, the ancient Greeks used the name of Byblos for the word "book," from which came "Bible" and many words containing "biblio." At this early date Byblos ranked above Tyre and Sidon and other flourishing centers of Phoenician culture.

Tripoli and Aradus also existed as coastal ports during this early period. A large maritime trade had been built by the Phoenicians. As shipbuilders they were without peer, and their vessels carried lumber and pine products to Egypt and other parts of the Mediterranean. It is supposed that Phoenician seamen sailed as far as Cornwall, England, where tin was mined.

The timber from the forests of Lebanon was a great source of wealth to the coastal cities, and they were not lacking in other industries. Glass-making was developed to a high degree. From a small shellfish (murex) they made a purple dye—the Tyrian purple beloved of the Romans centuries later.

Our alphabet is sometimes said to have been invented by the Phoenicians, but this is only partially true. There is no doubt that these people did evolve one of the earliest alphabets but they were probably helped by their knowledge of the alphabets of other peoples, gained through their activities as traders. However, it was because of the widespread commercial relations of the Phoenicians that languages using an alphabet, such as Aramaic, were transmitted to other peoples throughout the Middle East and as far as Persia.

Because of their riches and their location on the highway from the north to Egypt (they were also the terminal points of the long caravan route from India and China), the Phoenician cities came under the rule of a long line of conquerors. Around 3000 B.C. they were under the protection of Egypt, and then, in turn, they were subdued by the Assyrians, the Persians and Alexander the Great. At times, nevertheless, the cities were able to break away from outside rulers. One instance of this is when Tyre allied herself with Israel during the reign of Solomon, exchanging timber for grain and olive oil. Later the cities became part of the Roman Empire and the Romans built great temples in them. A famous one was to Jupiter, at Baalbek. With the break-up of the Empire, the region became part of the Byzantine realm, though by this time most of the greatness of the past had faded.

In the seventh century the Arabs gained power and later the area passed under Ottoman control, which lasted until the end of World War I. Lebanon was then made a French mandate. The country was declared a republic in 1926 under the mandate but was a republic in little more than name. During World War II the Free French forces ousted the Vichy Government in Lebanon and again pro-

KEYSTONE

ALL THE FAMILY WATCHES AS DAUGHTER MAKES BREAD

Pieces of dough are spread flat and then baked over a fire of twigs set between stones. Instead of loaves, the finished product in the tray (right) looks more like crisp pancakes.

306

claimed Lebanon a free republic. This became a reality on January 1, 1944. Even then French troops remained stationed in Lebanon and were not withdrawn until 1946.

The tiny Republic of Lebanon is almost squeezed into the eastern end of the Mediterranean Sea by its much larger neighbor, Syria. On the south Lebanon shares a short boundary line with the Republic of Israel.

Much of Lebanon is mountainous. The Lebanon Mountains parallel the coast for more than a hundred miles. In Biblical days they were covered with cedars. The highest peak in this range—Dahr el Qadib—near Tripoli in the north, is more than 10,000 feet high, and one near Beirut —Qurnet es Sauda—is only a little lower. The eastern border is rimmed by the Anti-Lebanon Mountains. Between these chains lies the narrow Bekaa, or Biqa', valley, watered by two rivers, the Orontes and the Litani (called Leontes in ancient days). The Orontes flows north for about 250 miles, entering Turkey and finally emptying into the Mediterranean. The Litani begins close by the Orontes, in the center of the valley, and flows south through deep gorges toward the upper Jordan. Because of the deep ravines, this river is of little use for irrigation.

A SHAWL INSTEAD OF AN OVERCOAT

On a chilly day this man of Beirut wears a camel's-hair shawl over his Western suit.

On the watershed of the rivers, at a height of about 3,600 feet above sea level, is the site of the ancient town of Baalbek (which the Greeks called Heliopolis, city of the sun) where Baal, the sun-god, was worshiped. There now remain only the ruins of its once huge temples. Baalbek was destroyed by an earthquake about the middle of the eighteenth century. The Arabs believe that it is the oldest city in the world and that Adam lived there.

Along the narrow coastal plains the climate is subtropical. Winters are mild, summers are moderately hot and there is plenty of rainfall. But in the mountains

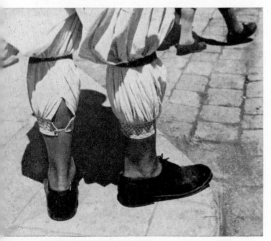

BLEND OF EAST AND WEST

Lebanese mix Eastern and Western dress with unconcern—old-time trousers and oxfords.

A CRUSADERS' CASTLE WEATHERED BY WIND AND WATER

The castle is in the harbor of Sidon, where some Crusaders landed. Deserted and crumbling for long years, the site was later used for a mosque. Its dome is visible in the center.

there is a great change even within as short a distance as five miles from the coastal plains. Here we find snow and cold winters. Snow stays unmelted on the Lebanon range about three months, and the peaks are usually covered with snow from December to June. It is said that the name "Lebanon" comes from a word *Leben* (whiteness) used in the old Aramaic language (spoken by Jesus) and refers to the view of the glistening mountains.

An average of forty-five inches of snow falls in the Lebanon Mountains each year. The Beirut-Damascus railway, which crosses the range, is covered with permanent snowsheds for several miles. The railway rises five thousand feet above sea level so steeply (in some places it was necessary to lay ten miles of winding track to advance two miles) that a cog rail is used for a quarter of the way.

In the Bekaa valley, winters are cool, and summers hot and dry. The rainy season starts in October, and the Bible refers to these autumn rains as the "former rains." The spring rains of April and May are termed the "latter rains." It is from December to March that the downfall is most heavy.

On the western slopes of the Lebanon Mountains, Mediterranean plants are found. Near sea level along the coast there are locust trees and stone pine. Wide areas are covered with brush. Farther up the mountains begin the woodlands, dominated by dwarf hardwood oaks. Still higher on the slopes is a belt of tall pines. At about four thousand feet the famous Lebanon cypress and cedar appear. There are also oaks and other leaf-bearing trees together with coniferous trees, including the rare Cilician silver fir. Extending nearly to the summits, stunted oak, juniper and barberry grow. The Lebanon cedars, you remember, were

THE STILL GRACEFUL COLUMNS OF THE TEMPLES AT BAALBEK
Though chipped and eroded, the stones have an impressive dignity. Baalbek is in the Bekaa
Valley and strange gods have been worshiped there: Baal, the sun-god, and later Jupiter.

TURKEYS PEER ABOUT CURIOUSLY ON THE WAY TO MARKET

The big birds stroll to market at an amiable pace. They are probably destined for the dinner tables
of luxury hotels; for they are hardly the usual diet in a Lebanese home.

used in building Solomon's Temple and
palace. Only a few of these cedars are
left, in groves considered sacred. Some
of the cedars are extremely old and are
nearly one hundred feet high and over
fourteen feet in diameter.

Beirut, the capital of Lebanon, is the
country's only modern seaport. In fact,
it is one of the main ports of entry in the
Arab world. Close by, in Khalde, is the
Middle East's largest airport. Mountains
rise almost directly behind the harbor, one
of the most beautiful in the world. With
its fine beaches, promenades and pine-
studded backdrop, Beirut is also a popular resort. In the modern hotel lobbies
one finds sheiks on holiday, rich merchants from other lands, cosmopolitan

SIGNS IN ARABIC AND FRENCH IN A BEIRUT ARCADE

There are fine shops in Beirut which sell exquisite imported goods. A French atmosphere lingers in the city and the French language is likely to be heard as often as Arabic.

diplomats, tourists, secret agents, adventurers and promoters. Political intrigue is rife. The atmosphere is French but a great many languages are heard. Many of the city's old streets are steep, winding alleys; but alley or avenue, Lebanese drivers ignore all hazards. Traffic moves at a terrific pace, made possible only by the drivers' lightning alertness. With what seems a natural bent for mechanics, the Lebanese love automobiles, the more powerful the better.

A mountain highway connects Beirut with Damascus, about sixty miles to the east. It is an exciting and sometimes hair-raising experience to motor around the hairpin curves, in the shadow of peaks or on the very edge of deep gorges. If one dares to look up from the road there are wide views of wild mountain scenery,

The people of Lebanon are about equally divided into Moslems and Christians. For this reason the president is usually a Christian, and the prime minister a Sunni (orthodox) Mohammedan. Chief of the Moslem group is the Sunni sect, although the Shiite sect is almost as large. The Druses may also be considered as a Moslem group.

However, the Druses seem to believe in a mixture of both Christian and Moslem ideas. Unlike Mohammedans, who do not believe in incarnation, the Druses believe that seventy incarnations of God

FISHING BOATS AT A QUAY ON ONE SIDE OF BEIRUT HARBOR

Ships from all over the world anchor in the harbor, and its shores are a semitropical playground. Behind the beaches and shore hotels rears a verdant backdrop of mountains clad with pines.

FREDERIC LEWIS

have occurred, the last one about 1000 A.D.; and Druses say there will be no more until the rest of the world is converted to the beliefs of the Druses, the "true children of God." These people are spread over much of the Lebanon and Anti-Lebanon mountains as well as through Syria. Among the most fierce fighters to be found anywhere, the Druses keep very much apart from their neighbors. They are jealous of their own customs and are especially hostile to Lebanese Christians, particularly the Maronites. In contrast with most other Mohammedans, the Druses are respectful of women. Women are allowed to join the men in religious services. They may also bring suit for divorce, an action unheard-of among orthodox Moslems. Having more than one wife is forbidden. Women must wear a veil but their sober black dress is

A BEDOUIN FAMILY COMES TO TOWN
Almost everywhere in the Middle East one will find Bedouins, the wanderers of the deserts.

relieved by scarlet slippers. Men wear a black robe with a white girdle. As a distinguishing mark from other Mohammedans, a white roll encircles the red fez. Druses are a tall people, with a fairer complexion than is usually found in the Levant.

Like the Druses, the swarthy Maronites are also mountaineers. They make up about a third of the population and form a distinct sect within the Roman Catholic Church. Their religious leader, under the pope, is called the patriarch of Antioch, which is in Turkey. He lives, however, in Lebanon. It is thought that some of the mountain folk were converted to Christianity about the seventh century and became followers of Saint John Maroun, from whom they derive their name. Like many people of a rugged land, the Maronites once engaged in bloody feuds but as a result of their relations with the Western world, their barbarous ways are vanishing. A national festival is held on September 14. The night before, bonfires are lighted and Maronite men and boys

313

A YOUNG GIRL OF THE DRUSES

The clothes she is wearing are light in color and have gay embroidery. When she is grown up, however, among her own people she will wear a black dress, crimson slippers and a veil.

show their bravery by leaping over the flames. At the same time there is an uproar of shouts and gunfire.

In Beirut and the larger towns living conditions are similar to those found in Europe; but village life is quite different. In most parts of the country the huts of the peasants are made of wattle or mudbrick or in part of stone. Interiors are bare of all but the merest necessities. In the far north and south poverty is severe. Villagers cannot afford to buy even rice, but live on lentils, bread and curdled milk.

Most of the villages are owned by a landlord and the people work for him. These landlords are the most important and influential groups in all Middle Eastern countries. There are, however, more freeholders in Lebanon than elsewhere. Possibly as many as one-half of the rural communities are freeholding peasants with small plots of land. Some of them spend part of the year tending to their crops and the balance working in factories. Methods of tilling the soil are still primitive but better results are obtained than elsewhere in this part of the world. It is not only the heavier rainfall but also a better-informed people that account for this. For instance, in places the western slopes are terraced to keep the soil from being washed away and to hold water. Though the land is cultivated intensively, not enough is grown to supply the country's needs and some grain is imported from Syria. Crops are diversified and include, in addition to various grains, olives, bananas and citrus fruits.

A Gateway for Trade

Despite the fact that two-thirds of the population is engaged in agriculture, trading is the most important economic activity. From the time of the Phoenicians to the present this seems to have been true. It is largely because Lebanon is one of the important gateways to the Far East. Today the country is a major center of foreign exchange and a place where goods are traded that never enter Lebanese territory. Beirut itself is the biggest gold market between Tangiers and Bombay.

The Lebanese factory worker is the best to be found in the Middle East, not excluding Turkey. After the fall of the Ottoman Empire, Lebanon gained rapidly in new factories. Unlike the experience of its neighbors, construction of new plants in Lebanon was due entirely to private enterprise and not to aid from the Government. A large number of small factories now produce various beverages, foodstuffs, cloth, razor blades, cement, soap, matches and other items. The silk industry, which had been a source of considerable wealth, was hurt by the invention of nylon, but is now reviving.

Electric power output is nearly 50 per cent greater than that of Syria, a much larger country. With mountain rivers such as the Litani, the possibilities for greater power generation are enormous. However, the country's known mineral resources are of no consequence. Since the country is already the most densely populated in the Middle East, further expansion appears quite limited. In fact, one of the reasons for the present relatively high living standard is that large amounts of money are sent back to relatives by those who have emigrated, especially to the United States (chiefly Detroit). Since the late 1890's, with little else to export, Lebanon has been exporting its population. It is said that almost every adult Lebanese has lived abroad or intends to; but they come home to retire— and usually bring with them the fastest, shiniest cars they can.

Pipelines from Iraq and Arabia

Two oil pipelines terminate on the Lebanon coast. One line originates in the Kirkuk oil fields of Iraq, with a branch going to Haifa in Israel and another branch ending at Tripoli. There are small refineries at both places. Another pipeline starts on the Persian Gulf, near the Bahrein Islands, crosses Saudi Arabia and ends at Sidon.

Schools and Colleges

Though the Government spends much more on national defense and internal police than it does on such matters as health and education, educational facilities in Lebanon are well above Middle Eastern standards. French Jesuits and American Presbyterians deserve a large part of the credit for this development. The Jesuits staffed numerous schools and founded the University of St. Joseph in Beirut in 1875. Earlier, in 1820, the Americans established several schools and a printing press. The Syrian Protestant College was chartered in 1863, under the laws of the State of New York, from where most of the money for its founding came. Eventually this college became the present internationally known American University of Beirut. For a campus, it has seventy acres of semitropical gardens, all overlooking the blue Mediterranean. No at-

KEYSTONE

A PRIEST OF THE MARONITE SECT

Most Christian Lebanese are Maronites, a distinct sect within the Roman Catholic Church. The priest's vestments include a chasuble, the beautifully embroidered outer garment.

315

DRAWING WATER FROM A WELL DUG BY THE CRUSADERS

Walled in by rough stones, the little well is on the summit of a mountain in a dry region where water is scarce. These women must make a long climb and clamber down heavily laden.

tempt is made to "Americanize" the students, which in a recent year were drawn from forty nations and twenty-one religious groups.

Lebanon has the framework of an educational system from the elementary grades through college. Almost 80 per cent of the Lebanese can read and write, compared with about 10 per cent in the rest of the Arab world.

Health standards are also higher. However, diet is hardly above the subsistence level for many of the people. Bread, milk, olive oil and fruits when in season are the basic foods. Sanitation is poor and disease prevalent. Malaria, typhoid, trachoma and other diseases are chronic. There are few doctors. Some headway in this field is being made, however. An antimalaria campaign has begun, there are a few classes for public-health nurses, and an effort is being made to improve water supplies and other sanitary facilities.

In Lebanon the conflict between the cultures of the East and West is especially sharp. It emerged with the end of the Ottoman Empire and the beginning of French influence. The attempts of the French to bring about a more orderly government, to improve education and health and to correct bad economic conditions met with great opposition from age-long traditions among the illiterate populace led by selfish landlords. Externals were changed but the basic social structure of semifeudalism held. This old order is breaking up and many serious problems arise in the process. To a considerable extent the valuable aspects of the traditional culture are lost while only material things are taken from the West. The forward-looking leaders of Lebanon are keenly aware of this problem. One such leader, Charles Malik—widely admired as Lebanon's delegate to the United Nations —has said that four developments are

PIX

LOOKING OUT OVER TRIPOLI TOWARD THE MEDITERRANEAN

Little of ancient Tripoli survives but the present-day city is thriving as the terminus of an oil pipeline from Iraq. This provides work and income for the city's people.

MULBERRY LEAVES FOR SILKWORMS

To add to the returns from their land, many farmers raise silkworms as a side line.

necessary within Lebanon and the rest of the Middle East: land reform, eliminating the present semifeudal system; replacement of bureaucratic administration with an efficient government; a high order of national leadership; and economic and political freedom for all.

It is interesting to note that one of the elements that has speeded the process of change has been the motion picture.

Another factor, mentioned earlier, is the number of Lebanese who emigrate and then return long years after. Though they remain loyal to their homeland, they cannot help but bring back new ideas.

Today the patriarchal family system—in which the father is all-powerful—is declining. At the same time the country is affected by the deep underlying ferment of Arab nationalism and by the challenge of its modern neighbor, Israel. Thus the peoples of Lebanon are not likely to find an easy solution to their difficulties.

By E. S. FERGUSON

FOOD FOR THE VORACIOUS APPETITES OF YOUNG SILKWORMS

The squirming caterpillars are kept on large, flat baskets in a dark room at a cool temperature. To keep up with their tremendous appetites, they must be fed every six hours.

ZAHLE, WHICH CLINGS TO A HILLSIDE IN THE BEKAA VALLEY

The delightfully cool summers of the valley make Zahle a refuge for people from the warmer coast.
They can reach the town easily for it is on the railway between Beirut and Damascus.

HIGH IN THE LEBANON MOUNTAINS A SKIER TRIES THE SNOW

Though Lebanon is usually thought of as a warm country, snow stays unmelted toward the tops of the ranges during the three winter months. Skiing on the firm crust is a popular sport.

TERRACED SLOPES ON THE EMERALD COAST OF LEBANON

The Emerald Coast—verdant with vegetation—is the narrow strip between the sea and the mountains. So that every bit of the fertile soil may be used, the slopes are terraced.

CEDARS OF LEBANON, TREES FAMOUS IN BIBLICAL DAYS

Few of the cedars, which King Solomon valued so highly, are left and the remaining groves are considered sacred. They grow in the mountains about four thousand feet above sea level.

321

THE COUNTRY

A republic in Asia, on the eastern shore of the Mediterranean, which was formed from five Turkish districts in 1920, administrated under a French mandate until 1941 and was finally given its full independence in 1944. The country is bounded on the north and east by Syria and on the south by Israel. It has an area of about 4,000 square miles and a population estimated at 1,300,000.

GOVERNMENT

Lebanon is governed by a president, a prime minister, and a Parliament having 77 seats which are distributed according to religious sects and not parties. The country is a member of the United Nations and of the Arab League.

COMMERCE AND INDUSTRIES

Although less than a quarter of its total area is under cultivation, Lebanon is primarily an agricultural state. Its chief food products, ranked according to the weight of their yield, are grapes, citrus fruits, wheat, onions, barley, potatoes, tomatoes, watermelons, maize, apples, pears and olives. Tobacco and cotton are also important crops. Besides processing crude oil piped in from Iraq, the country manufactures matches, soap, cigarettes, shoes and cotton goods—and weaves silk and woolen materials from imported yarn. There is a little mining of lignite. Tripoli is the terminus of an oil pipeline from Kirkuk, Iraq; and Sidon is the terminus of another pipeline from Abqaiq, Saudi Arabia.

COMMUNICATIONS

There are less than 500 miles of railway but the highways and secondary roads are good. Most of the passenger and freight traffic is handled by the hundreds of inexpensive bus and truck companies. Lebanon also has two national airlines and an international airport which is used by a number of foreign lines whose planes offer direct service to and from the Far East, European capitals, London and the U. S. A.

RELIGION AND EDUCATION

Various sects of Christians make up about half of the population, while the rest of the people belong to various Moslem sects. The Government maintains more than 1,000 primary and technical schools; and there are some 850 private and foreign schools. The country has two outstanding universities, the University of St. Joseph and the American University, both located in Beirut.

CHIEF TOWNS

Beirut, the capital, has a population of about 350,000; Tripoli, 65,000; Zahle, 26,000; and Saida, 20,000.

INTERNATIONAL BECHTEL

PLOWING IN THE OLD WAY BESIDE OIL STORAGE TANKS

The crude implement drawn by oxen and the tanks are symbolic of present-day Lebanon. It is at a crossroads in its history where ancient customs and modern ideas are meeting head-on.

THE STATE OF ISRAEL

New Nation with an Ancient History

When Moses led the Children of Israel through the wilderness, they dreamed of Canaan, their promised home, as a "land flowing with milk and honey." Perhaps it was never so rich as the phrase implies and in any case it lay almost barren for long centuries. Today the modern Canaan—Israel—is once again beginning to bloom. With the dream of a Jewish homeland realized, zeal inspired by faith and hope has wrought wonders. Some of this is suggested in the name given to immigrants' children born in Israel—*sabras*. *Sabra* means the "fruit of the cactus"—prickly outside and sweet within.

ON May 14, 1948, when thirty-five men and two women signed the new State of Israel's Proclamation of Independence, a gap of 1,942 years in the history of the Jewish people was bridged.

The solemn opening words of the document called attention to the historic link between the new Republic and the ancient kingdom of Judaea: "The Land of Israel was the birthplace of the Jewish people. Here they achieved independence and created a culture of national and universal significance. Here they wrote and gave the Bible to the world. . . ."

Under a mandate from the League of Nations, the future state of Israel was governed, as part of Palestine, by British administrators from 1923 to 1948. The first move toward independence took place on November 29, 1947, when the United Nations General Assembly passed a resolution to partition, or divide, Palestine into Jewish and Arab states. The resolution was to become effective upon the withdrawal of the British in 1948.

Real independence, however, was accomplished only after the Jews fought long and bloody battles against the numerically superior armies of Egypt, Lebanon, Iraq, Syria and Jordan—all members of the Arab League. Although the Proclamation of Independence was issued in 1948, just a few hours before British rule was supposed to end, Israel was at war with her Arab neighbors until 1949.

When armistice agreements were finally reached with the governments of Egypt, Lebanon, Jordan and Syria, Israel was left in control of 8,048 square miles

out of the total area of Palestine, 10,434 square miles. Thus, the Jewish state now controls 77 per cent of the territory of Palestine as compared with the 56 per cent allotted to it under the United Nations partition plan. This was the plan that the Arab League armies had tried to set aside.

Included within Israel's boundaries are the plains of Zevulun, Sharon and Judaea, a narrow, fertile region along the coast, where oranges and other citrus fruits thrive. From the plains rise the highlands of Galilee, on the north, and Judaea. The highest point in Israel is Jebel Jarmaq (3,963 feet), in upper Galilee.

In the midst of the north-central hills is the Plain of Jezreel (Esdraelon), between Mount Carmel and the Jordan Valley. Israel extends only to the western bank of the Jordan River. Besides the Jordan, there are intermittent streams, including the Kishon and the Yarkon. Since 1919 the swamps on the plains of Sharon and Jezreel and around Lake Hula have been reclaimed. To the south is the dry Negev, a triangular district with one point on the Red Sea. The Negev is being irrigated and settled on a large scale.

The modern port cities of Tel Aviv, Jaffa and Haifa are a part of Israel. In addition, the state controls a broad corridor through the bare limestone hills of Judaea linking the coastal plain with the city of Jerusalem.

The holy city of Jerusalem is divided. The Old City, walled, sacred to Chris-

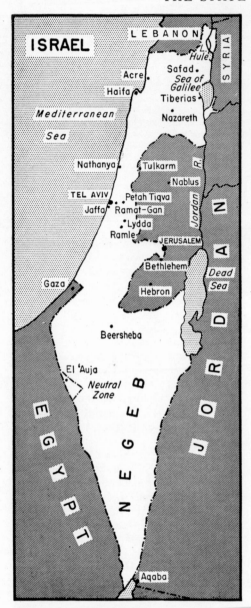

NEW NATION—HISTORIC LAND

tive powers. Rather, the real power is held by the prime minister and a cabinet of ministers. In turn, the prime minister and his cabinet are responsible to the Knesset. This body not only makes the laws but also keeps a close watch on all government activities. If the Knesset passes a vote of nonconfidence in the cabinet, which indicates disapproval of the cabinet's actions, the government then automatically falls.

The members of the Knesset represent all the different groups in the Israeli population. They include farmers from collective settlements, rabbis, city workers, lawyers, doctors and other members of the professions, and Arabs.

Equality for Israel's Minorities

In the early 1950's the minority races of Israel numbered 177,000 out of a total population of 1,607,000. Most of the minority groups are either Moslems or Christian Arabs. In the Proclamation of Independence the Jews guaranteed minorities "full social and political equality . . . without distinction of religion, race or sex . . . freedom of religion, conscience and culture."

Moslems and Christian Arabs live, for the most part, in Nazareth and the other villages of Galilee. They speak their own language and their way of life is little different from what it was before they became citizens of the Jewish state.

The official language of Israel is the language of the Old Testament: Hebrew. The Jewish holy days are national holidays and Saturday is the official day of rest. Minorities, however, choose their own day of rest and celebrate their own holidays.

Trains and busses do not operate from sunset on Friday to sunset on Saturday. Offices, factories and businesses are closed and work on the land is forbidden out of respect for Jewish religious laws. Israel, however, is not a theocracy—that is, a state ruled by religious law. There are no laws to prevent an individual from driving his car or working in his garden on the Sabbath.

tians, Jews and Mohammedans, is within the territory of the Hashemite Kingdom of Jordan. The New City, built outside the walls in the nineteenth and twentieth centuries, is governed by the Jews. The Israeli Parliament, the Knesset, and the offices of the government ministries are housed in the New City of Jerusalem.

The president of Israel has no execu-

The meat imported by the Israeli Gov-

AN IMMIGRANT FARMER in the Negev of southern Israel prepares the land for crops. The Negev is largely desert country, in the process of reclamation and settlement.

SHEEP-RAISING has been important to the Holy Land's economy since ancient times. The modern Israeli shepherd differs merely in costume from his counterpart of Biblical days.

VIRGINIA TOBACCO, now grown in Israel, is considered superior to the native leaf.

ernment is kosher—that is, slaughtered in accordance with Jewish ritual. However, nonkosher meat is available for those who desire it. Yom Kippur, the Day of Atonement, is a Jewish fast day and on this most holy of days the Israeli Army does not serve meals. Food, however, is left out for those soldiers who do not wish to observe the fast.

The question of religious observance is one of the most painful and difficult problems facing the leaders of the Jewish state. The Government's attitude is satisfactory neither to the orthodox rabbis, who want stricter observance, nor to those at the other extreme, who complain that the present laws already amount to religious coercion. In order to avoid a showdown on this delicate issue, the writing of a state constitution has been de-

ferred. Instead, in 1950, the Knesset enacted a series of fundamental laws which eventually will be combined into a constitution.

One of these basic laws, passed on July 5, 1950, is the Law of the Return. It states: "Every Jew has the right to immigrate to Israel." This law reaffirmed what had been said earlier in the Proclamation of Independence: "The State of Israel will be open to the immigration of Jews from all countries of the Dispersion."

Accordingly, since the gates of Israel were first opened to immigration, more than 700,000 Jews have poured into the new state. They came from every part of the world, but in particular from regions where Jews were in distress: eastern Europe, North Africa and other countries of the Middle East.

This mass immigration, especially of those peoples from undeveloped countries, had a tremendous impact on the infant state. It strained the country's resources almost to the breaking point as there were already grave shortages in housing, clothing, food, educational and

BUILDING a new collective farm, or *kibbutz,* in the Negev region near Beersheba.

KINGSWAY, the main thoroughfare of Haifa, is lined with many modern buildings. The city was founded by German settlers in 1869 and has the only deep-water harbor in Israel.

TEL AVIV'S PROMENADE along the sunny Mediterranean coast overlooks a fine bathing beach. Modern, industrial Tel Aviv ranks next to Haifa in importance as a port city.

A NARROW STREET in Nazareth that seems to have changed little since Jesus lived there in his youth. Yet the modern town is far larger than the ancient Galilean village.

328

MC LEISH

IN ACRE is this mosque, built by a Turk named Jezzar Pasha, who brought columns for its ornamentation from the ruins at Caesarea. Caesarea was the capital of Roman Palestine, but is now only a small village. Acre, a seaport situated on a promontory at the base of Mount Carmel, was regarded as the "Key of Palestine" in the time of the Crusades.

EWING GALLOWAY

ZION SQUARE, in the New City of divided Jerusalem, is the heart of Israel's capital. The historic Old City, containing most of the holy places, is only a short distance away.

ISRAEL OFFICE OF INFORMATION

A MONUMENT to Israel's impressive growth and progress. Hadassah Medical Centre in Jerusalem maintains the most up-to-date equipment and has a staff of excellent doctors.

medical facilities, transportation and other basic requirements. In order to insure equal distribution of the meager food and clothing supplies, rationing was put into effect immediately.

Sympathizers throughout the world recognized Israel's plight and contributed hundreds of millions of dollars in the form of grants and loans for her aid.

With this financial assistance the Israelis built scores of new towns and villages to replace the tent cities that newcomers were forced to live in at first.

For some years Jewish settlers have been developing the land, and in many places what was once barren soil has become rich productive earth. Rural villages, as a rule, take one of three forms. The *moshav ovdim* is a co-operative settlement of small privately owned holdings. The *kibbutz* and the *kvutsa* are communal settlements—that is, the land is held in common—usually affiliated with a political party. In the *moshav shitufi*, the land is also held in common but the profits are divided among the members.

In the past few years foreign and local investors have enabled the new state to develop a large number of factories and industries. At the south end of the Dead Sea, for instance, there is a large plant for extracting the mineral wealth from these waters. Potash heads the list of basic chemicals. Education, medicine and transportation are also taking long strides forward.

However, despite Israel's impressive growth, it will take a good many years to restore the standard of living to the level it had attained before the mass immigration began. The task of developing the new state is further complicated by the necessity of maintaining a large standing army to protect its many frontiers. Although the Arab-Israeli war was to have ended with the 1949 armistice, Israel's neighbors, Egypt, Jordan, Syria and Lebanon, are still hostile to the new country.

The armed forces of Israel are composed of all men from the ages of 18 to 45, and women up to the age of 34 who have no children. The older people belong to reserve units and are called up annually for short training periods.

The army of Israel is unique in the world. It trains its men and women not only to be good soldiers but also to be

EWING GALLOWAY

NOT FAR from Jerusalem is Ein Karim, the birthplace of John the Baptist. Today it is one of many villages in which immigrant Jews from all over the world find peaceful homes.

MC LEISH

ACROSS THE SEA OF GALILEE glides this boat with a bright blue sail. Its progress is assisted by the crew bending to their blue-and-white oars. Formerly the sea, which is thirteen miles long and eight miles wide, was crowded with shipping, for on its shore were several important cities, but of these only Tiberias remains today, so that usually only a few fishing boats are now to be seen upon its surface. The Lake of Tiberias is another name for this sheet of water, which, though deep set among steep hills, is often swept by sudden and violent storms.

BY THIS ANCIENT BRIDGE Roman legions crossed the River Jordan in the days of long ago. The bridge spans the river at a point about seven miles south of the Sea of Galilee, and was constructed by Roman engineers. The exact date of its construction is unknown. To the south of this ancient structure is a modern railway bridge, sixty-five yards in length, over which pass trains from Haifa, a port on the Bay of Acre, to El Hamme, a town in southern Syria. In Hebrew times the Jordan valley was regarded as a "wilderness." Only in Roman times was it at all populous.

FRUIT JUICES are one of the country's chief export items. In the pressing department of a food-processing plant, the juice extracted from oranges flows into enormous basins.

WOOLEN CLOTH from the rollers in this textile plant will reach many world markets.

good citizens. After their basic training, recruits spend several months in agricultural settlements where they are taught farming, geography, Hebrew, history and civics. Many of the recruits are newcomers to Israel and this process speeds up their feeling of identification with their new home. The classes also teach them trades and professions designed to make them useful citizens.

There is an intense interest in music, the theater and other arts in Israel, in villages as well as cities. Such conductors as Toscanini and Leonard Bernstein have led the fine Israel Philharmonic Orchestra. Folk dancing is a favorite recreation in the settlements.

Most of Israel's population is concentrated in the country's three largest cities: Haifa, Tel Aviv-Jaffa and Jerusalem. The Government, however, is making a determined effort to spread the population. New immigrants are urged to settle in outlying farm areas where their skills and labor will be of most benefit to the country.

By Moshe Brilliant

FREIGHT CARS haul material to a large cement factory. Financial aid, both foreign and domestic, has played a major role in the expansion of Israel's modern industries.

ISRAEL: FACTS AND FIGURES

THE COUNTRY

Palestine, formerly under British mandate, was partitioned into Jewish and Arab states in 1947. The Jewish portion became the State of Israel, bounded on the north by Syria and Lebanon, on the west by Egypt and the Mediterranean and on the east by Jordan. Area, 8,048 square miles; population 1,607,000, of whom about 1,430,000 are Jews.

GOVERNMENT

An independent sovereign republic since 1948, Israel is administered by a coalition government. In 1949 the Knesset, or Parliament, laid the foundation for permanent departments of government and in 1950 voted to delay adoption of a constitution for an unspecified period. The president, elected by the Knesset, holds office for five years.

COMMERCE AND INDUSTRIES

Agriculture is the chief occupation in those regions having sufficient rainfall. Barley, wheat, sorghum, olives, grapes and citrus fruits are among the principal crops. Poultry, sheep and goats are raised. Mineral resources include limestone, petroleum, gypsum, sandstone, rock salt, sulfur and potash. Petroleum refining, various manufactures and automobile assembly are among Israel's expanding industries. Chief exports: citrus fruits, fruit juices, textiles, chemicals. Imports: machinery, timber, grain, other raw materials.

COMMUNICATIONS

There are about 325 miles of railway and some 1,500 miles of all-weather roads. Regular airline flights are maintained to many world capitals. There is regular steamer service to and from Haifa and Tel Aviv-Jaffa. Telephone and telegraph lines total about 79,000 miles.

RELIGION AND EDUCATION

A special government ministry supervises the religious affairs of Jews, Christians and Moslems, with the affairs of each community under control of the respective authorities concerned. Education is directed by the Ministry of Education and is free and compulsory through the primary grades. Separate schools exist for Jewish and Arab students. The Hebrew University in Jerusalem and the Hebrew Institute of Technology in Haifa are among the institutions of higher learning.

CHIEF TOWNS

Jerusalem, capital (Israeli part only), 170,-000; Tel Aviv-Jaffa, 400,000; Haifa, 200,000.

THE BEAUTIFUL traditional costumes of Israeli women are not often seen in the modern
land. The headdress of this girl is decorated with overlapping coins. Her head shawl and
gown are elaborately embroidered with delicate designs. To complete the picture of former
days, the girl follows the Eastern custom of carrying a water jar balanced on her head.

© PHOTOCHROM

THESE THREE OLD JEWS, who are taking their leisure beneath the ramparts of Jerusalem, have seen the population of that city change considerably since they were young. Among the Jews who are citizens of Israel are some whose families have lived in Palestine for generations; but many more Jews have immigrated to their homeland.

SLENDER MINARETS dominate the skyline of Amman, the capital of Jordan. The main section nestles in a cup of hills. Outlying districts, with steep streets, clamber up the slopes.

THE CHURCH OF THE NATIVITY in Bethlehem marks the birthplace of Christ. The present shrine is built upon the ruins of a church erected by the Emperor Constantine in 330 A.D.

HASHEMITE KINGDOM

The Country beyond the River Jordan

The shape of the little Hashemite Kingdom of Jordan is something like that of a butterfly, though its "wings" are of unequal size. The larger one spreads out toward the south, and the other toward the northeast. Except for a few miles of coast on the Gulf of Aqaba, an inlet of the Red Sea, Jordan is surrounded entirely by other nations: Israel, Syria, Iraq and Saudi Arabia. As part of Palestine for many centuries, Jordan has a rich past. Here were the Biblical lands of Gilead, Edom, Moab and Ammon; and the little town of Bethlehem is within Jordan's present boundaries.

JORDAN is mainly an arid, hilly plateau rising about 3,000 feet above sea level. There is a steep drop of several thousand feet from this plateau on the east as it approaches the Dead Sea, which is 1,300 feet below sea level. This sea has no outlet, and the water that pours into it rapidly evaporates in the great heat. Consequently the sea is extremely salty and can support practically no life. In the south of Jordan are many mountains, and close by the seaport of Aqaba, Jebel Ram pushes up to a height of 5,396 feet.

Part of the boundary between Israel and Jordan is formed by the Jordan River, which flows south into the Dead Sea. The valley formed by this river and the Dead Sea is the deepest trench in the earth's surface. There are a few small streams in Jordan that drain into this turbulent river. One of the larger of these, the Zerka, has cut out a valley through which the automobile road from Jerusalem to Amman, Jordan's capital, runs.

The few cities in Jordan are located in the western part of the country, mainly in the northwest. To the east are deserts, a tremendous sea of sand that extends over a great part of Saudi Arabia. This desert country is called the "Land of Emptiness."

There is plenty of rainfall in the northwest of Jordan, but as you travel eastward, it decreases rapidly. Consequently, the land that can be cultivated lies in the small northwest area between the border of Israel and the railroad from Damascus, in Syria, to Amman. This railroad is an extension line from Damascus to the

north, and it runs to Ma'an in the south of Jordan. It is called the "Pilgrim Railway" because it carries a large number of Arabs making the pilgrimage to Mecca. The people were afraid of the railroad when it was first built, and for a long time they could not be persuaded to ride on it.

The poorness of the country can be seen from the fact that only about 5 per cent of the land can be cultivated. The peasant farmers, fellahin, farm nearly all of this available land.

Because of little rain over most of the country, irrigation must be used. One means of getting water is by *qanats,* or artificially built subterranean canals. In many places the natural streams disappear underground and run along the rock or hard layer below the ground surface. To get at this water, tunnels are dug, creating artificial underground streams, which carry the water to fields that are to be cultivated. The method of digging these water tunnels is very primitive. Every few hundred yards a well is dug down to the water, and a tunnel is extended toward the land to be irrigated. The earth from the wells is taken up through the wellholes and piled around the edges of the openings at the top. These well openings resemble miniature craters. When seen from an airplane, the land appears to have been peppered with hundreds of meteorites. Then you realize that the wellholes run in too straight a line for this to be possible. *Qanats* are also found in Syria, Iran and China. The United Nations is endeavoring to help Jordan with irrigation projects in order to gain more land that can be

A SHEPHERD leads his flock of sheep and goats through the streets of a town in Jordan. Eighty-five per cent of the people of Jordan make their living by agriculture or from their flocks. The skins, hides and wool of domestic animals give Jordan most of its exports. Because of low rainfall, only about 5 per cent of the land in Jordan can be cultivated without the aid of irrigation. The most fertile land lies in the northwest corner of the country. To secure food for their livestock, the shepherds must wander with their animals in search of grass.

340

MC LEISH

TWO TURBANED MOSLEMS watch the bustling crowd of traders, pilgrims and travelers that gathers at the Jaffa Gate. Jaffa is one of eight gates in a wall around the Old City of Jerusalem. All of Jerusalem that lies outside this wall is called the New City. Jerusalem has shrines of the Christian, Jewish and Moslem faiths, most of which are in the Old City.

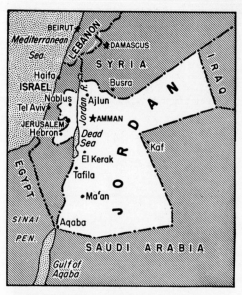

BUTTERFLY-SHAPED KINGDOM

made fertile for the raising of crops.

Jordan has little natural wealth. There are no industries and, therefore, very little trade. Some livestock is raised, and wheat, barley and grapes are the main crops grown. Vineyards, to which the hilly country is suited, are extensive. The surplus from the crops is exported to Syria, Iraq and, before the Palestinian war, to Israel. The break in relations between Jordan and Israel has been harmful to the economic life of both since there is no exchange of products between the two countries. Imports, which are mainly cloth, foodstuffs and livestock, come from the United States, Great Britain and Iraq.

There is only one port, Aqaba, located on the Gulf of Aqaba, which opens into the Red Sea. Here by this port, the boundaries of Jordan, Israel, Egypt and Saudi Arabia meet. In ancient times, Aqaba was important as it received valuable goods carried in ships across the Indian Ocean from India and other Far Eastern places. Large caravans were then made up to carry this merchandise on to Mediterranean ports and to Egypt. The ancient port is now being modernized and enlarged to handle a larger volume of goods. Since Jordan and other Arab countries refuse to carry on commercial relations with Israel, most of Jordan's imports now have to go by way of Beirut and Damascus, which is much more expensive than going across Israel.

Amman, Jordan's capital city, was called Rabbath Ammon during the time of Moses, when it was the capital of the Biblical Ammonites. Later it was rebuilt by a king of Egypt, Ptolemy Philadelphus, and given the name Philadelphia. Today it is a typical Arab city. The houses, usually made of stone, are low and look like little forts. The streets, through which all the odors of the bazaars are wafted, are crooked and very dusty. Several motion-picture houses give the city a modern touch, and other than these, sidewalk cafés with radios are the only form of entertainment.

There are few wealthy people in Jordan. Most of the population belong to nomadic tribes of Bedouins, who tend small herds of sheep or cattle to make a living. Often the tribes, sometimes including more people than the city of Amman, move over tremendous distances, even crossing boundaries into other countries. They move wherever there is a supply of water and pasture for their herds.

History as Old as the Bible

Even though Jordan is a new nation, the area has a long history dating from Biblical times. As Palestine, it was part of the Ottoman Empire from the sixteenth century until the end of World War I. After the war, it was, for a short time, under the rule of Feisal I of Syria. When Feisal was driven out by the French, Great Britain took control of the area under the Palestine mandate. It was then called Trans-Jordan, or Transjordania. In 1923, the British recognized the independence of Trans-Jordan with Abdullah, a member of the Hashemite family, as ruler. In return, Great Britain was given various privileges, including the keeping of troops in the country. At that time Jordan was one of the most backward areas in the Middle East. There was no orderly form of government, poverty was widespread and the Bedouins, paying little attention to international boundaries,

THE CHURCH OF ALL NATIONS, located in the Garden of Gethsemane between the Mount of Olives and Jerusalem, was built by donations from many lands. An olive grove surrounds it.

made continual raids upon the few settled villages.

The first thing Great Britain did was to bring under control the custom of raiding. Gradually the authority and efficiency of the government was built up, largely by means of the Arab Legion. This army, under the leadership of a Briton, Captain F. G. Peake, was composed of selected Arabs who were given intensive military training.

Since force had been the means of both acquiring land and keeping it, there were no written records of land ownership. With the introduction of law, records were made and a system of establishing boundaries was put into effect. It then became possible and necessary to tax the people to supply the government with a steady income. Because this income has never been enough to fully support the government, Great Britain has added to it by loans.

In 1946, Jordan became a kingdom and made a treaty of alliance with Great Britain. The Arab Legion of Jordan, under the direction of Major John Bagot Glubb, was fast becoming a well-disciplined fighting force. It gave a good account of itself in the Arab-Israeli war of 1948; and as a

WHO WILL BUY? Flat loaves of bread, fresh from the oven, in the market place of Amman.

MC LEISH

THE DOME OF THE ROCK in the Old City of Jerusalem was built by the Arabs in the seventh century. Mohammedans believe that the souls of sinners will be weighed here on the Day of Judgment. The Old City came under Jordan in the division of Jerusalem in 1948.

MARRIED WOMEN of Bethlehem wear a white veil draped over a tarboosh, or fez. Rows of coins ornament the hat, and from it are suspended silver chains. It is the custom for them to pull the veil over the tarboosh and also to secure it under the chin when they go out of doors. Over the richly colored dress, a short embroidered jacket is worn.

THE HOUSES IN JORDAN are made from blocks of stone, chipped and chiseled to a perfect smoothness by hand. The second worker from the right is checking his stone with a square.

result of the power shown by his army, King Abdullah became an important figure in the Arab world. His dream of a greater Syria seemed possible of realization. This plan and Abdullah's willingness to make a truce with the Israeli caused other Arab nations, especially Egypt and Saudi Arabia, to oppose him. In 1951, he was assassinated.

It is doubtful that Jordan could continue with an orderly government if British support were to be withdrawn, as Jordan does not have the means to support itself. Several plans have been proposed to improve the economic conditions of the country, one by the United Nations Economic Survey Mission in 1949. Progress, which compares favorably with other Arab countries, has already been made under the guidance of Great Britain. Education, though still poor, has been greatly extended. Health standards have been raised, as is shown by the steady decline in the death rate of infants. However, the great influx of refugees from Palestine has increased the country's difficulties. Foreign aid is being given to help care for these refugees, but a more permanent solution must be worked out.

By E. S. FERGUSON

JORDAN: FACTS AND FIGURES

THE COUNTRY

Bounded on the north by Syria, on the northeast by Iraq, on the east and south by Saudi Arabia and the Gulf of Aqaba and on the west by Israel. Total area, about 37,700 square miles; population, about 1,250,000.

GOVERNMENT

Independent since 1946, Jordan is a constitutional monarchy, with a king, a cabinet and a legislature consisting of two houses: a lower house elected by male voters, and a senate appointed by the king.

COMMERCE AND INDUSTRIES

Agriculture, including livestock-raising, is chief occupation. Crops include various grains and legumes, olives and grapes. Stock includes goats, sheep, cattle, donkeys and camels. Phosphates and potash are taken from Dead Sea. Copper and iron mined to a small extent. There are few industries other than handicrafts.

COMMUNICATIONS

There are about 422 miles of all-weather roads, and 1 railway crosses the country. Airfields are at Amman and Mafraq, and there are 2 small airlines.

RELIGION AND EDUCATION

Practically all the inhabitants are Moslems. There are about 750 government schools.

CHIEF TOWNS, POPULATIONS

Amman, capital, about 170,000; Hebron, 27,000; Nablus, 25,000; Bethlehem, 10,000; Ma'an, 10,000; Mafraq, 2,000.

THE DESERT RANGERS

The Beduins as They Are in Reality

The Beduin is a man of many countries. A pastoral nomad, he wanders from one oasis to another in search of good grassland and water for his flocks. Beduins are found throughout the deserts of North Africa, Arabia and Syria. They live as simply as the most primitive peoples on earth, yet many have an intelligence as quick and subtle as the most civilized men of the West. Outsiders find it hard to understand the changeable nature of the Beduin. At one moment hostile and the next a generous host, he earns respect at all times for his ability to wrest a living from the unyielding desert.

IN song and story the Beduin is often pictured as a picturesque fellow, leading a roving life much as gipsies do. This portrait is false. The Beduin's life is as monotonous as his diet of dates, camel's milk and camel flesh. Living in the hostile desert, his wandering is a matter of necessity, for he must constantly seek pasture, wherever a bit of grass grows, for his sheep and goats.

Camels, however, are his chief source of food, his beasts of burden and his medium of exchange. Without them, he could not live in the desert at all. If he is wealthy, by Beduin standards, he may own one or more horses, and lavishes great care on them.

The desert man's mental horizons are severely limited. He is bound by strict allegiance to his clan and his tribe. Yet through his nature there runs a rich vein of poetry. His intelligence is naturally quick; and it has been shown that when he is placed in a totally different environment, he can adjust himself to it with surprising ease.

In the northern area of the great deserts of the Nile one may find here and there Beduins who have at least an idea of modern ways of life. These are the wealthier tribesmen who, perhaps, have been successful in breeding and trading camels and horses. Some live in villages and differ greatly from their poorer desert brothers, who pitch their tents in the wilderness and lead a wandering life.

For many centuries the Beduin has been one of the best-known features of the East. His very name in Arabic means "man of the desert," and his range is a wide one. From Arabia and Syria, his original home, he spread over Mesopotamia and Egypt, and all along the northern coasts of Africa. At the present day he has wandered even as far afield as Persia and Turkestan. In all it is reckoned that there are about 1,500,000 of these desert gipsies, of whom those in Arabia and Egypt are perhaps the most widely known. Those of the former country com-

ARAMCO

KEEN EYES emphasize the strong features of a Beduin who lives in Saudi Arabia.

347

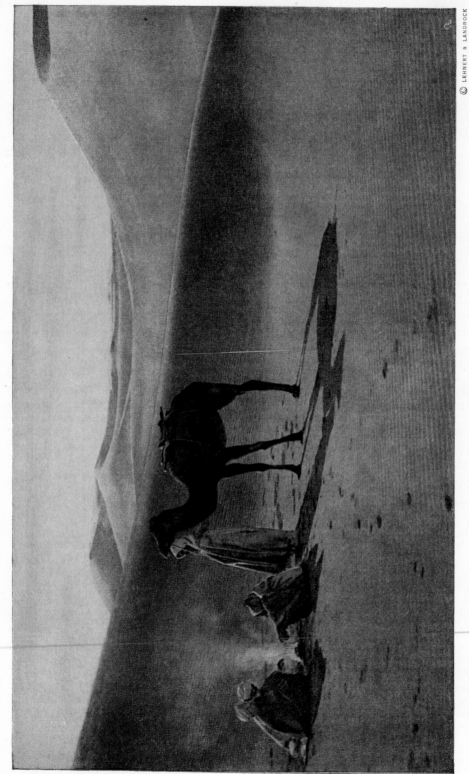

DESERT TWILIGHT shows a glory of color which does not last beyond a few seconds. Soon after, the day's fierce heat is radiated away through the clear dry air and the warmth of a fire is grateful. It is through such country as this that the Beduins wander with their flocks and herds from camp to camp, for the pasturage is scant and often gives out in twelve days. Indeed, the hard life of the desert is today driving many of them coastward to the cities where they often lose their special qualities and soon mingle with the rest of the population.

348

BEDUIN WOMEN, when they go upon a journey, are usually shut within a litter fixed upon the back of a camel. It is a Moslem practice that women shall be hidden from the public gaze, so they must travel swaying giddily to and fro on their unwieldy covered platform, which is fastened upon the camel's hump, and how uncomfortably hot and stuffy it must be inside.

THE LIFE OF A DESERT DWELLER DEPENDS UPON A STURDY MOUNT

Since ancient times the people of Saudi Arabia have been known for their horsemanship and fine steeds. An Arab horse is relatively small, sure-footed, with great physical endurance.

prise about one-fifth of the whole population, including in this estimate the territories of Iraq, Palestine and Syria. How this figure is arrived at one cannot say, for all attempts to get the nomadic tribesmen into a recent census were unsuccessful. The Beduins saw behind the census papers the threatening figure of the tax collector, and as they have never paid tribute to any government they refused to have their heads counted.

Of the higher class Beduins, most live in communities each of which, as has been said, is ruled over by a sheik. It is among such that the more picturesque features of desert life are to be seen. Here are larger and better equipped tents. The sheik himself will be garbed in clothes of fine quality while his tribesmen, in their parti-colored robes, will make a brave show. The national dress consists of the "abba," or camel's-hair cloak—striped gaily with colors or black and white—beneath which is a closely fitting tunic that may be of silk or cotton, according to the owner's means. This is gathered in by a leather girdle or a colored sash, in which a pistol or dagger can be stuck.

How the Desert Men Dress

As headdress is worn a square of cloth —again cotton or silk—brightly hued and striped. This is doubled over the head, the two long ends falling down upon the shoulders. A notable feature of this headgear is the twisted band of camel's hair, which is worn round the top of the head and helps to keep the cloth in position when the front part is pulled forward as a shade for the eyes.

Women's garments among the more settled tribes may also be brightly colored. A blue, red or yellow handkerchief serves for head-covering while the loose robe, fastening with a girdle, is striped or of a striking pattern. But out in the desert the women are drably clothed compared with their husbands. Unlike her Arabian sisters, the Beduin woman does not wear a face veil. Her custom is to cover the lower portion of her face with a corner of her shawl at the approach of a stranger. But she has a feminine weakness for neck-

laces and other trinkets especially for bangles round arm and ankle. Most likely too she will wear a talisman in her headdress, a small transparent stone set in beads, which is supposed to act as a charm against the "evil eye."

With her brown skin, her dark flashing eyes gazing at one from below a well-draped headdress, and with the pleasant jingle of her metal chain necklaces and ornaments, this daughter of the East is quite charming in her youth. But she ages too quickly for her life is one of constant toil with little pleasures.

Workaday Life of the Womenfolk

The Beduin man leaves all the domestic duties to his womenfolk. They grind the wheat in the handmill or pound it in the mortar. It is they who knead and bake the bread, make butter, carry water from the wells, work at the loom and mend the tent covering. To the women also usually falls the task of rolling up the tents when camp is broken and the tribe is moving on to some fresh pasturage.

One of our pictures shows a Beduin mother carrying her baby in the manner usual among this people. The youngster, wrapped in garments of bright colors, is swung over the mother's back in a shawl. At other times it may be set astride her shoulder. As a rule the little ones are strong and healthy for in their babyhood they are left to roll naked in the sun. As they grow up, however, numbers of them suffer from ophthalmia and other eye troubles brought on by dirt and inflammation from the sand or by the sun's glare. In some cases total blindness follows, and then they drift into the towns to join the ranks of the beggars who are so common there.

The Beduin at Close Quarters

If he be less presentable than his more prosperous brothers of the village, the Beduin of the desert, the true nomad who shifts continually from place to place, is even more truly a descendant of Ishmael in the Bible story. Romance and color fall away from this type the closer we get to him. Below middle stature, lean and wiry

BEDUIN GIRLS, like this attractive nomad maid of Tunisia who is shown here with her mother, are as fond of dolls as any young ladies of the same age in our country. It was the Arab conquests of the eighth century which took her forefathers from their original home in the wilder parts of Syria and Arabia along the coast of North Africa as far as Morocco.

BABY BEDUINS, carried pickaback in a shawl, soon get tanned a rich clear brown by the desert sun. So too do their mothers, for the Beduins are an independent folk and their womenkind do not always wear the face-veil. They cover the lower part of the features with a corner of their cloak when a man not of their own household is seen approaching.

353

in physique, he is clad in coarse garments; his tents are of poor quality, and his horses and camels are underfed and shamefully ill-used. With the poorest of these desert gipsies a few wretched goats are often their only livestock.

The Bedouin's treatment of his camel is far from what the "Ship of the Desert" deserves at his hands. It is true that the animal has few good points in his nature; he cannot be described as lovable. He is sulky and refractory and appears to be incapable of affection for his master—though this may only be the result of the treatment he receives. He is made to flop down for loading and unloading pur-

STANDARD OIL CO. (N. J.)

AN ARABIAN BEDOUIN AND HIS FAMILY RELAX BEFORE THEIR TENT

In Abqaiq, Arabia, a Bedouin employed as a watchman in the nearby oil fields builds his tent and clothes his family in the manner of his nomadic tribesmen. The large metal food can the boy to the right holds and the burlap sacking that has been used for the tent are typical of many objects from the modern West that have found a place in Arab life. The women are closely veiled.

THE BEDOUIN IS NO LESS MANLY FOR HIS LONG BRAIDS OF HAIR

A Bedouin of Al Kharj in the Nejd region of Saudi Arabia seems fiercely proud of his distinctive hair style. Al Kharj is one of the best farm regions of the Arabian peninsula. Modern irrigation waters date groves and fields of wheat, alfalfa and millet. Because of the abundance of feed, Bedouins have settled with their herds on the lands about Al Kharj.

poses by blows on the knees; there is no word of command, such as other draught animals learn to obey. When resting with heavy loads on his back, and when taking his food, the ill-fitting framework on which his burden is piled is not removed.

On the other hand he is quite indispensable to his master for he can travel far in a waterless region and can feed on the thorny plants that grow in the sand. His eyes are well protected from the sun by the thick upper eyelids with which he is provided, and when the fierce simoon wind rages across the waste he can close his nostrils to it and the blown sand particles.

A sand storm in the desert is one of the terrors of the nomad's life. When it breaks, the camels crouch down with their backs to it, the travelers seek shelter within

355

ARAB CHILDHOOD does not last very long, and for the girls it ends even earlier than for the boys. At the age of thirteen or fourteen the Beduin girl shown above will be considered to be grown up and a husband will have been found for her. But while she is yet in the playtime of her life she makes the very utmost of it as her cheerful smile suggests.

BEDUIN MOTHERS, though they usually have bright wrappings for their babies, often leave them entirely unclothed. It is a common sight in an encampment to see dusky-skinned infants left on their bare backs in the sand to kick in the sun. Notice the chains of metal trinkets that clash at every movement, and the number of different colors and patterns worn.

357

tent or other covering and the women who are fortunate enough to be in litters draw the cloth screens tightly around these for protection. To face the rushing wind, which brings along with it minute grains of sand, is a terrible experience. The Beduin's skin, hardened by exposure and screened by his cloak from the full force of the blast, enables him to bear it; but a foreigner, less accustomed to the elements, will come through the ordeal with his face badly cut and bleeding.

Shepherd and Robber by Turns

From time immemorial the Beduin has been a herdsman and a shepherd. It is the necessity of finding fresh pasturage for his flock that compels him to move from one spot to another. He will pitch his tent in some oasis in the desert with its water wells, until the scanty herbage has been exhausted, then the camp is broken and the journey onward is continued.

But such a peaceable existence as this has never satisfied the restless wanderer. The stern struggle for existence and ever-ready opportunity have made him an outlaw, a highwayman of the desert. To how many travelers and caravans has not the sudden cry of "Beduins" brought terror! The plundering of a caravan is a fierce joy to the Beduin. With rifle, lance and yataghan he descends upon his victims, and woe betide the trader who is not strong enough to beat off the marauders.

Why Caravans Are Looted

The Beduin on a foray is an enemy to be feared. He is merciless in the treatment of his captives and the ransom he extorts is heavy. The Arabs have a proverb which runs: "Entertain a Beduin and he will steal your clothes." So powerful are these marauding bands that they will levy toll even on the safe conduct of pilgrimages to Mecca. They regard the looting of caravans and travelers, indeed, in an original light—namely as the equivalent to the taxes and customs that are exacted in civilized countries. "The land is ours," they argue, "and if you trespass on it you must pay us compensation."

If, however, traveler or trader can show anything in the nature of a permit to enter the territory dominated by a tribe, such a document is generally recognized and respected. A permit of this kind can be purchased from a sheik, who will place some of his followers at the disposal of the travelers and thus pass them on from tribe to tribe across the desert.

Side by side with this lawlessness among Beduins there runs a regard for the laws of hospitality that is almost sacred. They are Mohammedans by religion, and the stranger who has eaten of their salt is safe from molestation. It might be well to amend the statement that they are followers of Mohammed for they are only nominally so. The tribes vary greatly in their religious customs and most of them disregard entirely the Prophet's command to pray five times daily and to make the pilgrimage to Mecca.

Supper in the Tent of a Sheik

Suppose now that we try to picture a sheik who is entertaining some guests. The Beduin camp has been pitched at an oasis. Outside the tent of their chief a little courtyard has been railed off with a hedge of brushwood. A fire blazes in the centre of this enclosure, partly for illumination as the tent is open on this side, and partly for boiling the water. Several of the womenfolk hasten to and fro, busy on the preparation of the coming meal. On the other side of the hedge are to be seen the dark figures of the kneeling camels.

The company gathered in the tent squats upon the mats and begins the meal, a mixture of meat, flour and hot oil, the bowl in which it is served being passed from hand to hand. An earthenware goblet of water makes the circuit of the tent in the same way. Rice is a favorite dish and of course there are dates and some sweetmeats, for the host is a man of position.

As an accompaniment to the feasting, one of the sheik's retinue who enjoys a reputation as a flute-player performs on his instrument. The chief guest—we will assume that he is a newcomer in this country—does his best to converse with his host, and is conscious occasionally of subdued laughter from the screened-off

A BEDOUIN CHILD TAKES A DRINK FROM A GOATSKIN WATER BAG

In a Bedouin camp at an Algerian oasis children take their turns at the goatskin water bag. In the desert water is not easily come by. Everyone must be careful not to waste a drop or to take more than his share, especially when the family is on the move, far from the next well. The Southern Territories of Algeria make up one vast desert broken by few oases.

portion of the tent in which the women have been placed. The more curious of these cannot be restrained from peeping at times over the screen to gaze upon the stranger.

Then, while hookahs and cigarettes are being lighted, coffee is served as a special token of friendship. During the evening, to add to the general comfort, a bowl is handed round in which are some live coals sprinkled with fragrant incense. Each of the company takes a good sniff at this as he passes it on.

With more pleasant converse and entertainment the evening slips away. The various guests make their salutations and depart; blankets are spread upon the tent floors, and soon the whole encampment, except for the watchers posted on the outskirts, is wrapped in sleep.

359

BEDUINS. Desert life, in spite of what is said in the imaginative stories of Arab chiefs, is not very healthful, nor are the desert folk overly clean. Opthalmia and other affections of the eyes are common, and this blind Beduin is only one of the many who wander into the towns to beg with a child as guide. He is in a market-place of Tunis in Africa.

ARABIA THE MYSTERIOUS

Its Arabs of the Desert and Its Holy Cities

The peninsula that we know as Arabia, the land of the Arabs, extends between the Red Sea and the Persian Gulf, somewhat in the shape of a baby's boot. Saudi Arabia, a kingdom that came into existence in 1932, occupies much the larger part of the peninsula. Yemen, whose present independence dates from 1934, is a mountainous triangle in the southwest corner. Along the southern edge is the Aden Protectorate, under British protection. In the southeast corner is Oman (officially the Sultanate of Masqat and Oman). Oman, as well as several sheikdoms along the Persian Gulf—Trucial Oman, Qatar and Kuwait— all have close ties with Great Britain. Much of Arabia is a desert, but there are many fertile valleys and beautiful oases.

THE peninsula of Arabia is familiar to us as being the birthplace of the Mohammedan religion and the home of many of its followers. In romantic stories, Arabia is sometimes pictured as a land of sandy wastes where bold sheiks, their robes streaming in the wind, dash across the desert on fleet Arabian horses. It all sounds very exciting, but the true picture is a little more prosaic.

Arabia has indeed many vast stretches of sand but there are arid wastes of stone and gravel with only occasional patches of grass and stunted bush—a desert of another kind. It is extremely dry and excessively hot so that only about one-third of its area is inhabited by settled people. The whole of Arabia, however, is not a desolate waste. There are oases of palm trees and expanses of green fertility amid the general desolation. Here and there, one may see broad green valleys dotted with bushes, where the Arabs and wandering tribes of Beduins graze their herds of cattle, sheep and camels.

The history of Arabia dates from the Creation, for Jidda (Jeddah) on the shores of the Red Sea and one of the principal Arabian ports, is said by the Arabs to have been the birthplace of Eve. In early times, Arabia was inhabited by many tribes who did not unite until the time of Mohammed in the seventh century A.D. Mohammed believed that there is but one God and he finally persuaded the people to give up their pagan gods, to accept his belief and to look to him as God's Prophet. At times, he fell into trances during which he said he was in communication with

God, and the messages, eagerly taken down by his listeners, form their Bible, known as the Koran. Among other things it commands a Mohammedan to be temperate, to pray five times a day—just before sunrise, just before noon, before and after sunset and when the day is closed—to fast from sunrise to sunset during the month of Ramadan, to give alms to the poor, and to make the pilgrimage to Mecca at least once during his lifetime.

At first, Mohammed did not have a large following but the numbers increased when he allowed the new religion to be promoted by means of the sword. The Arabs, or Saracens as they were then known, gathered under the green flag of Islam and determined to carry it throughout the world. Mohammed died in 653 A.D. but his successors carried out his plans and this vast empire at its zenith extended through Western Asia across North Africa and even into Spain.

However, as time went on, Arabia broke up again, and although the Turks conquered the territory in 1517 and held it until the War of 1914-18, some of the nomadic people were never subdued.

In the middle of the eighteenth century, there began what was known as the Wahhabi movement. It was named for its founder, Wahhab, who sought to purge the Moslem faith of its evils and to return to the true simplicity of the original Mohammedanism. In recent times, under the leadership of Ibn Saud, its object has changed from religious reform to nationalism and an increasing number of Arabians have been attracted to this cause.

361

© LEHNERT & LANDROCK

THE GREAT DESERT in the centre of Arabia is well named the Dahna, which means "empty quarter," for it is a waterless stretch of sand and rock that has only twice been crossed by white men, and rarely by an Arab. Here, on its western edge, where it is known as El Ahkaf, we see an Arab citadel, built, probably, to protect the oasis nearby from predatory Beduins. That there is water we can see from the scrub and few palm-trees. There may even be a stream, but if so it will be dry for most of the year, for that is the fate of all Arabian rivers.

CAMEL CARAVANS must serve the purpose of both freight and passenger trains between Medina and its port of Yembo, for there is no railway line, only a rough track crossing about 130 miles of sun-scorched steppe. It is a frequently used road, however, for Yembo is known, with reason, as the "Gate of the Holy City." Thousands of Mohammedan pilgrims arrive there every year bound for Mecca, the birthplace of Mohammed, and Medina, his burial place. A large escort was needed for every caravan until quite recently, for nomad tribes waylaid and robbed all ill-protected travelers.

A SAUDI ARABIAN CHIEFTAIN CLINGS TO HIS ANCIENT FASHIONS

The flowing robes of the desert people are still worn in Jidda, Saudi Arabia's Red Sea port. Light
covering, especially of neck and head, is needed for protection from the desert sun.

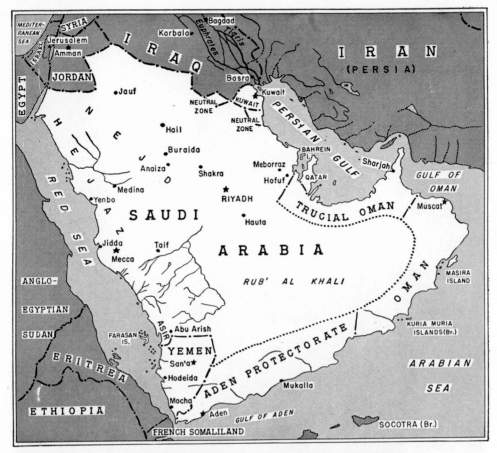

THE STATES OF THE GREAT ARABIAN PENINSULA

Ibn Saud took advantage of the first World War to free his domains from Turkish rule. Later he conquered Hejaz, extended his authority over the larger part of the peninsula, and renamed his kingdom Saudi Arabia. Colonel T. E. Lawrence, a British officer, who sympathized with the cause, did much at that time to develop a spirit of nationality among the Arabs.

Besides Saudi Arabia there are several smaller states, some of them under special treaty arrangements with Britain. In the southwest is the sultanate Yemen and the British colony and Protectorate of Aden. The sultanate of Oman and Muscat is on the Gulf of Oman. On the Persian Gulf are the Trucial Coast sheikdoms and Qatar, the Bahrein Islands and Kuwait.

Mecca and Medina are the two most important towns in Arabia from a religious and political standpoint. Mohammed, the founder of the Moslem faith, was born in Mecca, and to that city as many as 200,000 devotees make the annual pilgrimage to do honor to the Prophet. Medina, his burial place, is also a place of worship to which unbelievers are denied entrance. It is interesting to note that the religion is divided into two main factions, the Sunnis and the Shiites. The division arose from the fact that Mohammed died without leaving a successor as the temporal and spiritual head of the faith. For twenty-two years after his death Arabia was ruled by three successive Caliphs.

It was then that the two rival factions rose. The Sunnis claimed the right to nominate the Prophet's successor, while the Shiites contended that the divine right of succession lay with Ali, Mohammed's son-in-law, and his descendants. Arising thus, the dispute assumed such proportions that the rival sects still have an undisguised dislike for each other. Cer-

365

THIS WILD RAVINE, the Wadi Musa, on a ledge of which these men are standing, leads to the valley in which are the ruins of the rock-city of Petra. In ancient times this city was extremely prosperous, and controlled the trade route through it, although often captured and sacked by invading armies. To-day little remains except a few temples and tombs cut in the rock.

© E. N. A.

AN ANCIENT TRADE-ROUTE between Palestine and Arabia runs through this dark narrow gorge of the Wadi Musa near Petra. Although caravans are not so frequent to-day as they were before the Hejaz railway was built, many old-fashioned merchants and pilgrims still prefer to travel by foot or on horse or camel and robbers as in olden times still lie in wait for them.

LEVELING SANDY TUFTS TO MAKE WAY FOR IRRIGATED FARMS

A road-grader, ungainly master of ruts and tufts, chugs across a bare field near an oasis in the Nejd. Next, plows will turn the soil, and water will pour from irrigation wells, pumps and pipes. Crops will be sown and harvested. Once again science and technology in the hands of an eager people will have pushed farther back the wasted, dry frontiers of the desert.

MORE PLENTIFUL, LESS EXPENSIVE, THE IRREPLACEABLE OXEN

Arabs walk behind yokes of oxen, guiding primitive leveling tools. It is a long, hard day of work, but the effort brings the reward of a smooth field and a fine, porous soil. Though more and more tractors and other farm machines are being brought into Arabia for the development of the irrigated areas, draft animals still must shoulder much of the burden.

MELONS, STOREHOUSES OF WATER FOR DRY DESERT JOURNEYS

An Arab farmer and an American technical expert admire a harvest of watermelons, one of many crops grown on the model farms of Khafs Dhaghra. Nearby are the limestone pits, dug in the 1940's, that irrigate the vast Al Kharj oasis in the Nejd. Because they contain a great amount of water, melons are highly prized by desert travelers of the Middle East.

CARVED BALCONIES, many of them beautifully painted and decorated with Arabic scrolls, overhang the winding streets of Jidda (Jeddah), a Red Sea port. Mohammedan pilgrims on their way to the holy city of Mecca, come here by boat and then, in recent years, make use of the motor bus service to reach their destination. There are several foreign legations in Jidda.

MC LEISH

THIS RED STONE TEMPLE of El-Deir at Petra was not built up of separate blocks of stone but was hewn from the solid cliff. To-day it is the most splendid of the remains that tell of the city's vanished glory. It was fashioned by the Romans when they captured Petra in the hope of securing for themselves the wealth and commerce of its inhabitants

DHOWS AT ANCHOR IN THE HARBOR OF MANAMA, BAHREIN ISLANDS

Bahrein Islands fishermen spend much of their time in the dhow, the heavy craft with the leaning mast and the swinging yard from which is hung a large lateen, or triangular, sail. From Manama, capital of the islands, the fleets go out into the Persian Gulf, where they brave the hottest of suns, and come back laden to the gunwales with pearl oysters and fish.

IN THE MANAMA BAZAAR, MARKETING CENTER OF THE BAHREINS

A ragged canopy of burlap cools a street in the bazaar of Manama. People walk the sun- and shadow-striped way at a summer's pace, haggling at the shops and stalls for a comb, a gem, a watch—perhaps a typewriter or a phonograph. Sometimes the rarest, least expected goods can be produced from shelf or trunk. Then buyer and seller bargain on the price.

Prophet's son-in-law, but that by mistake he handed it on to Mohammed.

The population is more or less divided into the semi-permanent inhabitants of the coast and of the cities and towns, and the wandering tribes of the interior. The latter are constantly migrating for their life is a pastoral one and they must move their encampments in order to find fresh pastures for their flocks and herds.

The dress of the men and women is very much the same. It is designed to give both ease and dignity, and consists of a long linen shirt, baggy trousers of linen that are fastened at the waist with a cord, and a cloak with ample sleeves. In the cold weather the sleeves can be used as gloves by being drawn over the hands. Over this cloak is worn a mantle of bright-colored cloth with, perhaps, a collar of gold or silver work.

A colored handkerchief covers the head and is secured by a woolen band worn in a double circle round the head. For footwear the Arab uses sandals. An Arab when mounted is an imposing sight, with his cartridge belt round his waist, his rifle slung across his shoulder or over the back part of the camel saddle, with his dagger stuck in a belt and his cloak thrown back. Thus arrayed he looks the picture of romance and wild freedom. He has some curious customs regarding the cloak. When entering a town or village it must be worn properly and not thrown back, but when approaching a camp or caravan out in the open plains he waves it as a sign that he has no hostile intentions and that none need fear for life or property.

AVA HAMILTON

WATER VENDOR OF THE MIDDLE EAST

In Saudi Arabia water is so precious a commodity that the thirsty traveler must purchase it by the glass or cup from a merchant who plies his tireless way up and down the hot, dusty streets of the city, heavy urn slung on his back.

tain sects of the Shiites say that they doubt the divine character of the Koran, stating that it was given to the Angel Gabriel for transmission to Ali, the

HEADLEY

MECCA'S GREAT MOSQUE is the holiest place on earth to a Mohammedan. He turns towards it when he prays, no matter in what part of the world he may be. The black cube-shaped structure in the centre of the courtyard of the mosque is the Ka'ba, or Holy House, the chief sanctuary of the town of Mecca even long before Mohammed. It is covered with silk. Pilgrims must, as their first duty, walk or run around the Ka'ba seven times murmuring prayers the while. In the courtyard, it can be seen, is a well in which pious Mohammedans dip linen that is later made into shrouds.

THIS PILGRIM CARAVAN is on its way to the hill of Arafat which Mohammedans hold in the greatest reverence. It lies about thirteen miles east of Mecca. All those who make the pilgrimage to the Holy City go to Arafat. They travel on foot, donkeys, horses and camels. This Caravan has two files of camels; those on the right carry the baggage and provisions, those on the left bear "shugdufs," tents of carpets and curtains which protect the riders from the sun. Every Moslem, financially able, is bound to go to Mecca once in his lifetime, or provide a substitute.

375

MUSCAT, INDIAN OCEAN PORT AND CAPITAL OF THE SULTANATE OF OMAN

Glimmering in the hot sun, the white buildings of the town nestle beneath an old Portuguese citadel. It dates from the days when Muscat was in Portuguese hands, during the sixteenth century. White buildings reflect heat and are a necessity in a land where the temperature seldom goes below 90 degrees in the shade and often reaches 110 degrees. Muscat is the only port for steamships in the region, although the town itself is a rather quiet, sleepy place. Ships that stop there load dates, Arabian horses and wheat, the most valuable products of the region.

The houses vary according to the district. There are camps of tents and houses of limestone blocks quarried in the vicinity. Let us pay a visit to an ordinary city or town. It is a curious mixture of architecture. There are the dwellings of the rich, with solid walls and exquisite woodwork tracery and carving; houses of mud with flat roofs; reed huts and, upon the outskirts of the towns, the camps of those who have come in from outlying parts to barter and trade. Among the houses are mosques with tall white minarets, from the summits of which the "muezzin," or priest, will call the Faithful to prayer five times during the twenty-four hours.

We may best see the life of Arabia on a bazaar, or market day. Tents of matting are erected and are crowded with all kinds of marketable goods, from wool, cloth, reed mats, palm fibre and dates, to fruit of every description, cattle, sheep, implements and all that goes to make up commercial and pastoral existence in Arabia of to-day.

STANDARD OIL CO. (N. J.)

HAMMERING SILVER INTO USEFUL SHAPES

A silversmith of the Bahrein Islands follows the old ways of his craft in an open shop. With infinite patience he will beat the silver bar, held on the old-fashioned anvil, into a tray or dish or box.

Apart from the booths and tents, there are the permanent shops, which are roofed like arcades in our country. In them we may see tailors, potters, metal-workers, jewelers, dressmakers, carpet-sellers and members of most other trades and professions, with crowds of people always seeking bargains. Every now and then, donkeys heavily laden with merchandise or camels with loads sticking out at dangerous angles force a way through the crowd. They may often unceremoniously hurl passers-by into shop fronts, thereby upsetting the shopkeeper's goods, but no one seems to resent this treatment for it has all been a part of the bazaar for ages past.

In Arabia, religion plays an important part in the daily life of the people, and when the priest gives the call to prayer from the towering minaret all business ceases for the moment and everyone turns to wash their hands and feet before praying. At the conclusion of the prayer business is resumed and the clamor of buying and selling continued.

Marriage in Arabia is a simple affair for it demands no more than the presence of a priest and four witnesses. In the interior of the country it is still further shorn of ceremony, for the legal necessities of the occasion are satisfied by the presence of witnesses from both families, and, a feast having been given, the marriage festivities are over.

From the romantic aspect, the Arabs of the desert are the most interesting to us, for they are the riders of the plains and are forever on the move. The internal

377

ONE OF THE FORTIFIED GATES TO THE WALLED CITY OF SAN'A, CAPITAL OF YEMEN

San'a lies high in the mountainous interior of Yemen, 7,250 feet above sea level. It is a walled city with eight gates, and within are forty-eight mosques. San'a has been a trading center since ancient times. Tradition has it that San'a was one of the chief cities of the kingdom of the Queen of Sheba (or Saba), whose visit to King Solomon is recorded in the Bible. Today camel caravans, laden with coffee, indigo, safflower, madder, frankincense and myrrh, still plod the road between San'a and its port Hodeida, on the Red Sea, forty miles away.

THE BODYGUARD of the iman (king) of Yemen. Used to going barefoot almost from babyhood, the soldiers do not wear shoes even in uniform. They are nonetheless doughty fighting men.

THE ROYAL PALACE at Sana, Yemen's capital. The present-day city is in the shape of an irregular figure "8," and the extensive palace grounds are where the lines of the "8" cross.

decoration of an Arab tent is often carried out on artistic lines if the owner be moderately wealthy. The floor is covered with carpets, and on one side will be a divan formed of carpets and cushions for the host and his guests. The walls are hung with embroideries worked by the women, who are as clever with the needle as they are at rounding-up cattle and camels. Suspended along the walls will be guns, harness and clothes, and on the floor stand the numerous coffee-pots and cups.

The Arab diet is mainly mutton, rice and bread, with small cakes made from milk and a form of vermicelli. If the camp be near the coast, fish is included. Prawns served dry are very popular. Camels' milk is drunk, and the first thing a thirsty traveler does is to drain a bowl of it.

On the occasion of a big feast, such as the marriage of an important person or some political event, the meat and rice are cooked in a kind of steamer raised a few inches above the ground and are served with bread, cakes, fruit, dates, milk and sundry other dishes. The company disposes of the food without the aid of knives and forks, making use of the fingers as Nature intended. At the end of the repast brass and copper bowls are handed round, in which the guests wash their hands.

An Arab Tribe on the March

When on trek the Arabs have some interesting customs in connection with their camping grounds. They send one of their number ahead, and he reserves the site of the proposed camp by spreading a mantle over a bush in the centre of the chosen ground. Although there may be others moving in the same direction, no one will interfere with the selection, however good the pasturage or attractive its other qualities.

The tribe marches in a long cavalcade, with possibly several thousand head of camels, sheep, goats and cattle. The men are distributed along the convoy directing the line of march. The women and children and all the paraphernalia of the camp are on camels and donkeys, and at the head of the tribe rides the sheik, or chief.

The women are veiled and ride on camels in a sort of huge pannier—a basket-carriage placed on the camel's back —with two large wooden crescents at front and rear, the horns of which stand out on each side of the pannier. From them hang the long tassels and the gaudy embroidery of this queer carriage. These are its most attractive feature, for the pannier is very uncomfortable, and the unfortunate occupants are like hens cooped up in a form of rocking carriage, the motion of which varies in accordance with the ground over which the caravan is passing.

Camp Site Dependent on Water

The camp is always pitched by a well. Water is scarce in Arabia, and the site of a well is usually marked by cairns of stones erected on the surrounding heights, so that the weary traveler may know that water is at hand and he is near his goal. The camels are watered once in every four or five days, but they can exist much longer in cases of dire necessity. The loading and unloading are done by the women, while the men watch the process and drink coffee.

As an Arab caravan leaves its camp in the morning it is a sight that reminds us of the stories of biblical days. Even as the patriarchs and their followers marched across the desert, so in our time do the Arab tribes move across the deserts, their banner leading them on by day and a lamp at night.

Unchanging Ways of the Desert

Thus do the ways of the desert remain the same, for time has not changed the order of things that was in vogue three thousand years ago. Not only in this respect is the life unchanged, for even the drawing of water at the wells is done the same way as in the days of Abraham. A rope is attached to the leather bucket. which is lowered and drawn up by a camel descending and ascending an inclined plane. It is picturesque, but laborious, yet the Arab will not change it for any more modern and rapid system, for it is sanctified by time and a recognized institution of pastoral life.

Among the wild life of Arabia is the ostrich, but it is only met with in certain parts. There are also gazelles and hares and a variety of bustard. The cheetah, or hunting leopard, is found in those parts of the desert frequented by gazelles, its principal prey. Its speed is almost incredible when it gives chase. It covers the ground in a rush that must be seen to be realized. A cheetah that the writer

FRITZ HENLE

CANALS TO COLLECT RAIN WATER FOR THE DESERT TOWN OF ADEN

Aden has little fresh water, and these canals help to conserve the scanty rainfall. Drinking water is also obtained from artesian wells and by distilling sea water. The British-owned fortress town, built partly in the crater of an extinct volcano on a rocky peninsula, guards the southern entrance to the Red Sea. Its climate is normally hot and dry.

A WELL DUG DEEP BELOW THE DESERT SANDS OF SAUDI ARABIA
The well is about 120 feet below the surface, and the refreshing water is hauled up in goatskin bags.
It is then emptied into a trough, also of goatskin, from which the camels drink.

knew brought down an antelope in a run of six hundred yards, the quarry having a start of two hundred yards.

The Beduins, the true children of the desert, have changed least of all in Arabia. They are the wild freemen who harassed the caravans of pilgrims a thousand years ago and they still keep their old wild habits. As they ride along they note every fold in the ground, for it may serve them in case of an attack or a raid by other tribesmen, and they notice every tuft of grass and every bush as possible fodder for their herds or for some sign of foes in the neighborhood.

They guard their flocks and herds like the tribesmen of old. In the heat of the day they recline in the shade of a palm tree, if there be one, or beneath reed matting stuck up on poles. They know the ways of their sheep and goats, and during the noonday siesta we may see a mantle arranged upon sticks so that it resembles a man and serves as a substitute for the shepherd. From time immemorial the goats and sheep have grazed quite placidly round the dummy under the impression that it is their master, and so they do not stray, while the shepherd is enjoying his sleep in peace.

One of the chief occupations of the Arabs is that of camel-breeding and they understand this animal better than any other race. From its hair they make blankets, tents, ropes and even clothing. They drink its milk, eat its flesh and tan its hide for leather; but they have no affection for the beast that gives them so much. Without the camels the Arab would scarcely be able to live in the desert, but all his affection, if he has any, is lavished upon his horse, which is looked upon as a family pet.

The horse is, however, unsuited to life in the desert as is shown in the following story which is current among the Arabs: "The horse complained to Allah that he was not made for desert journeying. His hoofs sank into the sand, the saddle slipped off his back, he could not reach the